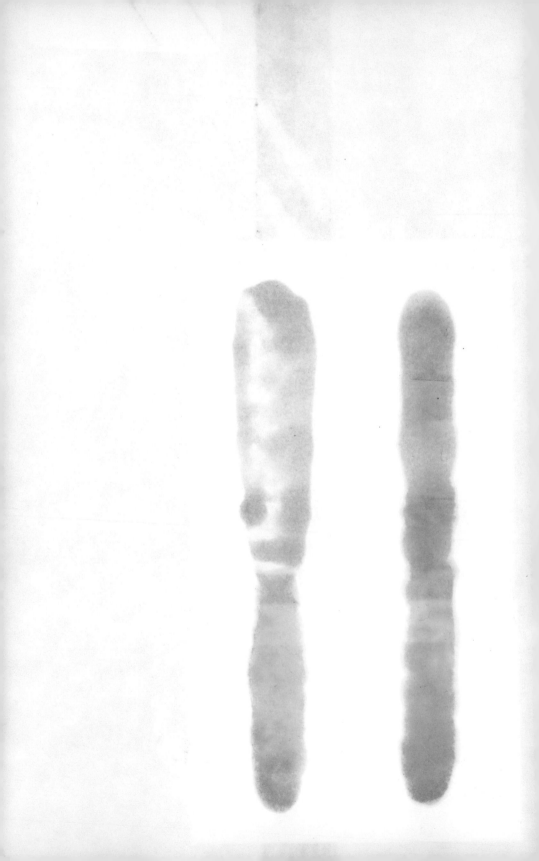

REGARDING TELEVISION

CRITICAL APPROACHES—
AN ANTHOLOGY

 The American Film Institute

The American Film Institute
Monograph Series

Ann Martin
Supervising Editor

REGARDING TELEVISION

CRITICAL APPROACHES—
AN ANTHOLOGY

Edited by

E. Ann Kaplan

University Publications of America, Inc.

The American Film Institute, established in 1967 by the National Endowment for the Arts, is an independent, nonprofit, national organization dedicated to advancing and preserving the art of the moving image.

The opinions expressed in this Monograph *are those of the authors and are not necessarily those of* The American Film Institute.

The American Film Institute *Monograph* Series is published by University Publications of America, Inc., Frederick, MD, in association with The American Film Institute.

The American Film Institute
2021 North Western Avenue
P.O. Box 27999
Los Angeles, California 90027

Library of Congress Cataloging in Publication Data

Regarding television.

    (The American Film Institute monograph series; v. 2)
    Bibliography: p. 139.
    1. Television plays—History and criticism—Addresses, essays, lectures.
2. Television broadcasting—United States—Addresses, essays, lectures.
I. Kaplan, E. Ann. II. Series.
PN1992.65.R4 1983   791.45'75'0973   83-17015
ISBN 0-89093-584-X

Table of Contents

Contributors

JEANNE ALLEN teaches film and mass media criticism and history at Temple University. She has published articles in *Screen, Journal of the University Film and Video Association, Quarterly Review of Film Studies* and *Cinema Journal* as well as in *The American Film Industry, The Cinematic Apparatus* and *The American Novel and the Movies*. She is currently working on a book-length study of the impact of industrialization on American mass culture.

ROBERT C. ALLEN teaches broadcasting and film at the University of North Carolina at Chapel Hill. He is the author of *Vaudeville and Film* (Arno, 1980) and, with Douglas Gomery, of *Film History: Theory and Practice* (Addison-Wesley, forthcoming). He has published articles on film, media and popular entertainment in *Cinema Journal, Quarterly Review of Film Studies, Wide Angle, Theatre Survey* and other journals.

WILLIAM BODDY is an Instructor in the Department of Communication and Theatre at the University of Notre Dame. He has written on film and broadcasting for *Ciné-Tracts* and the *Millennium Film Journal,* and is currently completing a dissertation on American television in the Department of Cinema Studies at New York University.

CHARLOTTE BRUNSDON teaches Film Studies at Warwick University, England. She was a member of the Media group and the Women's Studies group while doing research at the Centre for Contemporary Cultural Studies at Birmingham University. Her publications include *Everyday Television: 'Nationwide,'* written with David Morley.

JANE FEUER teaches film and popular culture at the University of Pittsburgh. She is the author of *The Hollywood Musical* (BFI/Macmillan Series, 1982).

SANDY FLITTERMAN is Assistant Professor in the English Department at Rutgers University. Her articles have appeared in numerous publications including *Screen, Ciné-Tracts, Film Quarterly, Wide Angle, Camera Obscura* and *University Publishing*. Her doctoral dissertation is entitled "Women, Representation, and Cinematic Discourse: The Example of French Cinema."

DOUGLAS GOMERY teaches film and broadcasting in the Department of Communication Arts and Theatre at the University of Maryland. He is the co-author of the forthcoming *Film History: Theory and Practice* (with Robert C. Allen), and the author of numerous articles on the history of the American film industry.

E. ANN KAPLAN teaches film and literature at Rutgers University. Her articles on women in film have been widely published in journals such as *Wide Angle, Millennium Film Journal* and *Quarterly Review of Film Studies,* and her two most recent books are *Women in Film Noir* and *Fritz Lang: A Research and Reference Guide*. Her forthcoming book is *Women and Film: Both Sides of the Camera* (Methuen, 1983).

TANIA MODLESKI teaches film and literature at the University of Wisconsin-Milwaukee and is the author of *Loving with a Vengeance: Mass-Produced Fantasies for Women* (The Shoe String Press, 1982).

MARGARET MORSE is currently on leave from her position as a Mellon Assistant Professor of Humanities and German and Slavic Languages at Vanderbilt University, to work as the Assistant Director of Liberal Studies of the University of San Francisco. She received her doctorate in German Literature and Aesthetics from the University of California at Berkeley.

ROBERT STAM is Assistant Professor in Cinema Studies at New York University, where he teaches courses ranging from French New Wave and Third World Cinema to Hitchcock and Buñuel and the Semiotics of Cinema and Television. He is co-author of *Brazilian Cinema* (Associated University Presses, 1982) and author of *The Interrupted Spectacle* (published in Brazil by Paz e Terra). He is currently collaborating on a dictionary of semiotic terms.

MAUREEN TURIM is an Assistant Professor in the Cinema Department at SUNY-Binghamton, where she teaches courses in film and video theory and history. She has published articles on visual perception and film analysis in *Wide Angle, Enclitic, Socialist Review* and *Semiotica*. She is currently working on a book to be titled *Flashbacks: Memory and the Subjectivity of History in Film*.

Acknowledgments

Charlotte Brunsdon's paper *"Crossroads:* Notes on Soap Opera" first appeared in *Screen* Vol. 22 No. 4 (Spring 1982).

Tania Modleski's paper "The Rhythms of Reception: Daytime Television and Women's Work," is part of her book *Loving with a Vengeance: Mass-Produced Fantasies for Women* (Hamden, CT: The Shoe String Press, 1982) and first appeared in *Tabloid: A Review of Mass Culture and Everyday Life* No. 4 (Summer 1981).

Introduction

E. Ann Kaplan

Some of the articles in this book (those by Jeanne Allen, Charlotte Brunsdon, Jane Feuer, Sandy Flitterman, Tania Modleski and Maureen Turim) were originally delivered as papers at a conference, "Perspectives on Television and Video Art," which I organized at Rutgers University in May 1981. The aim of that conference, as now of this book, was to gather together and make readily available new critical and theoretical approaches to commercial television. Some of these new approaches apply—with interesting results—the tools of semiology, psychoanalysis and structuralism that have dominated recent film criticism to television; others reflect methodologies specific to television, but differing substantially from the traditional American methodologies outlined by William Boddy in the first part of this book.

The kind of theoretical work that the essays reveal is long overdue in American television studies. While critics in England have been publishing work of the kind represented here for some time (see especially *Screen Education, Screen, Working Papers in Cultural Studies*, The British Film Institute *Television Monographs* and the work of Raymond Williams), the structure, form, content and context for British television are so radically different from those of its American counterpart that everything has to be rethought by critics in this country. Television scholarship is simply not exportable in the easy manner of film criticism.

Let me focus for a moment on why television studies in the United States have taken a radically different form from that of the work offered here, and also from the approaches that have dominated film studies in recent decades. Because film could be considered an art form in some of its modes (i.e., the avant-garde film, the foreign film), it weathered the disparagement of mass culture by humanities academics much better than did television during the 1950s. Dwight McDonald's famous essay on mass culture set the tone for the humanities critique in arguing that mass culture was debased "art"—trivial, cheap, meaningless.[1] This was in 1963, at the very moment when in England film and television were seen by some as worthy of in-depth study from a humanities point of view.[2]

The aesthetic position (namely, that art works had to manifest proven aesthetic greatness to be proper subject matter for university courses) ruled out study of most mass media forms in humanities departments. But history departments managed to teach some courses on the history of film, while people in literature and the other arts could get by if the focus was on the so-called art film—foreign and experimental works. Auteur theory, particularly in the form of Andrew Sarris' "Pantheon" of American directors, finally made it possible in the '60s and early '70s to teach at least the "accepted" American films, but the discourse on film was limited largely to the aesthetic, paralleling literary discourses.

This intellectual background explains why Hall and Whannel in their pioneering *The Popular Arts* felt obliged to redeem mass culture by ranking popular works along an aesthetic dimension. If mass culture courses were to be accepted by the establishment, the argument had to be that one could improve students' aesthetic tastes by contrasting high and low culture works; or that one could move students on to the better popular works, and give them greater aesthetic awareness, by examining mass culture in depth.[3]

Marxists, meanwhile, had their own objections to mass culture, arising largely out of the work of the Frankfurt School. From this point of view, the mass media are, both technologically and culturally, a product of the Industrial Revolution; the breakdown of traditional ties and community structures set in motion by the Industrial Revolution has left people isolated and vulnerable to external manipulation precisely through the agencies of the mass media spawned by the new technology. According to David Morley:

> This 'pessimistic mass society thesis' stressed the conservative and reconciliatory role of 'mass culture' for the audience. Mass culture suppressed 'potentialities' and denied awareness of contradiction in a 'one-dimensional world'; only art, in fictional and dramatic form, could preserve the qualities of negation and transcendence.[4]

Thus, although they approached the problem from an entirely different perspective, the Marxists nevertheless joined the proponents of high culture in denouncing the mass media. But while the humanists at this point did not really have anywhere to go with mass culture works (other than in the direction advocated by Hall and Whannel), a few Marxists produced work in the Frankfurt School tradition that provided an intelligent critique from a sociological perspective.[5] Much more common, however, was the work of mainstream social scientists who, in reacting against the Frankfurt School position, had a field day with television, particularly from the 1960s onward.[6] As David Morley points out in his excellent historical review of social science conceptions of mass culture, mainstream television research "can be said to have been dominated by one basic conceptual paradigm, constructed in response to the 'pessimistic mass society thesis' elaborated by the Frankfurt School." He goes on to say:

> In reaction to the Frankfurt School's predilection for 'critical' social theory and qualitative and philosophical analysis, the American researchers developed what began as a quantitative and positivist methodology for empirical radio audience research into the 'Sociology of Mass Persuasion'.[7]

Two broad strands of research followed: first, various models for the effect of the content of "messages" on audiences; and second, audience-based studies which emphasized the "needs" which audiences brought to or got from the "messages."[8] Most took the form of data collecting or of controlled experiments from which certain conclusions were drawn.

Thus, when communications departments got properly under way in the early '60s, it was naturally social science concerns and methodologies, including communications theory, that dominated the curriculum, so far as there was any general education in television theory.[9] Geared toward preparing students for careers in commercial television, these departments naturally focused on instruction in television technology and production. Little attention (as far as I can gather) was given to television aesthetics, to how meaning is produced, or to television as an ideological institution functioning within a complex consumer circuit that allows only for the production of carefully constricted meanings. In the social sciences, emphasis has remained on the impact of television on individual or group behavior, studied from an empirical perspective.[10] As John Downing has recently noted, while empiricist research sometimes produces interesting results, it is severely limited by the impossibility (within the framework) of making value judgements or of applying a critical stance to data collected or experiments performed.[11]

Thus, except for a few isolated people doing work in a vacuum, humanities scholars and Marxists by and large ignored television, leaving a void which communications departments and the social scientists naturally filled. This book aims to correct the one-sided disciplinary approach to television by offering articles written largely by people trained in film and in the humanities.

The book opens with William Boddy's useful evaluation of American writing on television. Boddy starts by looking at weaknesses in the work of television journalists, who fail to recognize the "artistic specificity of medium," and who often adopt the mistaken stance of "reviewer-as-cultural-crusader." Journalists have been slow to address issues of authorship, "treating programs as vehicles for performers, designs of producers or campaigns of network strategists."[12] In the second section of his essay, Boddy locates the reasons for this stance in the positioning of television in a particular tradition of popular culture and mass communications studies. He traces the way in which the second generation of communications research "has been concerned with modifying or refuting the earlier account of media manipulation and atomized mass audience," and has settled into "methodological refinements in design of empirical studies." The location of television studies in schools of journalism and communication, along with the crafts of reporting, advertising and public relations, has, Boddy argues, "certainly encouraged communications researchers to pursue questions of more or less direct utility to the communications industry."[13]

The next stage was the "uses and gratifications" research, which, Boddy notes, abstracted the audience "into bundles of *a priori* psychological functions," and provided no account of "the relationship between the unproblematic psychological determinants and the social order."[14] The model left no room for investigating either the determination of specific media forms, or the relationship between media and the social formation. Boddy demonstrates the inability of this functionalist communications research to develop cultural or political policy with a close look at Herbert Gans' *Popular Culture and High Culture*.

Boddy ends his essay by summarizing the problems with the dominant American communications theory model; it is now necessary, he says, to apply the theories of subjectivity and social process developed by culture critics to television. "Critical work on television as an industry," Boddy notes, "has to be located in the fields of history and economics," while the study of television programming should be approached through analysis of "both the agency of a particular symbolic form and an account of the social process of the construction of its meaning."[15]

It is precisely the kind of intervention in television studies which Boddy calls for that this book aims to provide. It is an intervention made possible by the introduction in literary and humanistic discourse of concepts from semiology, psychoanalysis and structuralism. While literary discourse had previously focused on form, style and content—on, that is, the *aesthetic* dimension of texts, as traditionally conceived—in the period following the work of Roland Barthes, Jacques Derrida and others, emphasis shifted to analysis of the production of meaning in a text, and to the relationship between text and reader. Texts are seen now as produced not so much by an individual author as by the dominant signifying practice within which they are embedded (whether it be written language, visual images or sound). These signifying practices embody the dominant ideology of a culture, which is communicated through the way in which texts construct the spectator in a particular position. A great deal of attention has thus been given to narrative, and to the way in which narrative codes work to implicate the reader in a certain fashion,[16] so as to ensure cultural hegemony.

Given the dominance of television as a cultural institution, it seemed important to the authors presented here to analyze the complex processes through which television, as a signifying practice, produces its meanings. The authors in the first section all theorize about live television programs: Jane Feuer about *Good Morning, America*; Robert Stam about the news; and Margaret Morse about sports.

Jane Feuer shows how the ideology of "liveness" is used to overcome fragmentation in a show like *Good Morning, America*: "David acts like a custodian of flow and regularity," Feuer argues, "the personification of a force which creates unity out of fragmentation."[17] Furthermore, she states that "this mode of address is embedded in a mutually reinforcing ideological problematic of national and family unity."[18] Hartman acts as the "father" of the *Good Morning, America* "family," sitting in his fictional living room and linking, through his person, in an electronic circuit, people in various parts of America whom he interviews on television monitors. The close-up device obscures the actual space separating David and interviewee, much as we, in our living rooms, are made to feel part of David's "space" by the mode of address and the reality-effects of "liveness." But David mediates all discourse. We are positioned, by the way the apparatus functions, so as to be sutured into David's space, participating in this way in the ideology of national and family unity. "Television," Feuer concludes, "in its liveness, its immediacy, its reality, can create families where none exist."[19]

Using psychoanalysis and semiology, Stam and Morse make a good case for an even greater degree of loosening of "the real" than Feuer showed; for the live programs paradoxically produce a fictional, phantasmic world that is pleasurable. Both show that the degree to which television uses reality-effects (a realist aesthetic) often varies in *disproportion* to its actual liveness; the live sports or news event is free to be phantasmic just because the spectator is "assured" of its "reality." Television, like film, has at once to satisfy the need for illusionism (i.e., that the television world will *look like* the external world) and the craving for the world of the Imaginary where the viewer can find identification with the Ego-Ideals of the pre-symbolic, pre-oedipal phase.[20]

Stam argues that television, despite its different viewing space and viewing situation, nevertheless encourages regressive and narcissistic attitudes similar to those found in the cinema. He argues that our position as protected witnesses of news events is essentially voyeuristic, and that it is a form of voyeurism geared to lessening our anxiety about the chaos in the external world. Television news, Stam argues, is self-enhancing, making us feel "better than" the people involved in disasters; furthermore, the presence of the reassuring anchor-people puts us in the position of "being taken care of."

From here, Stam goes on to argue for the essentially fictional nature of the news, its status as "story," and the newscasters' status as fictional characters; the whole creates "the predictable but renewable charm of the genre film,"[21] complete with suturing and the masking of discontinuous images. And it is in these devices of classical narrative that the news indeed brings about the "pleasure" Stam began by investigating.

Margaret Morse also investigates a particular kind of pleasure in live television—this time sports. Noting the increase in television spectatorship of sports programs, Morse is concerned with three basic questions: first, she examines the formal differences between sports in the arena and sport on television; second, she considers whether television sport has changed "the spectator's psychic experience of sport," or "the function of sport as a social imaginary";[22] and finally, she looks at what characterizes sport as a genre on television, and at any changes in the ideological or social function of sport when it is watched through the television mechanism rather than in the arena. In considering all three questions, Morse is particularly concerned with the fact that the discourse of sport takes the male body as object of the gaze in a society which has a strong cultural inhibition precisely against the look at the male body. "How is it," Morse asks, "that spectator sports can license such a gaze and render it harmless?"[23] She finds the answer in the careful balance of "play and display" that characterizes modern sport, and that permits an effective mechanism of disavowal through the focus on scientific enquiry into the limits of human performance.

In a manner similar to Stam, Morse shows how the world of television sport is a phantasmic one, "highly invested with desire and capital."[24] Nothing about the presentation strives for realism, but, on the contrary, all is set up for the creation of a surreal, imaginary world. Morse notes that:

> The most memorable shots are the ones shown in slow motion, where violent force and speed are invested electronically with grace and beauty. . . . To show the ecstasy of victory, slow motion may spill beyond the end of the game itself into the crowd, unanchored by any hermeneutic process, to become pure spectacle.[25]

The image of masculine power and perfection, Morse shows, is the commod-ity that television relies on to link sponsor and viewer, so that it is in the television stations' interest to maximize spectacle while including mechanisms of disavowal that prevent men from admitting their pleasure in gazing at their exhibitionist like. Morse concludes that the correspondence between images in sports programs and images sponsors provide to sell their products "centralizes and unifies the powerful social imaginary of civic and masculine identity and restricts the object of discourse on sport."[26] The strong identification with the male image of beauty and power remains intact and unquestioned, when supported by the images in the ads; for men can "forget" the actual discrepancy between the phantasmic images and their "real" selves and daily lives by believing they are acquiring the signs of masculinity through buying the objects advertised.

Following the articles on live television is a case study on Soaps. I chose to focus on Soaps as against other genres first, because relatively little has been written on the genre, and second, because Soaps raise particularly interesting questions in relation to women. Tania Modleski argues, in a pioneering essay, that there is an intimate connection between the form of Soaps and women's work in the home. First, women get a training from Soaps in how to "read" other people; the obsessive close-ups signify the emphasis on unspoken feelings that the viewer must interpret from the facial image alone, and, says Modleski, "This openness to the needs and desires of others is, of course, one of the primary functions of the woman in the home."[27] Second, the form of Soaps reflects the state of constant distraction that the housewife must learn to cope with, since she has to be ready to deal with needs, conflicts or crises as they arise among the many people she is responsible for. Thus, the Soap is constructed around multiple plot lines so that no one story can become too absorbing for too long a time; the little episodes from various "lives" are broken up by commercials, which, Modleski says,

> ... present the housewife with mini-problems and their resolutions, so that, after witnessing all the agonizingly hopeless dilemmas presented on soap operas, the spectator has the satisfaction of seeing *something* cleaned up. . . .[28]

Finally, the open form of the Soaps, i.e., the endlessly deferred resolutions and climaxes, fits the kind of rhythm women experience in their daily lives, where there is also no "resolution," but a constant process, constant repetition, constant return and duplication.

The next two essays pick up and expand in interesting ways on points raised by Modleski. Charlotte Brunsdon, in her discussion of the British soap opera, *Crossroads*, first discusses the way traditional narrative linearity, familiar in the classical Hollywood film, is replaced by the "continuities of moral and ideological frameworks which inform the dialogue" and which are aimed at "constructing moral consensus about the conduct of personal life."[29] Different characters have an opportunity to speculate about outcomes and judge others' behavior, and the viewer is thereby positioned so as to do the same thing. Second, Brunsdon analyzes the degree to which Soaps can be said to construct a specifically female spectator in terms of the competencies the dramas rely on for their meaning. She concludes that the texts imply a feminine viewer skilled in the "rules" of romance, marriage and family life.

Sandy Flitterman takes up the question of the relationship between the Soaps as narrative and the commercials as narratives, from the perspective both of their respective forms and of the cultural meanings they embody. She explores the differences between daytime and prime-time ads from the point of view of both frequency and content (social meanings) so as to show the appeal in the day to "the centrality of the family and the important function of the woman as nurturing support system," and the prime-time appeal to "a business sense traditionally defined as masculine."[30] Flitterman turns next to an analysis of commercials as texts, as modes of meaning production. Taking four well-known ads for in-depth study, Flitterman analyzes their narrative processes using Metz' syntagmatics. What she discovers is that each ad corresponds to one syntagma (the basic unit of narrative construction), while, of course, Soaps themselves, like any narrative, consist in many syntagmas. Her point is that "far from *disrupting* the narrative flow of daytime soap opera, commercials can be seen to *continue* it."[31] They prolong and maintain the overall impulse for narrative that Soaps satisfy, while providing units of satisfying closure in an overall form that itself frustrates closure.

Finally, in terms of social meanings, Flitterman reveals the idealized family present in the commercials, as against the families overwhelmed with apparently unresolvable problems in the Soaps. The commercials thus function interactively in Soaps, setting up a "dialectical alternation between the vision in the Soaps and that in the ads."[32] It is this interaction between social meanings in the two sets of narratives that results in commercials having "an important function in shaping society's values."[33]

While the three papers I've discussed look at Soaps very much from the perspective of their interest to feminist issues, the last article in this section, by Robert Allen, focuses first on Soaps as industrial product; second, on a semiological reading of the codes according to which the Soap, as text, is organized; and third, on the Soap audience. Allen accounts for the profitability of Soaps in terms of their low-cost/high-yield phenomenon, and describes the organization of production units that enables them to be cheaply made. Turning to the Soap as text, he comments on the difficulty of defining what the text is (since it is often comprised of *years* of individual programs), and then discusses the Soap as an open rather than the closed text Ellen Seiter has posited. After outlining the main codes according to which the Soap is organized, Allen claims that the very over-coding of the Soap, its quality as an open text (containing many possible readings within its lexical and syntactical limits) accounts in part for the increasingly diverse audience Soaps are attracting. Relying on studies of audience response, Allen shows that people use a mixture of codes in interpreting and responding to texts, combining knowledge of narrative codes with reliance on ideological ones; that is, viewers make sense of Soaps by "integrating them into (their) own field of knowledge, values and experiences."[34] Allen concludes that Soaps are interesting precisely because of their openness; they do not offer "a message or easily summarizable world," but rather "complex fields of semiotic possibilities which a variety of audience members can use in a variety of ways."[35]

Robert Allen's discussion of the Soap as industrial and social product leads into the next section of the book, which deals with television in its economic and technological dimension. We still know relatively little about the relationship between technological discoveries and forces in the government and big business. How, when and why do technological discoveries gain entry into the public sphere? To what extent is technology *per se* determining? To what extent do government, military or big business forces exploit or constrain technological invention in order to preserve their own interests? How was television, as a new technology, historically (and how is it still in the present) implicated in such a complicated social matrix?

Jeanne Allen's paper addresses these questions in relation to television in the decades before 1945. She explores some of the reasons why, although the technology was developed and television heralded as far back as the mid-1920s, it took two decades until it was truly mass marketed. She is particularly interested in the constraints put on the development of two-way television:

> . . . since two-way or genuinely interactive television represented perhaps one of the most explicit challenges or oppositions to the centralized and centralizing structures of commerce, government and the military which Raymond Williams cites as basic to broadcasting's development.[36]

She shows how at every point the interlocking of government and big business interests ensured that television would be one-way (the only big business desiring two-way television was AT&T), since in this form its potential for surveillance and control is much greater.

Jeanne Allen also comments on the professional and business collaboration between film and television from at least 1941 on, belying the public image of competition between the two media. The collaboration within potential competition is the theme of Douglas Gomery's article; he traces the complex history of relations between television companies and Hollywood companies, documenting for each period the precise nature of the business collaboration in what emerges as a fascinating story of interaction. Gomery concludes that:

> Movies presented on television, either theatrical or made-for-television, have created sizable profits for both the U.S. television industry (stations and networks), and the U.S. motion picture industry (the Hollywood producers). . . . Television is a far more cost-effective way to reach potential movie viewers than was the neighborhood movie house.[37]

The book ends with a paper by Maureen Turim on video art as a medium for the future. At the conference at Rutgers, a whole session was devoted to viewing video art with the idea of showing the medium's capabilities outside its commercial forms and usages. Turim usefully analyzes the links between video and avant-garde art movements in film and music, thus placing video in a "respectable" art tradition, but goes on to point out the differences between video and forms like music and painting—differences that in part account for negative responses to video as art. The automatic, mechanistic aspects of video lead to focusing merely on special effects; or to "exploring the capabilities of technology," producing only a "catalogue of possible imaging techniques"; or, finally, to simply mimicking images produced by artists in other media such as painting.[38]

In the second half of the paper, Turim examines the areas that make video ideal for artistic exploration: namely, "visual perception, the imaginary and the density of discursive presentation."[39] She links each of these to a major issue of contemporary theory—the psychophysiology of perception, psychoanalysis and semiotics. Turim concludes that as an art of our future, video is "only as narcissistic as we let ourselves be, only as inherently commercial as our minds become." We have to learn to see the video apparatus "not as an entity whose inherent properties determine its limitations but as a tool for diverse art-making projects."[40]

This book goes to press at a time when commercial television is undergoing enormous changes due to the introduction of cable television and pay television, and the likelihood that independent television companies will expand. It is possible that the phenomenon of video art may work beneficially in showing the capacity of the medium for meaningful work of a higher technical and intellectual level than commercial television usually offers. Meanwhile, the essays here help to explain our fascination with commercial television and the mechanisms through which television, as an apparatus embedded in ideology, functions to implicate the spectator in a positioning that reinforces repressive social modes.

E. Ann Kaplan
September 1982

I wish to thank Ann Martin for her scrupulous final editing, her careful attention to detail, and for being helpful and supportive throughout the project.

NOTES

1. Dwight MacDonald, "A Theory of Mass Culture," in *Mass Culture: The Popular Arts In America*, ed. Bernard Rosenberg and David M. White (Glencoe, IL: The Free Press, 1957), pp. 59-73. For example, MacDonald says: "Mass culture is imposed from above. It is fabricated by techniques lived by businessmen; its audience are passive consumers [sic], their participation limited to the choice between buying and not buying. The lords of Kitsch, in short, exploit the cultural need of the masses in order to make a profit and/or to maintain their class rule." (p. 55.)

Earlier texts important as background to MacDonald's position are F[rank] R[aymond] Leavis and Denys Thompson, *Culture and Environment* (London: Chatto and Windus, 1937); and José Ortega y Gasset, *The Dehumanization of Art*, trans. Willard Trask (Garden City, NY: Doubleday, 1956), and *The Revolt of the Masses* (New York: W.W. Norton, 1960).

For a critique of the elitist cultural argument see Herbert J. Gans, *Popular Culture and High Culture* (New York: Basic Books, 1974); this text has a useful and extensive bibliography of books and articles involved in the debate, especially from a sociological perspective. See also John G. Cawelti, "Beatles, Batman and the New Aesthetic," *Midway* Vol. 9 No. 2 (Autumn 1968), pp. 49-70.

2. See in particular Stuart Hall and Paddy Whannel, *The Popular Arts* (London: Pantheon Books, 1964); and a series of British Film Institute Monographs edited by Paddy Whannel, such as A.P. Higgins' *Talking About Television* (London: British Film Institute, 1966), Jim Kitses and Ann Kaplan's *Talking About the Cinema: Film Studies for Young People* (London: British Film Institute, rev. ed. 1974), and *Film Teaching*, ed. Paddy Whannel and Peter Harcourt (London: British Film Institute, 1968), which contains essays by Stuart Hall, Roy Knight, Albert Hunt and Alan Lovell.

3. See, for example, their comment that "We must also stop talking about the various kinds of art and entertainment as if they were necessarily competitive. Popular music, for example, has its own standards. Ella Fitzgerald is a highly polished professional entertainer who within her own sphere could hardly be better. Clearly it would be inappropriate to compare her to Maria Callas. . . . Equally it is not useful to say that the music of Cole Porter is inferior to that of Beethoven. The music of Porter and Beethoven is not of equal value, but Porter was not making an unsuccessful attempt to create music comparable to Beethoven's." (*The Popular Arts*, p. 38.)

4. David Morley, *The 'Nationwide' Audience: Structure and Decoding*, BFI Television Monographs/No. 11 (London: The British Film Institute, 1980), p. 1.

5. See the work of Theodor W. Adorno and Walter Benjamin, particularly in the 1930s; more recently, see Richard Hoggart's *The Uses of Literacy: Changing Patterns in English Mass Culture* (London: Chatto and Windus, 1957).

6. For an idea of the amount of material on radio and television see William E. McCavitt, *Radio and Television: A Selected Annotated Bibliography* (Metuchen, NJ: The Scarecrow Press, 1978). Although McCavitt only provides a selection from the total volume, the proportions of his categories are nevertheless revealing. Out of 229 pages, only 18 are filled with items relating to

my concerns here. Most items come under "Regulation," "Public Broadcasting," "Technical," "History," "Production," etc. Even the items apparently relevant, such as "Research and Theory," "Responsibility and Society," and "Criticism" either were sociologically oriented or, in the case of "Criticism," involved television journalism rather than proper scholarly approaches.

7. Morley, p. 2.

8. Ibid., pp. 3-6.

9. Work in mass culture and communications started much earlier than the departments themselves, researchers coming from disciplines such as sociology or psychology. The earliest departments were focused mainly on journalism, but the real enlargement of the area of study into full-blown communications departments is relatively recent. For a typical text in the field, see John R. Bittner, *Mass Communication* (Englewood Cliffs, NJ: Prentice-Hall, 1977).

10. Typical recent studies of this kind are: Leonard O. Eron, L. Rowell Huesman, Monroe M. Lefkowitz and Leopold O. Walden, "Does Television Violence Cause Aggression?", *American Psychologist* Vol. 27 No. 4 (1972), pp. 253-263; George Comstock, Steven Chaffee, Natan Katzman, Maxwell McCombs and Donald Roberts, *Television and Human Behavior* (New York: Columbia University Press, 1978); and Charles Atkin, Bradley Greenberg, Felipe Korzenny and Steven McDermott, "Selective Exposure to Television Violence," *Journal of Broadcasting* Vol. 23 No. 1 (Winter 1979), pp. 5-13.

11. John Downing, "Communications and Power," *Socialist Review* (forthcoming).

12. William Boddy, "Loving a Nineteen-Inch Motorola: American Writing on Television," in this volume, p. 2.

13. Ibid., p. 5.

14. Ibid.

15. Ibid., p. 9.

16. See particularly here Roland Barthes, *S/Z*, trans. Richard Miller (New York: Hill and Wang, 1974).

17. Jane Feuer, "The Concept of Live Television: Ontology as Ideology," in this volume, p. 17.

18. Ibid., p. 18.

19. Ibid., p. 20.

20. For the theoretical underpinning of these concepts, derived from semiology and Lacanian psychoanalysis, see essays in *Edinburgh '77 Magazine* No. 1 (1977), especially those by Rosalind Coward, "Lacan and Signification: An Introduction," pp. 6-20; Christian Metz, "History/Discourse: Notes on Two Voyeurisms," pp. 21-25; Stephen Heath, 'Screen Images, Film Memory," pp. 33-42; and Claire Johnston, "Toward a Feminist Film Practice: Some Theses," pp. 50-59. See also the issue of *Screen* devoted to Psychoanalysis and Cinema (Vol. 16 No. 2 [Summer 1975]), which includes articles of particular interest by Christian Metz ("The Imaginary Signifier," pp. 14-76), and Stephen Heath ("Film and System: Terms of Analysis, Part II," pp. 91-113).

21. Robert Stam, "Television News and Its Spectator," in this volume, p. 33.

22. Margaret Morse, "Sport on Television: Replay and Display," in this volume, p. 46.

23. Ibid., p. 45.

24. Ibid., p. 49.

25. Ibid., p. 51.

26. Ibid., p. 61.

27. Tania Modleski, "The Rhythms of Reception: Daytime Television and Women's Work," in this volume, p. 70.

28. Ibid., p. 71.

29. Charlotte Brunsdon, "*Crossroads:* Notes on Soap Opera," in this volume, p. 79.

30. Sandy Flitterman, "The *Real* Soap Operas: TV Commercials," in this volume, p. 86.

31. Ibid., p. 93.

32. Ibid., p. 94.

33. Ibid., p. 95.

34. Robert Allen, "On Reading Soaps: A Semiotic Primer," in this volume, p. 104.

35. Ibid., p. 105.

36. Jeanne Allen, "The Social Matrix of Television: Invention in the United States," in this volume, p. 110.

37. Douglas Gomery, "Television, Hollywood, and the Development of Movies Made-for-Television," in this volume, p. 127.

38. Maureen Turim, "Video Art: Theory for a Future," in this volume, p. 133.

39. Ibid., p. 134.

40. Ibid., p. 137.

Loving a Nineteen-Inch Motorola: American Writing on Television

William Boddy

In America, popular literature on television seems as ubiquitous as the medium itself. Publicity images, newspaper reviews, trade magazines, star biographies, profiles of popular programs, coffee-table nostalgia books and popular accounts of the industry crowd the newsstand and bookshelf. Writing on television and its video offspring has exploded in recent years; more than ever, people are reading about the ever-present apparatus *cum* art form. By any standards, however, American writing on television, from journalistic reviewing to scholarly research, has been marked by a parochialism and triviality hardly equal to the medium's proclaimed social importance.

The peculiar position of television in American intellectual life and the specific situating of television studies in American academia have served to isolate television research and its popular literature from the contributions of contemporary social theory and cultural analysis and to keep television criticism in its well-worn paths.

Popular histories of television have constructed a number of enduring myths of the medium, like those of the 1950s "Golden Age" of live drama and newsman-crusader Edward R. Murrow, and the 1970s network programmer as superstar. Such figures, invoked and sustained in the popular literature, have tended to obscure more promising paths of historical enquiry with anecdotal clutter and accepted wisdom.

Practical problems attend the writing of television history. Like the critic of television, the historian is confronted with the endless stream of hetero-geneous programming which floods the medium. Only with the recent

1

founding of program archives and the introduction of inexpensive video tape recorders has the historian been able to separate television forest from tree. Basic reference works have only recently begun to reflect and help direct such enquiry. Like earlier contemporary commentators of Hollywood's studio era, television critics have been slow to address the issue of creative authorship in the medium, more often treating programs as star vehicles or cannon fodder for the ratings wars of network strategists. The auteurist project is new to television historiography, introduced, significantly, through the work of two British researchers.[1] In any event, much more needs to be known about the aesthetic conventions and production conditions of specific television program forms before work in authorship can be much more than a compiling of credit lists. More sophisticated work on authorship waits on a more complete aesthetic and historical understanding of the medium.

If recent works in television history do promise the tools for a more rigorous and informative view of the production of television programming, a similar sophistication is only rarely evident in television criticism. Journalistic criticism of television has its roots in radio reviewing and reporting on the one hand, and in film criticism on the other; the mix of gossip, press release and moralistic preaching has been familiar to all of them. The daily television critic faces frustrations of space and deadlines, and the frequent difficulty of gaining access to material for previewing. More importantly, the critic typically must take on the simultaneous tasks of program reviewer, industry reporter, celebrity columnist and social critic. Traditionally, television critics were drafted into the lowly-esteemed job from every journalistic beat, without specific preparation in dramatic criticism. Confusion seems at the heart of many television critics' task, not only between the poles of criticism and publicity, but also in a deeper equivocation in the very term "television," at once a disorderly collection of discrete programs, a technological device and an enormous industry. In the semantic confusion, the possibility of articulating television's aesthetic specificity seems doomed. A critic complained in 1969 that "television . . . is not one of the arts but a mere transmitter of them. How do you love a 19-inch Motorola or a network vice-president?"[2]

Television criticism has clearly overrepresented what used to be known as "quality" programming: prime-time drama, network "specials," documentaries and imported drama on public television. News programs, talk shows, dramatic serials, non-network material, children's programming and television commercials have all been slighted or completely excluded from critical commentary. The reviewers' emphasis on the discrete dramatic program or event deflects critical attention from those program forms which seem most characteristic of the medium.

In part reflecting their difficulty in coming to terms with notions of the artistic specificity of the medium, critics have often tended to view television in monolithic terms as a social institution. Emblematic of reviewer as cultural crusader is Jack Gould, broadcasting and television critic of the *New York Times* from 1942-1971. Described by a fellow critic as a "sharp reporter but a menace as a reviewer," Gould was scored in a 1959 Fund for the Republic report on television criticism as "short on aesthetic and long on morals."[3] One temptation of the television critic has always been to use the occasion of the program nominally under consideration for the venting of generalized cultural complaint or commentary. Such occasions rarely make for incisive criticism. The *New York Times'* enduring policy, under Gould and his successor John O'Connor, seems to be, in Robert Sklar's words, "to make television appear so boring that *Times* readers will lose interest in the medium."[4]

It would be misguided to seek the roots of the general weaknesses of television criticism in the policies of individual publications or reviewers. Daily broadcasting critics have always been, in Charles Siepman's phrase, "the retail agents of research";[5] the real problems lie elsewhere. The faults of television's journalists, critics and popular historians are symptomatic of more deep-seated weaknesses in academic work on television in the United States. The nature of the theoretical and empirical research which constitute television studies in America (and frame the everyday encounters with television in the popular press) reflects television's particular academic context in the study of popular culture and mass communication in America. An examination of this intellectual and institutional positioning may help explain the present state of television's popular literature.

Rolf Meyersohn wrote recently that "until the 1930s, there was no systematic effort to understand or even describe popular culture sociologi-cally."[6] The dominant tradition of television and media studies in postwar America emerged from a confrontation with this early work on popular culture. The study of mass media as part of a project of cultural criticism was brought to America in the 1930s by Max Horkheimer, Theodor Adorno and other Frankfurt School refugees. These left-wing culture critics used earlier emblematic of 20th-century culture. Leo Lowenthal, summarizing the critical position of the research at Horkheimer's Institute for Social Research, noted: commodity capitalism. The Frankfurt School critics saw the possibilities for contestation or negation of the social order traditionally offered by high art thoroughly restricted by the new mass culture and its media. Like many contemporary conservative social theorists, the Marxist culture critics felt a deep pessimism about the replacement of the interpersonal ties of community (family, neighborhood, workplace) by the impersonal relations created by urbanization and industrialization. The media audiences, unprotected by the weakening primary ties of traditional community, were seen as passive objects of direct manipulation by the new tools of mass persuasion. The critics' fears grew from the success of the tabloid newspaper and of broadcast advertising in the United States and the rise of fascist culture in Europe. Their pessimistic view of the new media audiences as an atomized mass found an echo in the rhetoric of the new advertising and public relations industries. Nineteen-twenties ad man Bruce Barton literalized the critics' fears in his description of the new radio audience as "human atoms, separated by hundreds of miles, yet acting at that hour as if some invisible hand united them with a common expectation."[7]

The culture critics viewed the operation of this invisible hand of commodity capitalism in the new media with undisguised horror. The organization of popular taste along the demands of the consumer market was a crucial condition of the alienated consciousness the Frankfurt School critics saw as emblematic of 20th-century culture. Leo Lowenthal, summarizing the critical position of the research at Horkheimer's Institute for Social Research, noted:

> The starting point is not market data. Empirical research . . . is laboring under the false hypothesis that the consumer's choice is the decisive social phenomenon from which one should begin further analysis. We first ask: What are the functions of cultural communication within the total process of a society? . . . We would insist on finding out how taste is fed to the consumers as a specific outgrowth of the technological, political and economic conditions and interests of the masters in the sphere of production. We want to investigate what 'likes' and 'dislikes' really mean in social terms.[8]

The early culture critics undoubtedly slighted the peculiarities of particular forms of popular culture in pursuit of a global theory of mass society. Their opposition of the producer of popular culture against a vision of the autonomous creator of high art betrayed a deep-seated cultural nostalgia and elitism. Furthermore, the model of media influence they elaborated, where effects are simple, direct and powerful, was subject to extensive revision at the hands of researchers who followed them. It would be a mistake, however, to collapse the American culture critics of the 1930s into the tradition of conservative critics of "mass society." Even though their vision of the media as all-powerful manipulators of an atomized, passive audience is untenable, the critics did offer an account of the media linking social structure, subjectivity and cultural form.

Nearly all American work in culture and communication since the 1930s has pulled away from the culture critics' interrogation of social process and culture form into more narrowly-conceived empirical studies. Communication research has almost single-mindedly taken the second path of an opposition Paul Lazarsfeld offered in the 1940s between cultural criticism and what he called administrative research. The postwar emphasis on quantitative communications studies—Lazarsfeld's "administrative research"—set the dominant intellectual context of television studies in the United States.

The new generation of communication researchers has modified or refuted the earlier accounts of media influence, but its chief concern has been the pursuit of methodological refinements of empirical studies. While still concerned with media effects, such studies sought to specify the conditions and means under which the media would have their greatest persuasive effect. Television and media studies in the United States are generally taught in schools of journalism or communication, and the positioning of television research alongside the crafts of reporting, advertising and public relations has encouraged communication researchers to pursue questions of more or less direct utility to the communication industry. As Paul Lazarsfeld noted in 1949:

> Communication research is an expensive undertaking. It could not go on if the communications industries were not contributing funds, and they would not contribute funds if they did not see some practical result.[9]

While pursuing methodological refinements, American communication research since the 1930s has turned its attention away from questions of theory and cultural form.

The culmination of the second generation of communication research came with the "uses and gratifications" model of the 1950s and 1960s. The celebrated inversion of the model of media effects—no longer what the media do to people but what people do with the media—seemed to offer a way beyond the passive, monolithic audience of the earlier researchers. Using the tools of the controlled experiment, content analysis and the audience survey, the new researchers sought a model allowing for an active, heterogeneous audience. With the new "sciences" of demographics and psychographics, researchers hoped to account for both individual audience differences and the role of intervening subgroups and opinion leaders in media's influence.

Much of the uses and gratifications research has been the academic equivalent of advertising's market research, where the pursuit of ever-finer distinctions and profiles of potential markets and individual consumers has led the way to an increasing penetration of commodities in everyday life. What the new communication researchers gave up, however, was the theoretical leverage to inquire into either the specific determination of particular media forms or the relation of media to social process. The uses and gratifications model tended to abstract the audience into bundles of *a priori* psychological functions or reified aggregates, reducing theory to correlations among free-floating variables, essentially nôn-falsifiable. The model provided no account of the relationship between their unproblematic psychological determinants and the social order.

The theoretical weaknesses of the functionalist uses and gratifications school stand out most clearly when offered to support positions of public policy. The proliferation of narrowly constructed empirical studies generated a confusion of divergent findings without the theoretical rigor necessary for generalization and policy making. An example is the contradictory responses to the Surgeon General's 1972 report on television violence; there were enough conflicting data in the huge study to supply both sides of the public debate with ammunition for years.

The most striking attempt to bring the social scientists' uses and gratifications model to broad issues of public policy was Herbert Gans' *Popular Culture and High Culture* (1974). Gans attacks the earlier cultural critics for their elitism, ascribing their posture to their threatened intellectual and class status in postwar egalitarian America. The critics were, for Gans, guilty of bad faith. In place of their aesthetic dismissal of popular culture, Gans sets up a non-evaluative typology of five separate "taste cultures." The various taste cultures are organized through Gans' elaboration of the uses and gratifications model; they are abstract social aggregates united by their common uses of general media forms. Moving beyond the traditional cognitive models of the audience, Gans adds "aesthetic urges," wish-fulfillment, self-realization and enhanced leisure time as constituents of taste cultures.[10]

Gans defines leisure negatively, as an escape from the working day and the achievement of a "minimum of boredom."[11] The terms proposed here reproduce the rhetoric of the modern consumer society, for example in Gans' celebration of the housewife who, breaking free of the dead weight of tradition, finds self-expression in decorating her home according to plans in mass-market women's magazines.[12]

Against Lowenthal's warning to the analyst of consumer behavior, Gans begins, and ends, with market data: "In a democratic society, a policy-relevant value judgement must begin with the notion that taste cultures are chosen by people and cannot exist without them." Gans refuses Lowenthal's interrogation of the social meaning of consumer tastes by arguing that the moguls of the media industries are so close to public taste as to function as their "representatives," "even if they are also tough-minded and cynical business men and women at the same time."[13] If Gans here rejects investigation into the issues of agency and democratic access to the means of cultural production, he also has difficulty in accounting for cultural change in any but a circular manner. Explicitly citing George Gerbner's work in uses and gratifications, Gans argues that changes in the "fashions" of popular culture forms follow changing uses and gratifications of the audience.[14] Aesthetic determination and historical agency completely fall away in this non-falsifiable schema.

Gans' model of marketplace pluralism, where the consumer function defines cultural and social processes, views the media as neutral instruments of social consensus, "channels which the various interest groups and subcultures of American society try to fill with news which presents their viewpoints positively and those of their opponents negatively."[15] The state apparatus in Gans' pluralist model intervenes to ensure "subcultural" programming, adjudicating impassively the demands of competing interest groups.

Prevented from aesthetic or political judgements upon the different taste cultures, and theoretically ill-equipped to interrogate either social structure or the market organization of popular taste, the only policy options available to Gans' model are bland calls for greater market choice. Culture is evacuated from the arena of political action for Gans in his mechanical and non-reciprocal linking of taste cultures to economic and educational status. "The educational and economic prerequisites of high culture use are such that it will always be the culture of a small public," Gans claims.[16] Furthermore, "democracies must and do function even when citizens are not educated."[17] Instead of a policy of democratizing access to the cultural apparatus, or challenging the market's definitions of audience "tastes," Gans merely argues for more market options: a few more channels on television and programming for the poor funded by federal anti-poverty agencies. The unchallenged marketplace assumptions and the calls for a consumerist "cultural pluralism" make Gans sound at times like nothing so much as a cable entrepreneur plying a credulous city council: "Subcultural programming would enable audiences to find content best suited to their needs and wants, thus increasing their aesthetic and other satisfactions, and the relevance of culture in their lives."[18]

Gans' relegation of the politics of cultural practice to the invisible hand of the market are echoed in a different context in the traditional American academic view of international communication. The cry of "free flow of information" evades analysis of the unequal access to the means of communication and the legacies of colonialism and economic inequality. Nations, like Gans' taste cultures and interest groups, will find expression and self-realization in the marketplace, or not at all.

If Gans' *Popular Culture and High Culture* demonstrates the importance of dominant functionalist communication research in developing cultural or political policy, the roots can be found in a fundamental theoretical impoverishment. Progress toward a genuine theory of television will only come about through a reconceptualization of basic terms by questioning the institutional and disciplinary frames connoted by the very words "communication" and "mass media."

The positivist bias in traditional television research, as Raymond Williams and others have pointed out, has construed communication as a process of transporting unproblematic *a priori* messages in neutral media vehicles between abstracted human agents. The specification "mass" in relation to this mechanistic schema, aside from the term's frequently pejorative political connotations, suggests an unhelpful opposition between the processes of signification in television and other media and those of interpersonal communication. "Mass" communication messages are seen as socially and technologically mediated, while face-to-face encounters are privileged by implication as transparent, "natural," beyond social and historical determinations. The term "mass communication" sets up undigested or spurious affinities among divergent cultural practices on the basis of technological or institutional characteristics, while it suppresses common ties with other cultural signifying practices, like speech, non-verbal communication, figurative representation, literature, or systems of dress.

In the dominant American model, communication becomes a cognitive, instrumental process, its privileged mode that of persuasion. The complex determinations of television discourse become ahistorical constructs of imputed audience psychology matched with unproblematic readings of the medium's manifest content. Such an impoverished view of cultural process has produced hopelessly global models of communication, like the schematic diagrams found in traditional undergraduate textbooks, where boxes and arrows link sender and receiver, stimulus and response, in ever more intricate and uninformative design.

If dominant American research on television has lost the theoretical grasp on subjectivity and social form offered by the Frankfurt School culture critics, recent work in social theory offers television studies a way out of its impasse. Critical work on television as an industry must be more rigorously grounded in the study of its history and economics. Always marked by significant vertical integration, the communication industry in the United States is undergoing significant horizontal integration, a change which must be reflected in the way television studies is constructed as a subject. The heretofore generally separate cultural industries—motion pictures, broadcasting, publishing and cable—are increasingly merging with the industries of telecommunications and data processing. The "information society" promised by AT&T is indisputably nearer; the transformation of information and culture into rigorously packaged commodity forms has taken a qualitative leap. At the same time corporations and technologies are remaking the workplace, especially the world of the white collar worker. The growing consolidation and importance of the culture-information industries in the American economy make more urgent the analysis of particular conditions, routines and ideologies of the producers of contemporary culture. Recent theoretical work on culture and social formation may help to inform such economic and historical studies of media institutions.

Similarly, challenges to the traditional models of national development and media allow the re-posing of the problems of international communication. Work in the analysis of capitalism as a global political and economic system, for example, can help challenge the models implied by "stages of development" and "free flow of information," and bring new analytical tools to the problems of cultural sovereignty and nation-building. Again, historical events make such reformulations especially timely. Direct satellite broadcasting threatens to obliterate national systems of broadcasting and trivialize the notion of national sovereignty in communication. Satellite broadcasting would open entire continents to transnational corporate advertising and programming. Remote satellite sensing would give First World energy corporations access to resource information beyond the means of the surveyed country. The growing technological capabilities make increasingly untenable the prevailing assumptions of world consensus and the role of media in national development. The rising objections of Third World nations to existing exchanges of technology and information have resulted in the growing isolation of the United States in international bodies like the United Nations. Research on international communication must proceed from an appreciation of the increasingly geopolitical significance of communication and economic development, and national sovereignty.

If a more rigorous theoretical account of social process in relation to the infrastructural role of domestic and international communication is needed to inform and position historical and economic analyses, social theory needs to be reinvested into the study of television programming as well. Repudiating the instrumental model of communication, such textual analysis needs to consider both the agency of a particular symbolic form and an account of the social process of the construction of its meaning. Such studies should address communication as a socially-constrained system of textual production and reception, not as a reified exchange through neutral media between abstract social beings. The integration of social theory could see the media not as the neutral arena of competing social groups, or merely the stakes of political struggle, but as the site of the production and engagement of political struggle as well. Until the media are conceived as something other than the transparent instruments of pre-existing messages, little work on the specific ideological agency of television can begin.

Such work on television and ideology needs to be sensitive to the specific conditions and procedures of the medium's production and reception. Among these peculiarities are the particular time structures of television programming. Issues of segmentation and flow are crucial from the level of the television season, the weekly and daily schedules, to the alternation of program and commercial within the individual television work.

The way in which television as an apparatus positions the spectator-subject, and the ways in which such subject construction relate to partriarchy and the social formation have to be accounted for in the varieties of television programming. Television researchers need to explore television's specific use of direct address, the live broadcast, its conventions of realism, and the construction of a structured hierarchy of image, dialogue, voice-over and printed text. Finally, one of the most striking qualities of television discourse, its complex structures of intertextuality, has to be worked out.

There is reason to hope that such an ambitious program of research in television may not be unthinkable. Recent teaching and writing in television studies reflect a changing sociological profile of the field. An important part of this shift is the increasing attention researchers and theorists in film and literary studies have shown the medium. Television historians are showing growing concern with issues of theory and historiography, and critics and theorists display a new receptivity to European theories of social formation and textual analysis. Finally, recent work in artists' video has moved away from the hermeticism of many earlier American videomakers who repressed the implication of broadcast television in their work. Some of the most interesting recent video work productively engages with many of the same issues (such as segmentation, intertextuality and representation) raised in textual analysis of commercial television.

Emerging work in television studies in America, then, challenges the dominant positivist tradition of communication research, in favor of what Lazarsfeld called cultural criticism. If recent theorists reject the model of "administrative research," there is nevertheless little sense of a return to the earlier Frankfurt School theories of subjectivity and culture. Much of the new work, following Brecht, Benjamin and Enzensberger, rejects the pessimism and theoretical closure of the earlier culture critics. Instead, the new cultural critics recognize the social contradictions within the prevailing uses of media, and with them the grounds for cultural intervention. Their recent contributions from social theory, historiography and textual analysis offer hope for a *theory* of television worthy of the name.

NOTES

1. Christopher Wicking and Tise Vahimagi, *The American Vein: Directors and Directions in Television* (New York: E.P. Dutton, 1979).

2. Richard Burgheim, "Television Reviewing," *Harpers* (August 1969), pp. 98-101.

3. Ibid., p. 100.

4. Robert Sklar, *Prime-Time America* (New York: Oxford University Press, 1980), p. 149.

5. Quoted in Peter E. Mayeux, "Stated Functions of Television Critics," *Journal of Broadcasting* Vol. 13 No. 1 (Winter 1968-69), p. 37.

6. Rolf Meyersohn, "The Sociology of Popular Culture: Looking Forwards and Backwards," *Communication Research* Vol. 5 No. 3 (July 1978), p. 331.

7. Quoted in Charles Henry Stamps, *The Concept of the Mass Audience in American Broadcasting* (New York: Arno Press, 1979), p. 41.

8. Leo Lowenthal, "Historical Perspectives on Popular Culture," in *Mass Culture: The Popular Arts in America*, ed. Bernard Rosenberg and David M. White (Glencoe, IL: The Free Press, 1957), p. 56.

9. Paul Lazarsfeld and Frank Stanton, eds., *Communication Research 1948-1949* (New York: Harper and Brothers, 1949), p. xvii.

10. Herbert J. Gans, *Popular Culture and High Culture* (New York: Harper and Row, 1974). p. 67.

11. Ibid., p. 131.

12. Ibid., p. 59; see also Christopher Lasch, "Mass Culture Reconsidered," *democracy* Vol. 1 No. 4 (October 1981), pp. 11-14.

13. Gans, p. ix.

14. Ibid., p. viii.

15. Ibid., p. 39.

16. Ibid., p. 136.

17. Ibid., p. 144.

18. Ibid., p. 133.

The Concept of Live Television:
Ontology as Ideology

Jane Feuer

Not much has been written on the aesthetics of television. One of the reasons for this becomes obvious as one sets out to correct this lack: no one is entirely sure exactly what the entity "television" is. At the level of the economic and cultural base, debate rages over whether the technology is cause or effect. In his book on television, Raymond Williams addresses this issue at some length and with some success, concluding that communications technology in general and specifically television "is at once an intention and an effect of a particular social order."[1] At the level of aesthetic superstructure, an even more difficult contradiction arises: Is television a thing-in-itself (i.e., a specific signifying practice) or is it merely a means of transmission for other processes of signification (cinema, news, "live" events)? And related to this: Should an aesthetics of television be historical and descriptive (based on received network practice) or speculative (based on an assumed essence of the medium)? The differences between television and its supposed linguistic sister, cinema, are too great not to see television as a qualitatively different medium, but granted this, what is specific to the diversity *within* television? These are the terms in which the dilemmas tend to be posed. Both network advocates and alternative video enthusiasts alike tend to argue from an assumed "essence" of the medium as if the history of that medium were not inexorably linked to what one assumes to be its essence.

One of the few sustained attempts at a speculative television aesthetics falls victim to just such a lack of historical consciousness. Herbert Zettl's aesthetic reflects the confusion of essence with history that also dominates industry discourse. In turn Zettl reinforces industry practice through his widely-used textbooks for television production courses, thus creating a closed circuit validating received television aesthetics. Zettl's view is that the essential nature of television is related to the concept of live television. Unlike film, which freezes events in frames, television in its very essence (that is to say the essence of its technology) consists of process. The ontology of the television image thus consists in movement, process, "liveness" and presence:

> While in film each frame is actually a static image, the television image is continually moving, very much in the manner of the Bergsonian *durée*. The scanning beam is constantly trying to complete an always incomplete image. Even if the image on the screen seems at rest, it is structurally in motion. Each television frame is always in a state of becoming. While the film frame is a concrete record of the past, the television frame (when live) is a reflection of the living, constantly changing present. The live televised event and the event itself exist in the same present. This is impossible with film. But as a record of the past, film affords us great control in the re-creation of an event. . . . Obviously, the filmic event is largely *medium dependent*, while television in its essence (live) is largely *event dependent*. [emphasis Zettl's.] While film can reflect upon our world or pretend to being current, it is totally deterministic; the end of the story is fixed as soon as the reel is put on the projector. Live television, on the other hand, lives off the instantaneousness and uncertainty of the moment very much the way we do in actual life. The fact that television can record images and then treat them in a filmic fashion in no way reduces the aesthetic potential and uniqueness of television when used live.[2]

Zettl's phenomenology of television echoes André Bazin's "realist" ontology of cinema without admitting, as Bazin does, that "realism" is based on artifice. To equate "live" television with "real life" is to ignore all those determinations standing between the "event" and our perception of it—technology and institutions, to mention two. Nevertheless, it is difficult to demonstrate the ideological nature of such an aesthetic.

For, from a certain technological and perceptual point of view, television *is* live in a way film can never be. Events *can* be transmitted as they occur; television (and videotape) look more "real" to us than does film. The point at which Zettl's argument slides from technological "fact" to ideological "interpretation" is difficult to determine. It is not enough to point out, as I intend to do shortly, that network practice scarcely ever (indeed never in pure form) exploits television's potential for "unmediated" transmission (assuming that the very selection and treatment of events did not in itself preclude total presence). For this merely leaves things on Zettl's own terms (i.e., the essence is live but it just hasn't been exploited yet). One has rather to critique the "live" aesthetic at the base of its philosophical assumptions. Zettl's logical development from the nature of electronic scanning to that of being in a "state of becoming" is itself philosophically and ideologically determined. In order to have an argument at all, Zettl must first personify the apparatus, animate and humanize physical processes. Thus his whole argument is founded upon a metaphor. Moreover, it is possible that we perceive video as more "real" because the industry tells us it is "live." Perhaps the ideology at least in part determines the perception. Ontology and ideology are confounded at the very base of Zettl's argument in his attempt to posit an "essence" which is ideologically neutral.

It is at this basic level of the ideology of the television apparatus that Stephen Heath and Gillian Skirrow attempt to critique received notions about television current affairs programming. Heath and Skirrow argue that, due to its electronic nature, television is far more capable of affirming its own mode as one of absolute presence than is film, even though the vast majority of television programs are not broadcast "live." They argue convincingly that by postulating an equivalence between time of event, time of television creation and transmission-viewing time, television as an institution identifies all messages emanating from the apparatus as "live." The live program is thus taken as the very definition of television. In this way, television as an ideological apparatus positions the spectator into its "imaginary" of presence and immediacy.[3]

Heath and Skirrow define the ideology of the television apparatus according to its temporal, electronic dimension, but suggest that other factors are involved, such as the closeness, availability and interpellative nature of the television image itself. Indeed, as television in fact becomes less and less a "live" medium in the sense of an equivalence between time of event and time of transmission, the medium in its own practices seems to insist more and more upon an ideology of the live, the immediate, the direct, the spontaneous, the real. This is true of both program formats and metadiscourse (references to the "Golden Age" of live television, "Live from New York, it's Saturday Night," the many local spots glorifying "instant" camera news coverage, "live" coverage of the Olympics, etc.).

Television's self-referential discourse plays upon the connotative richness of the term "live," confounding its simple or technical denotations with a wealth of allusiveness. Even the simplest meaning of "live"—that the time of the event corresponds to the transmission and viewing times—reverberates with suggestions of "being there" . . . "bringing it to you as it really is." The contradictory television coinage "live on tape" captures the slippage involved. From an opposition between live and recorded broadcasts, we expand to an equation of "the live" with "the real." Live television is *not* recorded; live television is *alive*; television is living, real, not dead. From asserting its reality to asserting its vitality, television's metadiscourse generates a circuit of meanings from the single term "live." The very lack of precision in the meaning thus generated helps rather than hinders the process.

Yet American network television, in the very process of technological advancement, has nearly destroyed even the simplest meaning of "live" transmission. Videotape, though perceptually equivalent to "live" transmission, preserves the event, eliminating uniqueness and thus aura.[4] The introduction of computerized editing equipment is making video editing as flexible as film editing. Curiously, the most sophisticated new technology— such as computerized graphics and instant replay techniques—was developed precisely for the purpose of recording and freezing those "live" sports events that were supposed to be the ontological glory of the medium. Anyone who watched the 1980 Olympics had to be aware that the idea of an event happening *once* is no longer a part of this highly packaged occasion. Clearly, in terms of this simplest conception of the "live," current American network television is best described as a collage of film, video and "live," all interwoven into a complex and altered time scheme. Why, then, does the idea of television as essentially a live medium persist so strongly as an ideology?

Raymond Williams invokes the concept of "flow" as a way of explaining the effect of immediacy and presence the experience of television gives. The defining characteristic of broadcasting, both as technology and as cultural form, Williams argues, is one of sequence or flow. Thus the "true series is not the published sequence of program items but this sequence transformed by another kind of sequence" (advertising, previews, etc.).[5] Television becomes a continuous, never-ending sequence in which it is impossible to separate out individual texts. Heath and Skirrow amend Williams' concept of flow to that of "flow and regularity," i.e., within the planned flow, certain elements, such as series and commercials, predictably recur.[6] The experience of flow, I believe, relates as well to the television viewing situation. The set is in the home, as part of the furniture of one's daily life; it is always available; one may intercept the flow at any point. Indeed the "central fact" of television may be that it is designed to be watched intermittently, casually, and without full concentration. Only the commercials command and dazzle; and these only if you stay to watch them. (We shall see that some television formats are explicitly designed not to be watched as a totality.) Television, then, because of the property of flow, seems "real" in another sense; unlike cinema, it is an entirely ordinary experience, and this makes it seem natural in a way going to the movies no longer does.

Yet "flow" as Williams describes it is pure illusion. It would be more accurate to say that television is constituted by a dialectic of segmentation and flow. Television is based upon program segments, advertising segments, trailer segments, etc. Williams says the property of flow makes it impossible to "segment" the flux of television for analysis. Yet he could just as easily have said that in television, segmentation is not a process of an analyst isolating fragments from the flow. For, unlike narrative cinema, segmentation is already a property of the text. Williams should more accurately say that television possesses segmentation without closure, for this is what he really means by "flow."

Flow as such is neither natural nor technologically determined. It is an historically specific result of network practice: "flow charts" are constructed by network executives prior to being reconstituted by structuralists. Flow, as a seamless scanning of the world, is valorized at the expense of an equally great fragmentation. Television exploits its assumed "live" ontology as ideology. In the concept of live television, flow and unity are emphasized, giving a sense of immediacy and wholeness, even though network practice belies such unity, even in—especially in—"live" coverage of events such as the Olympics.

One could imagine a rather Bazinian coverage of the Olympic games, but in fact Olympic coverage follows network practice rather than determining it. "Whole" events are segmented and fragmented through excessive commentary used for narrativization: the figure-skating pairs competition becomes the saga of the young couple's unrealized dream. We cut back and forth between discrete events. Boring events such as cross-country skiing ("boring" being the equivalent of "not designed for television") are enlivened through time-lapse editing. Instant replays and slow motion endlessly analyze the unique and spontaneous events in the name of the broadcast. The ideology of liveness overrides all of this. Network television never truly exploits its capacity for instantaneous and unmediated transmission. Only the ideological connotations of live television are exploited in order to overcome the contradiction between flow and fragmentation in television practice.

One program in particular has always seemed to me to epitomize this concept of an ideology of liveness overcoming fragmentation. This program—ABC's *Good Morning, America*—is perhaps the ultimate product of flow calculated to position the spectator. *Good Morning, America* is consciously charted for intermittent, early-morning viewing patterns, with planned repetitions as people go off to work. Moreover, *Good Morning, America* was calculated to hit a precise "target" audience: middle to lower middle class, slightly ethnic mix, largely female. According to *TV Guide:*

> No program in television's brief history has been constructed with as much self-conscious care as *Good Morning, America*; every minute is the product of exhaustive attitudinal research.[7]

The *TV Guide* article goes on to say that television executives believe that, with the influx of cable and cassette programming, the stuff of present-day morning shows (national and local news, features and highly-produced "coping" segments) will be "the future of American television in network form."

Good Morning, America is constructed around the most extreme fragmentation—a mosaic of film, video and "live" segments emanating from New York, Washington, and Chicago, with features on how to clean fireplaces and how to use an electric blanket, news of the Iranian crisis and the Olympics, ads for Sears soft contact lenses and Lucky's pinto beans, not to mention Rona Barrett's review of *Cruising*, Joan Baez' visit to Cambodia, and the last in a series of "great romances." All of these (and more) were part of a broadcast I videotaped for analysis during the 1980 Olympics. But it is not so much the variety of content that distinguishes the *Good Morning, America* format; it is rather the extreme spatial fragmentation which characterizes the form of the show, regardless of the content on any given day. Analysis of the flow of the program I studied reveals constant alternation of media (live, film, video) and of locale. Both commercials and programming alternate local and network sources. The local weather forecast is inserted within the network forecast. Segments emanate from New York, Chicago, Lake Placid. Yet all this is unified by the presence of David Hartman—the ultimate father figure—in the anchor chair. David's function—aside from participating in the segments—is to remind the viewer both what time it is (and thus of the "live" nature of the broadcast) and of what will occur in future segments within a clearly designated future time. The show is obsessed with its own liveness, as symbolized by the logo with the time and upcoming segment in a box. David acts as custodian of flow and regularity, the personification of a force which creates unity out of fragmentation.

An understanding of David's role in "anchoring" the flow of *Good Morning, America* can profit immensely from work done on a comparable British television program, the BBC's *Nationwide*.[8] In *The 'Nationwide' Audience*, David Morley adapts Steve Neale's distinction between the "ideological problematic" of a text and its "mode of address." The former, according to Morley, refers to "the field and range of its representational possibilities," whereas the "mode of address" involves the text's relation to, and positioning of, its audience.[9] As I understand this distinction, the opposition is not simply one of form versus content in the traditional literary sense. Rather, the mode of address relates specifically to spectator positioning; the ideological problematic refers not merely to the dominant set of issues raised by a text—its overt agenda—but also to hidden agendas and structuring absences. For example, Morley found that many working-class groups reject the overall tone of the program (its mode of address) while sharing its ideological problematic of populism which they articulate as "common sense." The distinction aids in an analysis of differences between responses of "real" audiences and the anticipated reaction of an "ideal" viewer constructed by the analyst from the text itself.

At first glance the flow of *Good Morning, America* would seem to be wholly contained in the realm of "mode of address," since the show's conventions for spectator positioning function above and beyond any particular discourse conveyed therein. Rather than undertake a detailed study of the flow of a particular program, I would like to analyze the way in which the circuit of address on *Good Morning, America* propagates an ideology of "liveness" overcoming fragmentation. I shall go on to argue, however, that this mode of address is embedded in a mutually reinforcing ideological problematic of national and family unity.

Every morning, *Good Morning, America* makes use of a monitor situated in David Hartman's fictional living room to interview subjects in different locations and to summon up other members of the *"Good Morning, America* family"—Steve Bell with the news (in Washington) or John Coleman with the weather (in Chicago). The use of the internal monitor for "live" interviews seems to be something of a metaphor for the show as a whole as it brings the nation together. The interviews—regardless of content—are shot from the same camera positions and depend for their effect on the confusion of David's space with the space of the interviewee with the space of the spectator. The typical sequence of shots during interviews seems at first to be a variant of the shot/reverse-shot pattern of classical Hollywood editing. We are given a look at each subject from the other's point of view, thus "suturing" our own subjectivity into the text.

But a closer examination reveals that the reverse shot from the point of view of the subject onto David—the "answer" shot—is deficient. For although we frequently see the internal monitor from a position over David's shoulder it is impossible to frame David over the subject's shoulder (at least from any camera position within David's New York studio). Instead of placing us within the world of the show, the fragmentation of space actually places the viewer *outside* the system, subject always to the mediation of David's look. Although at the beginning of each segment the shot over David's shoulder reveals the boundaries of the internal television monitor, the cut *into* the space of the internal television makes it seem as if the interviewee and David were occupying the same space. But in fact the camera taking the close-ups of the interview subject has to be in the studio with that subject, far away from David's "live" glance. As we cut back and forth between the internal monitor (its edges eliminated in close-ups) and David, the distinction between "live" (in the sense of in the same space, "being there") and "live at a second remove" (same time, different spaces) is obliterated. The editing creates a temporary illusion of David and the subject being in the same "live" space together, a space that we as the audience share. For if the internal monitor can bring the presence and immediacy of the subject into David's living room, cannot *Good Morning, America* thrust its own presence into *our* living room?

The sleight of hand the live flow conceals is this: David mediates our vision of the interview subject and the subject's discourse whereas we do not control David's discourse. (By "David's discourse" I mean the flow of shots as chosen by the director; the "real" David Hartman controls only the questioning process which is in turn controlled by the written and unwritten rules of television journalism.) David sets the circuit of address: he may look into the internal monitor and he may look at us; but the guest looks only at David—so that David mediates all discourse. The format denies the possibility of direct address from the interviewee to spectator (only members of the *Good Morning, America* family may address us directly) while the "live" flow and, especially, the cuts to within the internal screen maintain an illusion of directness and presence. What control over the discourse we *do* have in common with David was revealed on March 26, 1980, when, in a moment of self-reflexivity, David switched off Steve Bell on the monitor when Steve ribbed David about his ineptitude at baseball! But the *raison d'être* of the flow of *Good Morning, America* is to prevent us turning off David except at times designated by *Good Morning, America's* discourse.

John Caughie, in articulating the Heath/Skirrow position on the mode of address of the television apparatus, has argued that flow "strives to ease unification and repress contradiction, to allow a plurality of content to disguise a singularity of representation."[10] This would seem a perfect description of the mode of address of *Good Morning, America*. No matter what the ideological position of the interviewee, it will be sifted through the "televisualizing" screen of David's discourse, which is, of course, the discourse of American network television with its notions of "fairness" and "showing both sides."

In terms of mode of address, then, I have argued that notions of "liveness" lend a sense of flow which overcomes extreme fragmentation of space. This, in turn, allows *Good Morning, America* to insinuate itself into our lives. But must the real spectator assume the position the text structures for him/her? David Morley argues that the view of spectator positioning advanced by Heath and Caughie attributes far too much potency to flow and to the ability of the televisual discourse to construct subjects (as if those subjects were not already situated within their society's flow of ideologies). *The 'Nationwide' Audience* significantly qualifies those readings which see the text as a "hypodermic" shot directly into the consciousness of the spectator; Morley argues convincingly from his data that audiences coming from different class positions may accept the "mode of address" without accepting the "ideological problematic" and vice versa.[11]

Although I am perfectly willing to submit my reading of *Good Morning, America* to empirical testing, I am not certain what I would be "testing" *for*. For—at least in the case of *Good Morning, America*—the mode of address *is* to a great extent its ideological problematic. It would not be accurate to say that the show "carries" certain ideologies which the viewer may then accept or reject. *Good Morning, America's* mode of address both produces and reproduces its ideological problematic of family unity and national unity-within-diversity. According to an ABC vice-president, "The image of David...is one of traditional values; he's perceived as a family man."[12] It does not take a psychoanalytic reading to see that members of the show's family are meant as an ideal family for us, an idealized bourgeois nuclear family with a daddy and (various) mommies, brothers and sisters, fragmented by space but together in time through the power of the television image itself. It is a family similar to many American families in its fragmentation, its mobility, its alienation, yet the *Good Morning, America* family is unified as a direct (it is implied) consequence of television technology. That is to say, television brings families together and keeps them together.

This self-referential component of *Good Morning, America*'s ideological problematic was clarified for me during a segment in which Henry Fonda and his children were "sketched" in separate but intercut filmed interviews in which they spoke "candidly" about each other. Back in the studio, David and the current mommy, Joan Lunden, rhapsodized over what a close family, a "real family," the Fondas were, even though, said Joan, "they don't see each other." Had the Fondas been on live television instead of film, they might actually have "seen" each other on monitors placed in their respective studios.

Television valorizes the nuclear family through its discourses, yet here we have the perfect illustration of the way the medium itself is implicated in the ideology of family unity.

Television, in its liveness, its immediacy, its reality, can create families where none exist. In *Everyday Television: 'Nationwide,'* Charlotte Brunsdon and David Morley refer to the functions of "links and mediation" provided by *Nationwide*'s "self-referential" discourse:

> . . . at many points the *Nationwide* discourse becomes self-referential— *Nationwide* and the *Nationwide* team are not only the mediators who bring the stories to us, but themselves become the subject of the story. This is the 'maximal' development of one consistent thread in the programme—the attempt to establish a close, personalised relationship between the *Nationwide* team and the audience.[13]

Much of *Good Morning, America*'s self-referential discourse acts toward promoting the ideology of family unity, as when we followed the early years of the "*Good Morning, America* baby" or when Joan Lunden herself became pregnant, a subject for frequent discussion in the linking segments. The viewer is enmeshed in the flow of this idealized fiction of family life; and here, I believe, is where the flow and unity of the show may obscure the manipulation implied by its mode of address.

It seems to me the ideology of "liveness" must surely act to suppress contradictions. However, I have difficulty theorizing the level at which this occurs, nor am I able to name *what* it is that occurs when viewing subjects watch *Good Morning, America* under "normal" early morning viewing conditions in the home. The phenomenon I am describing operates somewhere in that netherworld between "effects" and "unconscious work." Although empirical studies of responses of different stratification of audiences (such as Morley's study) can capture the response (or lack of it) to the overall "tone" of a program, I am not convinced that they are articulating responses to the program's mode of address at the level I am situating it.

The problem of testing for responses to the ideology of liveness is further complicated by the fact that *Good Morning, America* itself is based on surveys seeking to give the people what they want. The program's researchers, however, are scarcely interested in the audience as subjects for ideology—they are interested in them as subjects for consumption of the products advertised on the show. Since the audience is *already* "targeted" (a revealing phrase) by class and sex, presumably the "content" of the show is already geared toward those likely to accept its ideological problematic. But how can we determine whether or not the program's mode of address remains opaque to its targeted "ideal" audience, if indeed the ideology of liveness is not precisely an "effect" at all, but rather a generalized ideological stance toward the medium itself?

In trying to figure out how "oppositional readings" of a program such as *Good Morning, America* by its intended audience might occur or perhaps already occur, we remain caught in a hermeneutic circle. Is the spectator positioned by the apparatus, or is the spectator relatively free, and if so, what permits us to analyze texts in the way I have done above, and why is *Good Morning, America* so successful? Or perhaps this manner of articulating the problem is itself the problem?

NOTES

1. Raymond Williams, *Television: Technology and Cultural Form* (New York: Schocken Books, 1975), p. 128.

2. Herbert Zettl, "The Rare Case of Television Aesthetics," *Journal of the University Film Association* Vol. 30 No. 2 (Spring 1978) pp. 3-8.

3. Stephen Heath and Gillian Skirrow, "Television: A World in Action," *Screen* Vol. 18 No. 2 (Summer 1977), pp. 7-59.

4. Walter Benjamin, in "The Work of Art in the Age of Mechanical Reproduction" (in *Illuminations* [New York: Schocken Books, 1969], pp. 220-221), defines the term "aura" as follows: "Even the most perfect reproduction of a work of art is lacking in one element: its presence in time and space, its unique existence at the place where it happens to be... One might subsume the eliminated element in the term 'aura' and go on to say: that which withers in the age of mechanical reproduction is the aura of the work of art."

5. Williams, p. 90.

6. Heath and Skirrow, p. 15.

7. Ron Powers, "How the Networks Wage War For Breakfast-Time Viewers," *TV Guide* (January 12, 1980), pp. 2-6.

8. See Charlotte Brunsdon and David Morley, *Everyday Television: 'Nationwide,'* BFI Television Monographs/No. 10 (London: British Film Institute, 1978); and David Morley, *The 'Nationwide' Audience: Structure and Decoding*, BFI Television Monographs/No. 11 (London: British Film Institute, 1980). These works heavily influenced the revision of the present paper.

9. Morley, p. 139.

10. John Caughie, "The 'World' of Television," *Edinburgh '77 Magazine* No. 1 (1977), pp. 74-82.

11. Morley, p. 138.

12. Powers, p. 6.

13. Brunsdon and Morley, p. 18.

Television News
and
Its Spectator

Robert Stam

Let us take as our point of departure something so obvious that it is often taken for granted, but something which in reality should astonish us: the fact that television news is *pleasurable*. No matter what its specific content, no matter how "bad" the news might be or how "badly" the newscasters or their presentations might offend our individual sensitivies or ideological predilections, watching the news is pleasurable. Even on a hypothetical day of worst-case scenarios—huge jumps in inflation and unemployment, imminent food shortages, nuclear leaks slouching invisibly toward our metropolitan centers—the viewing experience itself would still afford pleasure. Our first question, then, is: *Why* is the news pleasurable?; and our second, intimately linked to the first, is: To what extent can contemporary theoretical models and analytical methods elaborated largely in relation to the fiction film also illuminate television news? How can contemporary methodologies—psychoanalytic, semiotic, dialectical—disengage the operations of television news as part of what Stephen Heath, in another context, has called a "pleasure-meaning-commodity-complex"? What are the specific pleasures of the news and how can we account for them?

Epistemophilia, the love of knowing, provides but a partial explanation. We would have to ask why people *prefer* to know the news through television, and why even those who already "know" the news through alternative media *still* watch the news. Taking our cue from recent work by film theorists such as Christian Metz, Jean-Louis Baudry and Jean-Louis Comolli, we may begin with the pleasuring capacities of the television apparatus itself.[1] By "apparatus," these theorists mean the cinema machine in an inclusive sense —not only its instrumental base of camera, projector and screen but also the spectator as the desiring subject on which the cinematic institution depends as its object and accomplice.

Metz argues in "The Imaginary Signifier" that the cinema spectator identifies first of all with his or her own act of looking, with

> himself as a pure act of perception (as wakefulness, alertness); as condition of possibility of the perceived and hence as a kind of transcendental subject, anterior to every *there is*.[2]

The "primary identification " then, is not with the events or characters depicted on the screen but rather with the act of perception that makes these secondary identifications possible, an act of perception both channeled and constructed by the anterior look of the camera and the projector that stands in for it, granting the spectator the illusory ubiquity of the all-perceiving subject.

The televisual apparatus, quite apart from its "programming," affords pleasures even more multiform and varied than those afforded by the cinema, for the viewer identifies with an even wider array of cameras and looks. The viewer of the evening news, for example, identifies with 1) film cameras and their footage shot around the world (films commissioned by the network, film from other sources, and library and archival material); 2) video cameras and their magnetic residue of images and sounds on tape; and 3) tapeless video cameras directly transmitting images and sounds (the anchors speaking the news in the studio or correspondents on location transmitting via remote). This last category is important, for television, unlike the cinema, allows us to share the literal time of persons who are elsewhere. It grants us not only ubiquity, but *instantaneous* ubiquity. The telespectator of a lunar landing becomes a vicarious astronaut, exploring the moonscape at the same time (technically a fraction of a second later) as the astronauts themselves. The viewer of a live transmission, in fact, can in some respects see better than those immediately on the scene. Multiple cameras facilitate a gratifying multiplicity of perspectives, and video tape and switcher provide the privilege of instant replay, whether of football touchdowns or political assassinations. The televisual apparatus, in short, prosthetically extends human perception, granting an exhilarating sense of visual power to its virtually "all-perceiving" spectator, stretched to the limit in the pure act of watching.

Television's "liveness" guarantees other gratifications. Live transmission makes possible real, as opposed to fabricated, suspense. Will the space mission get off the ground? Will the assassination victim survive? Unlike the cinema, television has to *tell* us, by superimposed captions, whether it is live or recorded. Talk shows *seem* to be transmitted live even when they are prerecorded, whence our occasional double take when an anachronistic allusion makes us realize that we are watching a rerun. Although live transmission forms but a tiny proportion of programming, that tiny portion sets the tone for all of television. In the news, the *part* of direct transmission—the anchor's report, conversations, occasional live special events— metonymically "contaminates" the *whole* of the news. The titles themselves—*Eyewitness News, Action News, Live at Five*—advertise this aliveness as the telos toward which the news presumably tends. In fact, this vivacity is largely fraudulent. The "fast-breaking news" is filmed hours or days before the newscast, and prerecorded correspondents' reports are fastened by rhetorical glue ("Well Walter, the feeling in Washington is . . .") to the directly transmitted studio reports that dominate the newscast. But this illusory feeling of presentness, this constructed impression of total immediacy, constitutes one of the news' undeniable satisfactions.[3]

The first pleasure of the news, then, is narcissistic. Television's heterogeneous resources—film, video tape, direct transmission—confer perceptual powers superior to those of the relatively sluggish and time-bound cinema, a medium that television both "includes" and surpasses with its ability to "cover the world." John Cameron Swayze anticipated this globe-trotting motif, at an earlier stage of technology, by the exotically picaresque title of his *Camel News Caravan*, and contemporary news programs call attention to it by their spherical-line globes and illuminated maps. We become, by virtue of our subject position, the audio-visual masters of the world—television transforms us into armchair imperialists, flattering and reaffirming our sense of power.

The technological supports of this intoxicating sense of power seem, at first glance, remarkably precarious. What do we see on television? We do not see John Chancellor, for he is in a studio in New York; we do not see a picture, for there is no photography involved. We see only a visual configuration, a suggestive aggregation of ionized data, what Yeshayahu Nir calls "immediate iconic presence, conjured up by an electronic scanner's promenade across a screen."[4]

Yet this low-definition image of television, often cited as a token of its "inferiority," in no way inhibits narcissistic identification. It might even be argued that in some respects identification in a medium varies in *inverse* proportion to its representational adequacy. The doubly imaginary nature of the cinema (imaginary in what it represents and imaginary by the nature of its signifier), Metz argues, heightens rather than diminishes the possibilities of identification. The impression of reality is stronger in film than in theater precisely because the phantomlike figures on the screen easily absorb our fantasies and projections.[5] Television, by this same logic, allows a more powerful identification because its signifier entails an even higher degree of imaginariness. It constitutes quintessential illusion, and it is hardly surprising that Marshall McLuhan, from a very different theoretical perspective, insists that its impoverished images, which are ultimately "not even there," make it a "cool" medium in which viewer involvement is all the more "hot" and intense.

Both cinema and television are simulation apparati which not only represent the real but also stimulate intense "subject-effects." For Baudry, the shadowy images on the screen, the darkness of the movie theater, the passive immobility of the spectator and the womblike sealing off of ambient noises and quotidian pressures all foster an artificial state of regression not unlike that engendered by dream. The cinema, for Baudry, constitutes the approximate material realization of an unconscious goal perhaps inherent in the human mind: the regressive desire to return to an earlier state of psychic development, a state of relative narcissism in which desire could be "satisfied" through an enveloping simulated reality in which the separation between one's body and the exterior world, between ego and non-ego, is not clearly defined.

Baudry's cinescopic theory must be "scanned," admittedly, for the purposes of television. Many of the factors that nourish narcissism and regression, which foster the "realer-than-real" effect of which Baudry speaks, simply do not operate in television, at least not in its present conditions of reception. Even apart from the theoretical ambiguities in Baudry's position—the quasi-idealist positing of a trans-historical eternal wish inherent in the psyche, the monolithic model of cinema which fails to allow for either a modified apparatus or for filmic texts which "wake up" and dephantasmize the spectator, the hegemonic slighting of the aural track—his schema requires substantial modification for television. For a complex series of social and historical reasons, the cinema continues to be associated with the privileged space of theater—latter-day heir to the sacred space of ritual, games and tragedy—while television is tied to the mundane surroundings of the average home. Its relatively aura-less presence accompanies our domestic routines. While the ciné-spectator is likely to sit "spellbound in darkness," watching in semi-reverential silence, the telespectator is more likely to be active, mobile and verbal. The lights are more likely to be on, and the viewer exercises a certain control over channel, sound, volume, contrast, and whether or not to turn the apparatus off.

On the other hand, one should not underestimate television's own persuasiveness or its powerful encouragement of regressive and narcissistic attitudes. The smaller screen, while preventing immersion in any deep enveloping space, encourages in other ways a kind of narcissistic voyeurism. Larger than the figures on the screen, we quite literally oversee the world from a sheltered position—all the human shapes parading before us in television's insubstantial pageant are scaled down to lilliputian insignificance, two-dimensional dolls whose height rarely exceeds a foot. The very availability of television, meanwhile, entails a special kind of identification: while the fiction film works its magic over the course of an hour or two, television casts its spell over a protracted period. The ephemeral intensity of the cinematic hare ultimately yields to the slow-working efficacy of the television tortoise; it is not Plato's cave for an hour and a half, but a privatized electronic grotto, a miniature sound and light show to distract our attention from the pressure without or within.

The privileged position of the television spectator has both psychoanalytic and political implications. Television, like the cinema, is founded upon the pleasure of looking (scopophilia) and the pleasure of hearing (Lacan's *"pulsion invocante"*) and both media allow us to see without being seen and hear without being heard. Quite apart from any specific voyeuristic content in the news itself (*Eyewitness News* reports on topless bars, scandals concerning celebrities, etc.) our situation as protected witnesses itself has voyeuristic overtones. Our privileged position triggers a fictitious sense of superiority, and in an atomized and hierarchical society where individuals are prodded to dreams of differential status and success, the recital of the misfortunes of others inevitably elicits an ambivalent reaction—mingling sincere empathy with mildly sadistic condescension.[6] In an economic situation where the fear of downward social mobility becomes an overriding concern, reports of industry layoffs can lead to a bizarre sense of There-but-for-the-Grace-of-God relief: "At least *I* still have a job!"

News programs are designed, on some levels, to enhance the self-image of His or Her Majesty the Spectator. The "bias" in the news often derives less from corporate manipulation or governmental pressure, although both undeniably exist, than from this inbuilt need to flatter the audience. Images of Iranian mobs implicitly contrast an objectified *Them* with a glorified *Us*, presumably as rational and humane as they are supposedly mindless and fanatical. (Europe constructed its self-image, Sartre explains in his Preface to Fanon's *Wretched of the Earth*, on the backs of its equally constructed Other: the "savage," the cannibal, the African.) Newscasters often neglect to specify the obvious for the same reason; Network News does speak of junta-style repression in Latin America, for example, but it does not usually point out that the repression is partially financed by the viewers' tax dollars. The omission does not necessarily derive only from complicity with established power or from ignorance of the facts, but also from the fact that an explicit statement that "you the viewer are in some way responsible for the atrocities you have witnessed" would not flatter and thus might hurt ratings.[7]

Apart from "primary identification" with the apparatus itself and with our own act of perception, television offers a gold mine of "secondary identifications" with the perceived human beings on the screen. Television news parades before us innumerable candidates for identification: the anchors, the correspondents, politicians and celebrities, the characters in the commercials and the "little people" featured in the news.

At the apex of the identificatory hierarchy: the anchors. The term connotes weight and seriousness, symbolic figures who will keep us from going adrift on a stormy sea of significations. The anchors are authentic heroes, whose words have godlike efficacy: their mere designation of an event calls forth instant illustration in the form of animated miniatures or live-action footage. It has become commonplace to call them the Superstars of the News (the correspondents and reporters being minor stars and starlets), comparable in charismatic power and box office appeal to the great stars of the cinema. Almost invariably male (women being relegated to the late-night or weekend ghettoes), the anchor is Commander-in-Chief, symbolic Father, Head of the Space-Team and the Time-Team.

The anchor personae are, clearly, artful constructs. Newscasters are actors and it is quite logical that some of them should be awarded roles in fiction films—Mike Wallace in *A Face in the Crowd,* Howard K. Smith in *The Candidate.* Although newscasters play themselves, in their own name, rather than fictional characters patently not themselves, their work does involve a kind of acting. Changes of tone of voice reflect sequential changes in subject matter, and often a final summing-up recapitulates the different stances adopted throughout the newscast. The Network News style of acting, an idiosyncratic synthesis of Stanislavsky and Brecht, is above all minimalist, consisting of the orchestration of barely perceptible smiles and the delicate lowering or raising of eyebrows in conjunction with slight variations in tone or stress. The performance is built on a series of negations, a willful non-acting which simultaneously implies the presence and the denial of normal human emotions and responses (whence the scandal and admiration at Cronkite's tears over the assassination of John F. Kennedy, tears that quickly took on the status of myth precisely because of the exceptional glimpse they provided of human vulnerability behind the newscaster's mask).

"Audiences forget that movies are written," Joe Gillis tells Betty Schaefer in *Sunset Boulevard,* "they think actors make up their lines as they go along." Television audiences, similarly, forget that the news, like the fiction film, is writing (scenario, text) received as speech. Even the most "off-the-cuff" lines are often fabricated by a team of writers and researchers. The newscaster's art consists of evoking the cool authority and faultless articulation of the written or memorized text while simultaneously "natural-izing" the written word to restore the appearance of spontaneous communi-cation. Most of the newscast, in fact, consists of this scripted spontaneity: newscasters reading from teleprompters, correspondents reciting hastily-memorized notes, politicians delivering prepared speeches, commercial actors representing their roles. In each case, the appearance of fluency elicits respect while the trappings of spontaneity generate a feeling of unmediated communication.

The minimalist acting of network newscasters—the special patterns of stress and inflection, the stilted body language (assumed by North American cultural codes to connote professional competence) and the facial expressions at once intense and bland, a studied expressionlessness open to the most diverse projections—combine to trigger an effect of neutrality. The faces become empty icons, as blank and meaningless as Mozhykhin's visage in the celebrated Kuleshov experiment. We suspect the blankness to be an act, since the behind-the-scenes books tell us of the commercial break tantrums of prestigious anchors who quickly resume a tone of calm and dignity once back on the air. In reality, the calculated ambiguity of expression forms part of a commercially motivated political strategy. Since a given piece of news might be cheered by one sector of the audience but deplored by another—presidential union-busting pleases management but not labor—and since the audience is heterogeneous, traversed by tension along class, ethnic and sexual lines, any undisguised expression of approval or disapproval would inevitably alienate part of the audience. The rhetoric of network diplomacy, consequently, favors a kind of oracular understatement, cultivating ambiguity, triggering patent but deniable meanings, encouraging the most diverse groups, with contradictory ideologies and aspirations, to believe that the newscasters are not far from their own beliefs.

In "A Short Organum for the Theater," Brecht denounces the bourgeois theater's deplorable habit of allowing the dominant actor to "star" by getting the other actors to work for him: "He makes his character terrible or wise by forcing his partners to make theirs terrified or attentive."[8] The news, similarly, fabricates its own star hierarchy. The superiority of the anchor, as we have seen, is structured into the news itself. But lesser newscasters also star. Their lines too are written, and their suave objectivity is underwritten by rehearsals and editing. Their forged articulateness, furthermore, contrasts with the inarticulateness of the "people in the street." A ritualistic montage during political campaigns, for example, features a series of voters expressing their preference for one of another of the candidates under consideration—"I like Carter, I think he's done a good job. . . . " "I sort of like Reagan; he looks like someone you can trust. . . . "—utterances striking largely for their apolitical and affective nature.[9] Like language, the news is built on differences. An ideologically-informed and perhaps largely unconscious binarism in the news pits discursive adults (the newscasters, the politicians, the managers) against a stammering child-populace, authoritative rationality against mindless affectivity, the voiced against the voiceless. The atrophied political sense apparent in these electoral montage segments corresponds, admittedly, to a real tendency (often fostered by television itself), yet it hardly accounts for the almost total absence of articulate and politicized everyday Americans (as opposed to the diverse incarnations of the Professional Manager) on Network News. Like Brecht's star actor, the professionals get the others to work for them. While they star, the people play the supporting roles, when they are not mere backdrop or passive audience.[10]

The anchors and reporters of Eyewitness News are also cast for stardom. Since the news comes to us with a human face, they must be photogenic, or at least charismatic. Techniques formerly exploited for testing commercials and spotting potential rock hits are enlisted in the search for what is called the right "news flesh." "Tellback" techniques register positive and negative reactions. Guinea pig audiences are wired with electrodes that measure pulse and perspiration as indices of galvanic response to potential newscasters. "News presenters" without journalistic qualifications are hired if they pass the "skin test," and what they lack in talent or background is fabricated through image-building hype. A Baltimore station even presented a series dealing with the secret fantasies of its news team. The news, especially at the local level, is as much about the newscasters as it is about information.[11]

The individual acting styles of these local newscasters cohere into a larger representation called the "happy news team." Indeed, local Eyewitness News programs feature a kind of ensemble playing as cohesive as that of a Renoir film. A contrived atmosphere of self-conscious informality fosters this impression: the address is integrative; good-natured kidding implies that we all belong to a larger community sufficiently at ease to kid and joke. The happiness of the news team, we know, is a construct favored by media consultants ("news doctors") who recommend it as a tactic to boost ratings, and many icy calculations form a part of the fabrication of "warmth."

Eyewitness News exemplifies the insight (developed by Hans Magnus Enzensberger, Richard Dyer and Fredric Jameson, among others) that to explain the public's attraction to a medium, one must look not only for the "ideological effect" that manipulates people into complicity with existing social relations, but also for the kernal of utopian fantasy reaching beyond these relations, whereby the medium constitutes itself as a projected fulfillment of what is desired and absent within the status quo. As Jameson puts it:

> The works of mass culture, even if their function lies in the legitimation of the existing order—or some worse one—cannot do their job without deflecting in the latter's service the deepest and most fundamental hopes and fantasies of the collectivity, to which they can therefore, no matter in how distorted a fashion, be found to have given voice.[12]

Indeed, Eyewitness News is susceptible to the same kind of analysis applied by Richard Dyer to the musical in his essay "Entertainment and Utopia." For what could be more utopian than this world of ludic productivity, where professionals seem to be having the time of their lives, where work is incessantly transformed into play? In the round of storytelling and easygoing chatter, laughter becomes the rhetorical glue between people and segments. Technical foul-ups elicit gales of laughter both from the on-screen newscasters and from the off-screen crew on the periphery of the set. In this electronically extended family romance, paternal figures preside benignly over a multi-ethnic symbolic family which stands as a metaphor for the larger

community. Desirable as the amiable camaraderie of this racial Utopia may
be, its fictional element must be acknowledged.

Just as all films, including documentaries, can be said to be fiction films,
so all of television, including the news, is inflected by fiction. But it hardly
requires a semiotician to point out the fictive nature of the news, for the
newscasters themselves, like journalists before them, consistently designate
their work as fiction. They promise "tonight's top *stories*" not "tonight's top
facts." Indeed, the industrial managers of the news virtually require a discourse with the attributes of fiction. Reuven Frank, president of the NBC
News Division, explains:

> Every news story should, without any sacrifice of probity or responsibil-
> ity, display the attributes of fiction, of drama. It should have structure and
> conflict, problem and dénouement, rising action and falling action, a
> beginning, a middle and an end. These are not only the essentials of
> drama; they are the essentials of narrative.[13]

The fictive nature of the news, or, more precisely, the nature of the news as a
construct whose procedures resemble those of fiction, helps shed light on our
initial question as to why the news is pleasurable. For stories, as a constitutive
element in human life, are pleasurable because they impose the consolations
of form on the flux of human experience. In this sense, all news is good news,
in the same sense that all stories are good stories because they entail the
pleasurability of fiction itself.

A typical news program can be seen as a weave of fictions: the individual
stories, the mini-fictions called commercials, the ongoing drama of the slow
revelation of the newscasters' personalities and the saga of their relation to
each other and to us as spectators. The news involves macro-fictions, larger
syntagmatic units such as the protracted story of American humiliation in
Iran on "this, the 100th day of captivity for the American hostages" (with
their homecoming orchestrated as the happy ending) and micro-fictions like
the one-liners that close off the news day.[14] It is almost as if the art of
storytelling, which Walter Benjamin thought to be in deep crisis, were being
resurrected by an unlikely medium. And much of the pleasure of the news
derives from systematic adherence to the teleological norms of storytelling.

At times, the news has more than the attributes of fiction: it literally is
fiction. Following the same logic that led J. Stuart Blackton to film the sinking
of the *Maine* in the bathtubs of New Jersey, networks have presented footage
of military operations in Viet Nam "as if" they were taking place in Cambodia.[15] At other times, the footage is authentic but its combination is fictional,
as when library material and freshly-shot location footage are molded into an
illusory continuity. Or a single track can be fictitious, as when library sound
aurally buttresses the image track. Instant matting via chromakey, meanwhile, performs a kind of "creative geography," making it appear that the
weatherwoman actually in the warm studio is strolling near the icy lake in
Central Park.

But even apart from such clearly fictional instances, the news generally cultivates the pleasing aspect of fiction. News programs, especially local news programs, deploy what Barthes would call "hermeneutic" teasers, pieces of partial information designed to stimulate interest: "Coming Up: A Man Murders Wife and Lover... Actress Attempts Suicide: Details in a Minute." The stage-by-stage unfolding of the story, the orchestration of enigmas and building to a climax suggest a narrative striptease. Just as a detective story teases us with the enigma of a murder, or Hitchcock teases us with the problematic etiology of a character's unconventional sexual behavior, news titillates our curiosity and keeps us tuned in and turned on.

Television news also deploys what Barthes in *S/Z* calls "reality-effects": strategic details designed to elicit a feeling of verisimilitude. Like the 19th-century mimetic novel, the news orchestrates authenticating details which create the optical illusion of truth. The representational accuracy of the details is ultimately less important than the mere fact of their presence. Walter Cronkite's last-minute scribbling and paper shuffling was, presumably, pure reality-effect, since he in fact read fixed texts from a teleprompter. The noisetracks of newscasts, to take another example, often include the sounds of teletype, even though a well-equipped contemporary newsroom does not use teletype. The sounds, perhaps an elegiac homage to print media, also aurally signify work, urgency and round-the-clock newsgathering. Those formulaic shots of correspondents posed in the White House driveway, finally, imply that the correspondent has just emerged with the news, yet in fact there are many roads to a presidential story and no guarantee at all that the correspondent physically entered the White House or even that he is actually standing in front of it.

Television news is a signifying practice with recognizable ordering procedures, an organized discourse rather than unmediated life. The news reduces the infinitude of available news items to a highly limited and predictable set of stories which it then produces and manufactures. The quite fantastic congruence of the three network news programs derives not only from shared "referential frames" and their common symbiotic relationship to established power, but also from the paradigmatic and syntagmatic operations that manufacture the news as narrative discourse.

The news, like the cinema, places images in sequence, and thus goes from shot to narrative. While newspaper readers have the freedom to fashion their own syntagmas, to determine their own itinerary through the printed text, the telespectator is obliged to follow a predetermined sequence. The news, in this sense, exhibits a certain syntagmatic orthodoxy. National Network News proceeds from "important" national or international stories through lesser stories and human interest features to a final anecdote providing an agreeable feeling of closure. Eyewitness News routinely begins with top local or national stories and proceeds to human interest, sports and weather. It would no more begin with sports and proceed to top local news (unless a major sports event *became* the top local news) than diners in a restaurant would begin with dessert and conclude with an appetizer.

Thus the news, on some levels, has the predictable yet renewable charm of the genre film. Informational material, neatly fashioned with beginnings, middles and ends, is poured into predictable narrative moulds provided by the surrounding televisual and cinematic intertext. The murders reported on Eyewitness News (forever playing the B-film to the high-art seriousness of Network News), murders that amount to narrativized visualizations of statistics, differ from the murders in police or mystery shows mainly in the fact that they happened to occur in the three-dimensional world. Subjective shots suture us into the perspective of rapists and assassins. The viewer becomes voyeur and accomplice, domestic private eye, subconsciously applauding a spectacle of death and abuse.[16]

Since the news partially adopts the procedures of fiction, it is hardly surprising that it draws, to some extent, on the continuity codes of the fiction film. Cinema's way of telling stories—the specifically cinematic organization of time and space aimed at the reconstitution of a fictional world characterized by internal coherence and the appearance of flawless continuity—was partially inherited (with limitations that we shall examine subsequently) by television news. The filmed segments, especially, tend to respect this conventional decorum. New scenes are presented by a choreographed progression from more distant to closer shots (long shot of the Capitol building, then to the reporter framed next to the dome, then to the hearings room, then a zoom-in to the face of the witness). Continuity editing sutures potential gaps and continuous sounds aurally mask discontinuous images. Interviews are handled in a ritual alternation of over-the-shoulder two-shots and semi-profile medium close-ups of the interlocuters. Interview questions, often filmed or taped *after* the answers have been given, are reinserted in their logical rather than factual position in the sequence. And off-screen glances, implied to be between interviewer and interviewee or between the newscasters themselves, stitch together the newscast as a whole.

The music track also affords pleasure and guarantees continuity. Network News eschews commentative music, exploiting instead an electronic theme, a percussive *musique concrète* which opens and closes the program, and which is faded in and out to smooth the transitions between news reports and commercial breaks. The "music" programmatically evokes the electronic modernity of the newsroom, providing a tonal analogue to the urgency of fast-breaking news transmitted direct. The noises simultaneously evoke the clatter of old-fashioned teletypes and the electronic bleeps of computerized newsgathering. The music of local Eyewitness News, meanwhile, is more likely to pay tribute to its dual inheritance of journalism and show-biz, molding modernistic fanfares with aural evocations of the newsroom activity.

Local news is more straightforwardly musical, with themes drawing on eminently urban musical forms such as jazz or disco, and is more likely to play with music for ironic effect, superimposing "It's Beginning to Look a Lot Like Christmas" on images of uncollected garbage, or accompanying space shuttle footage with the opening chords of *Thus Spake Zarathustra*.

While insisting on certain shared continuity procedures between television news and the conventional fiction film, we would be wrong to posit an absolute identity between the two media. In fact, as the Glasgow University Media Group points out in *Bad News*, television news inherits two distinct and in some ways contradictory discursive logics: the filmic and the journalistic. Filmic procedures are indeed present, especially in the filmed correspondents' reports, but they are constantly jostled by journalistic codes and procedures. This journalistic heritage of the news gives the lie to the myth of television's "visual imperative." In fact, television news is relatively impervious to the hegemony of the visual, for its images, more often than not, simply illustrate the spoken or written commentary. The soundtrack is in many respects more essential than the image track; the news' Echo speaks louder than its Narcissus. Since the news consists largely in newscasters speaking the news in the studio, we can grasp its essentials even when we merely hear it from another room. The news, furthermore, rather like the cinema immediately after the advent of sound, tends toward slavish devotion to the talking head, to a veritable worship of the human voice speaking in synchronous sound. In this sense it is phono- as well as logocentric, cultivating a televisual "metaphysics of presence."

In an otherwise excellent and incontrovertible article, William Gibson reaches the hasty conclusion that the fundamental aesthetic of television is naturalist:

> ... why do these symbolic visions look so real? The answer begins with the aesthetic of television news, Naturalism. All network news camera placing, filming and editing are conducted with the goal of completely erasing or minimalizing all signs of camera placing, filming, and editing. The Naturalist film code seeks to hide the fact that it is film and instead presents itself as unmediated reality.[17]

Gibson goes on to generalize about the medium:

> Network news is not the only network program to conceal its symbolic fabrications in naturalistic film. Most movies and most television series and even most commercials also present themselves as *unmediated* reality.[18]

No section of the television world, Gibson goes on to argue, shows any awareness of the existence of any other part:

> For a television program to present itself as "life," it must for that very reason deny that there is any other "life." For a television show to refer to other shows or commercials would be to call attention to its own existence as a program, rather than "live." ... Such are the dynamics of Naturalism.[19]

But while the charge of naturalism applies, as we have seen, to certain features of the news, specifically to the illusionistic continuity codes of filmed reports, that charge must be revised and even reversed when extended to the news as a whole or to television in general. And here we approach the limits of the analogy between television news and the classical fiction film.

The naturalism of the filmed reports, first of all, is not total. We can dismiss one fissure in this illusion—the visible presence of the microphone— as 1) a solution to the problem of what the correspondent is to do with his or her hands, and 2) a prop or reality-effect, an iconic signifier denoting "television correspondent." But the fact that the correspondent addresses us directly cannot be so easily dismissed. Whereas the classical fiction film inherited the "fourth wall" convention from naturalistic theater, whereby the actors were not to regard or address the spectators lest they be disturbed in their position as Peeping Toms, television news more typically involves direct address by both anchor and correspondent. Although individual filmed reports may be edited as stories, they are framed as conversation, a fact whose implications, as we shall see later, are complex and far-ranging.

The view of the news aesthetic as *fundamentally* (rather than incidentally) naturalist and illusionist is misguided on a number of grounds. It is misguided, first of all, for a practical reason. Illusionistic continuity is often simply impracticable in the news; obviously not all stories permit the luxury of fiction film procedures. In such instances, it becomes virtually impossible to efface the marks of enunciation. But by a curious kind of associational boomerang, it is precisely the presence of these marks of enunciation—the blur created by the hurried movement of the camera, the inadequate focus, the awkward framing—that convinces us of the scene's authenticity, for we associate them with reportorial work on live, actual, unpredictable events. (Which is why fiction films, from *Open City* through *Battle of Algiers* and *Medium Cool*, pointedly incorporate the traces of improvised, on-the-spot filmmaking into the films themselves as guarantees of verisimilitude.)

The view of television news as naturalist in style is misguided, secondly, because of the nature of the pro-textual event. Illusionism in the cinema is designed to convince the spectators that what they are seeing and hearing corresponds to "something that happened." But spectators of the news *know* that something really happened, first of all because it almost invariably *did*, and secondly because alternative media such as radio and the print media have already alerted them that it did. The telespectator's credence, consequently, is less dependent on illusionistic trickery. The news is thus freed to play with what normally would be considered anti-illusionist effects. Assassination footage can be replayed in slow motion, stopped, frozen and decorated with illustrative circles because the viewer does not doubt for one instant the reality of the event.[20]

It is only by a highly artificial feature, furthermore, that we separate the news from the commercials. The "flow" of the news program includes the commercials. Indeed, on one level, the commercials *are* the news. That sponsors have the right to interrupt essential information, for example about a narrowly averted nuclear disaster, itself conveys a powerful ideological effect. Coca Cola is the real thing, eternal; the news is factitious and ephemeral—such is the ontology of the commercial. At the same time, the news and the commercials reciprocally influence each other, so that the commercials imitate the news and vice versa. Mobil Oil, to take one example, seats an imitation anchorman at an imitation news desk, backed by an imitation newsroom map of the world, and has him express the Mobil *Weltanschauung*. Trading on the widespread trust of the news as institution, Mobil hopes to transfer that confidence to itself and its policies. (The fact that Mobil advertises on the same program that features oil news is infinitely more important that any verifiable "bias" in the news presentation itself.) The news, meanwhile, imitates the commercials by advertising itself, its news teams and upcoming news specials, and by exploiting some of the same manipulative procedures—image enhancement, secondary identification, mini-narrative structures.[21]

Both commercials and the news fit into generic moulds thrown up by the cinematic and televisual intertext, and this intertext is not intrinsically or invariably naturalist but often, surprisingly, self-referential and reflexive. Far from being hermetically sealed off from one another, there is constant circulation between the programs. The news itself does features on the popularity of shows like *Dallas* or *General Hospital*, and Walter Cronkite has a cameo appearance on *The Mary Tyler Moore Show*. At least two shows— *Mary Tyler Moore* and *Jessica Novak*—have been set in newsrooms, while the short-lived *Fly and Bones* featured the Smothers Brothers as television reporters. In the world of sitcoms, Archie Bunker, like Ralph Kramden and many others before him, performs in a television commercial, while the real-life Carroll O'Connor made commercials for Jimmy Carter. Variety shows like *Carol Burnett* or *Saturday Night Live* constantly "carnivalize" commercials and other shows. Talk shows not only display cameras and video switchers as part of their credits but also incessantly turn to talk about television itself. Johnny Carson mocks his own monologue as self-consuming artifact, while the video cameras show his producer just off-stage. Television enjoys its own "bloopers" and regularly rebroadcasts them. It even recounts its own history in *The Golden Age of Television*, and looks at itself in the mirror of *Entertainment Tonight*. In countless ways, in sum, television is self-referential and self-cannibalizing.

Television, in fact, often seems positively Brechtian rather than naturalist. Many of the distancing features characterized as Brechtian in Godard films typify television as well: the designation of the apparatus; the spatial co-presence of multiple images within the frame; the inclusion of two-dimensional materials; the direct address to the spectator; the commercial "interruptions" of the narrative flow; the juxtaposition of heterogeneous slices of discourse; the mixing of documentary and fiction modes; the subverting of visual hegemony through a dominant soundtrack; the constant recourse to written materials; the creative incorporation of errors.

Yet we know that if television is Brechtian, it is Brechtian in a peculiarly ambiguous and often debased way. While authentic Brechtianism elicits an active thinking spectator rather than a passive consumer of entertainment, most television is as narcotic and culinary as the bourgeois theater that Brecht denounced. Brecht's goal was not to satisfy audience expectations but to transform them, whereas the central impulse of commercial television (notwithstanding the creative and critical contribution of its artists) is to transform only two things: the audience's viewing habits and its buying habits. Brecht's goal was not to *be* popular in box-office terms but to *become* popular—that is, to create a new public for a new kind of theater linked to new modes of social life—whereas commercial television's goal, at least from the point of view of its managers, is to be popular in the crudely quantitative terms of "ratings." Rather than trigger "alienation effects," commercial television often simply alienates. It domesticates the horrible rather than estranging it; it often obscures the causal network of events rather than revealing it.

While television does occasionally suggest the *possibility* of authentic Brechtianism—one thinks of certain features of *The Mary Tyler Moore Show*—many of its many distancing devices, when looked at more closely, turn out to be, if not naturalist, at least anti-Brechtian.[22] The commercial interruptions that place the news "on hold," for example, are not pauses for reflection but breaks for manipulation, intended not to make us think but to make us feel and buy; rather than providing demystifying jolts, they continue the narcotic flow. The self-referentiality of commercials also serves an anti-Brechtian purpose. Commercials which parody themselves or other commercials do not demystify the product or expose hidden codes; rather, they serve both to differentiate their sponsor from other, presumably less candid sponsors who do not "confess" their commercial's status as artifact, and to weaken the spectator's defenses. From Arthur Godfrey through Johnny Carson, good-natured kidding of commercials has helped rather than hurt sales, for the humor signals the spectator that the commercial is not to be taken seriously, and this relaxed state renders the spectator more open to its message. In fact, the commercial is in deadly earnest—it is after the spectator's money.

Both the news and the commercials share one Brechtian feature which deserves a longer and deeper look: a penchant for direct address. Most of the news consists of talking heads speaking directly to the camera. Nothing, on the surface, could be farther removed from the illusionist aesthetic. A cardinal rule of the classical fiction film is that the actor must never acknowledge the camera/audience. The fictive events must unwind magically, indifferent to the presence of the audience. Illusionism hides the source of enunciation, masking its discourse as "history." The news, on the other hand, offers the image of a person, who would seem to be the source of enunciation, at a close social distance speaking directly to us.

What can we say about this apparent contradiction between illusionistic aspects of the filmed reports and the news' penchant for the same direct address favored by Brecht and Godard? First, the contradiction is real—the direct address segments *are* less illusionistic than the filmed reports. Second, this direct address is correlated with power. Newscasters share with advertisers, entertainers and politicians this privilege which implies immense political, narrational and discursive power. This power is correlated, furthermore, with lack of mediation. (Presidents, anchors and advertisers address us directly in relatively close shots, correspondents address us from a slightly greater distance and regard us somewhat less insistently, and the "others" are filmed as they might be in a fiction film.)[23] Thirdly, this direct address is itself a fiction. It is fictional in its apparent spontaneity—the implication that the newscaster has authored his or her own remarks without preformulated sources or editorial elaboration. The newscasters, furthermore, speak to an audience not present in the flesh, all the while cultivating the tacit assumption that what is said was formulated just for that audience, as if each spectator or group of spectators were the only one.

Although the apparent structure of the news is one of discourse, then, this discourse is itself fictional; it is itself *histoire*. The news is fiction, but the fiction is displaced. The "stories," although they exploit fictional procedures, are not ultimately fictional; the fiction lies, rather, in the fictive nature of the relationship between newscaster and audience. The news does not begin with "Once Upon a Time" and conclude with "They Lived Happily Ever After"; it begins with "Good Evening" and ends with "Good Night." It is framed, in other words, as a simulation of face-to-face two-person communication; the newscaster singlehandedly imitates the characteristic rhythms of dialogue. The "communication" is unilateral, not a reciprocal exchange between two transmitter-receivers but rather a powerful transmitter enjoying direct access to millions of subjects. On one level, then, we can even *reverse* the illusionistic formula. If illusionistic fictions disguise their discourse as history, television news, in certain respects, wraps up its history as discourse.

That this displaced fiction effect actually works is attested to by the immense credence given the news. Polls have shown Walter Cronkite to be the most trusted man in America and the news to be one of the country's most trusted institutions. The pseudo-intimacy of the global village fosters a confusion betweeen the actual newscasters and their fictive personae, or, more accurately, it installs a phantasmatic relationship between the viewer and the news celebrity. People who scarcely know their own neighbors are convinced that they know the newscasters. Ted Koppel reports receiving letters which address him as if he were father, son or lover. In a social situation of interpersonal loneliness, television becomes a meal and bedtime companion, part of the existential fabric of our lives, and newscasters become friends and confidantes.

Television news promotes what might be called—in both psychoanalytic and political terms—the regime of the "fictive We." In psychoanalytic terms, television promotes a narcissistic relationship with an imaginary other. It infantalizes in the sense that the young child perceives everything in relation to itself; everything is ordered to the measure of its ego. Television, if it is not received critically, fosters a kind of confusion of pronouns: between "I" the spectator and "He" or "She" the newscaster, as engaged in a mutually flattering dialogue. This fictive "We" can then speak warmly about "Ourselves" and coldly about whoever is posited as "Them." This misrecognition of mirror-like images has profound political consequences. Oil corporation commercials tell us: "We Americans have a lot of oil." The "We" is clearly fictive; most of us own no oil; we buy it at exorbitant prices in the wake of a stage-managed energy crisis. Shortly after the ill-fated "rescue attempt" in Iran, to take another example, Chuck Scarborough of New York's *Channel 4 News* began his newscast, "Well, we did our best, but we didn't make it." The "We" in this case presumably included the newscaster, the president, and a few aides. It certainly did not include the majority of Americans, even if their "support" could be artfully simulated after the fact. Television news, then, claims to speak for us, and often does, but just as often it deprives us of the right to speak by deluding us into thinking that its discourse is our own. Often it gives us the illusion of social harmony, the ersatz communication of a global village which is overwhelmingly white, male and corporate.

The televisual institution, to slightly paraphrase Metz, is not just the televisual industry (which works to boost ratings, not to diminish them), it is also the mental machinery—another industry—which viewers "accustomed to television" have internalized historically and which has adapted them to the consumption of television as it is. The social regulation of the telespectator's metapsychology has as its function the setting up of "good object" relations with television (including television news) if at all possible, for television is watched out of desire, not reluctance, in the hope that it will please. The psychology of the spectator is linked to the financial mechanisms of television news and its possibilities of self-reproduction as Heath's "pleasure-meaning-commodity-complex." Psychoanalytic methods help disengage its relation to desire; semiotics helps disengage its procedures of meaning; and a critical and dialectical Marxism can disengage its status as purveyor and exemplification of commodity fetishism and its place within competing class discourse.

Only such a multi-dimensional approach can fully answer our original question: Why is the news pleasurable? Television is a libidinal as well as technological apparatus, a machine for erotic as well as financial investment. For its own self-reproduction within a capitalist system, the news must establish a good object relation with its spectator. Viewers have to "like" the news or they will not watch it, and they have to watch so that they can be sold again to sponsors. Television thus manufactures its own audience as well as the news. Through the pleasuring capacities of the apparatus, through the procedures of fiction, through attractive newscasters as the erotic subtext of the news, it manufactures itself as a good object. At the same time, to remain a good object, it must also somehow connect with the mass of people who are its audience and represent their larger social wishes and desires, for the kernel of utopianism also forms part of its constant solicitude and seduction.

It is for this reason that we would be wrong to regard television, or its news, as monolithically regressive. Manipulation and exploitation are present, but so are resistance and critique. As a matrix in which dominant and oppositional discourses do constant battle, television can never completely reduce the antagonistic dialogue of class voices to the reassuring hum of bourgeois hegemony. Television can numb consciousness, but it also drags colonial wars into the hearts of imperial beasts. While it at times amplifies the discourse of power, it also can make us aware of how social policies impinge on human beings. Television is not only its industrial managers, it is also its creative participants, the people who appear in the news, and we the audience who can resist, apply pressure to, and decode its messages. But one of our first theoretical tasks is to understand not only the alienation, but also the utopian promise of its mechanisms of pleasure.

NOTES

1. For discussions of the apparatus, see Jean-Louis Baudry's "Cinéma: effets idéologiques produits par l'appareil de base," *Cinétique* No. 7-8 (1970) (published in English translation by Alan Williams as "Ideological Effects of the Basic Cinematographic Apparatus," *Film Quarterly* Vol. 28 No. 2 [Winter 1974-1975], pp. 39-47), and his "Le Dispositif: approches métapsychologiques de l'impression de réalité," *Communications* No. 23 (May 1975), pp. 56-72 (published in English translation by Bertrand Augst and Jean Andrews as "The Apparatus," *Camera Obscura* No. 1 [Fall 1976], as well as his *L'Effet cinéma* (Paris: Albatross, 1978). See also Christian Metz, "Le Signifiant imaginaire," *Communications* No. 23 (May 1975), pp. 3-55 (published in English translation by Ben Brewster as "The Imaginary Signifier," *Screen* Vol. 16 No. 2 [Summer 1975], pp. 14-76), and his "Le Film de fiction et son spectateur: étude métapsychologique," also in *Communications* No. 23 (pp. 108-135), and translated by Alfred Guzzetti as "The Fiction Film and Its Spectator: A Metapsychological Study," *New Literary History* Vol. 8 No. 1 (Autumn 1976), pp. 75-105. Jean-Louis Comolli's "Machines of the Visible" is included in *The Cinematic Apparatus*, ed. Stephen Heath and Teresa de Lauretis (London: St. Martin's Press, 1980).

2. Metz, "The Imaginary Signifier," p. 51.

3. The fact of live transmission also slightly alters Metz' conception of the cinematic experience as a missed rendezvous between an exhibitionist and a voyeur, in which the actor-exhibitionist is present at the filming but absent at the screening, while the spectator is present at the screening but absent at the filming. On its own terms, Metz' conception entails the problem that the film, if not the actor, is present at the screening, a fact equally true of television. But through live transmission, television at least allows the putative voyeur and exhibitionist to share the *time* of the performance.

4. I would like to express my deep appreciation to Yeshayahu Nir of Hebrew University for his stimulating comments and helpful suggestions. He will doubtless recognize certain of his examples and insights in the "shared discourse" of this essay. I would also like to thank Ann Kaplan and Brian Winston for their suggestions.

5. Jean-Louis Comolli, in "Machines of the Visible," speculates that the extreme eagerness of the first cinema spectators to recognize in the filmic images—devoid of color, depth, nuance— the literal double of life itself, derived precisely from this sense of a lack to be filled. Is there not, Comolli wonders, "in the very principle of representation, a force of disavowal which gives free reign to an analogical illusion that is as yet only weakly manifested in the iconic signifiers themselves?"

6. The cinema's most vivid object-lesson in both the illusory superiority and the voyeuristic nature of the cinematic/televisual situation is, perhaps, Alfred Hitchcock's *Rear Window*, in which the Jimmy Stewart character (significantly a mass media photojournalist) spies on his neighbors across a Greenwich Village courtyard. Stewart's eye wanders from window to window, as if he were changing channels from sit-com to police serial to soap opera. Hitchcock brilliantly undercuts his scopophilic protagonist by having the world he is watching, supposedly from a safe distance, invade his space and quite literally grab him by the throat.

7. Robert MacNeil of *The MacNeil-Lehrer Report* recalled that during the war in Vietnam, footage of American soldiers cutting off Vietnamese ears had been rejected for the program because newscasters pointed out that the evening time-slot coincided, for many families, with dinner time. Apart from this "culinary" censorship, however, he might have also pointed out that such imagery would not have flattered the American self-image as morally superior to the Vietnamese.

8. Bertolt Brecht, *Brecht on Theatre*, ed. John Willett (New York: Hill and Wang, 1964), p. 197.

9. This inarticulateness contrasts sharply with the peasants and workers interviewed on the street in Guzman's *The Battle of Chile*; their off-the-cuff remarks show a sophisticated grasp of domestic and international politics.

10. The non-professionals in the news—the interviewees on the street, the bystanders waving in the background, the individuals featured in human interest stories—at times nourish their own dreams of stardom. Indeed, the general familiarity with such media performances would enable most of us to adopt the correct persona if called upon. Jean-Luc Godard and Anne-Marie Miéville, in some of their television work, make a gesture toward taking this seriously by presenting "ordinary people" more or less directly to the viewer. The scandal of *Six Fois Deux* consists precisely in this conjunction of ordinary people with a deliberate lack of directorial mediation or editorializing. Two schizophrenics speak, but they are neither named nor labelled as schizophrenics. No editing betrays an authorial attitude, and no newscasterly wrap-up tells us what to think. Thus Godard-Miéville hypostatize an existing feature of television—its fondness for popular vignettes—while at the same time radicalizing and subverting it.

11. For more information about the exploitation of sexual appeal in local news, see "Sex and the Anchor Person," (*Newsweek* [December 15, 1980], pp. 65-66) by Harry F. Waters with George Hackett; and Richard Corliss on "Sex Stars of the Seventies," (*Film Comment* Vol. 15 No. 4 [July-August 1979], pp. 27-29).

12. Fredric Jameson, "Reification and Utopia in Mass Culture," *Social Text* No. 1 (Winter 1979), p. 144.

13. Quoted in Edward J. Epstein, *News From Nowhere* (New York: Random House, 1974), pp. 4-5.

14. That the story of America's humiliation was partially a media construct becomes obvious when we recall that the imprisonment of the crew of the *Pueblo* in North Korea received no such buildup, nor did their homecoming elicit a heroes' welcome. The media treatment of Iran, in any case, certainly helped create an atmosphere in which the American public was quite ready for Ronald Reagan and increased defense expenditures.

15. Epstein, p. 22.

16. Christian Metz holds the fiction film itself partially responsible for the mental and motor passivity of the spectator. Norman Holland, similarly, argues in *The Dynamics of Literary Response* (New York: W.W. Norton, 1975) that the "willing suspension of disbelief depends partially on the knowledge that he or she will not be expected to act as a result of the fiction, a convention that allows a relaxation of the reality principle—the critical faculty through which we continually check what is presented as 'non-fiction' for its truth—and thus results in a pleasant blurring of what is fiction and what is self."

17. William Gibson, "Network News: Elements of a Theory," *Social Text* No. 3 (Fall 1980), p. 103.

18. Ibid., p. 106.

19. Ibid.

20. Much of the news, on the other hand, is highly pre-packaged, consisting of staged presentations or "pseudo-events": press conferences, hearings, speeches, poll results. The singularity of the Sadat assassination was, in a sense, the fact that a pseudo-event (a president reviewing his troops) was brutally interrupted by a "real" event.

21. The commercials, like the news, draw on the cinematic-televisual intertext. McDonalds' commercials draw on the codes of the musical comedy, creating an atmosphere of whimsical group-singing magically transcending spatial distance. Toy commercials incline to single frame

animation and computer ads draw on science fiction. Headache remedies (see especially Excedrin commercials from the mid-seventies) pay homage to deep-focus realism à la Orson Welles, foregrounding the potion while the characters play out oedipal dramas in the "deep space." Perfume, deodorant, and jewelry commercials tend toward Lelouche romanticism (soft focus, sensuous dollies, liquid dissolves), their 30-second plots racing from meeting to *coup-de-foudre* and implied *jouissance*. Jeans commercials, meanwhile, are more straightforwardly pornographic.

22. Two shows reveal both the critical potentialities and frequent degradation of Brechtianism on television. *The Mary Tyler Moore Show*, with its quasi-theatrical sets, archly distanced acting and its constant appeal to the spectator's intelligence, exhibits aspects of an authetic Brechtian-ism. The short-lived *Jessica Novak*, on the other hand, exploits both the image of the "new woman" (often equated with "sexually aggressive") and public curiosity about the behind-the-scenes truth about the newsroom and the newscasters in a show whose apparent reflexivity masks a regressive illusionism. In *Jessica Novak,* the self-referential becomes the self-reverential as the protagonist embodies Television, which is the real hero—the *deux ex machina* that solves the problems, saves lives and heals families. The attention paid to television processes becomes merely another reality-effect, an index of profession and milieu.

23. Whence the outrage when one of the "others"—an Iranian woman militant (triply "other")—proposed to address the American public directly during the hostage crisis. The proposal elicited an instant outcry that the militants were trying to "use" the media—as indeed they were—but the accusation implied that television and its audience were not being "used" every day of the year.

Sport on Television: Replay and Display

Margaret Morse

Introduction

> Play and display are precariously balanced in sport, and, once that balance is upset, the whole character of sport in society may be affected.
>
> —Gregory P. Stone in "American Sports: Play and Display."[1]
>
> Man is reluctant to gaze at his exhibitionist like.
>
> —Laura Mulvey in "Visual Pleasure and Narrative Cinema."[2]

The discourse on sport is like no other in our culture insofar as its object is the male body; its currency is statistical comparison of performances, of exchange rates and ownership, of strategies for deployment of bodies and of the particular weaknesses, quirks and gradual submission to injury, illness and aging of those bodies.[3] At the center of this discourse is an *image* of fascination, the perfect machine of a body-in-motion choreographed with others as a vision of grace and power: "Now, there's an athlete!"

Despite the inroad of women as active participants into some spectator sports such as tennis and into all sports as spectators and even to some extent as commentators,[4] sport remains a masculine preserve, a place of "autonomous masculinity,"[5] freed even from dependence on woman-as-other to anchor identity. "This is a game for *men only!*" the color-man emphasized in a recent *Monday Night Football* telecast.[6] His words were meant to underscore the evenly matched power of the opponents and to add to the excitement of the game by emphasizing the uncertainty of the outcome; but they also drew attention to the male body in the only situation in which it is a legitimate object of the male gaze.

The strong cultural inhibition against the look at the male body can be attributed to a deep-seated reluctance to make the male the *object* of scopophila (i.e., erotic pleasure in looking). The look at another is both a privilege and an instrument of power, potentially a tool of mastery and degradation. Yet the gaze at "maleness" would seem necessary to the construction and constant replenishment of a shared cultural ideal of masculinity. How is it that spectator sports can license such a gaze and render it harmless?

The answer lies in the nature of modern sport itself as a careful balance of "play and display," which allows the operation of a very effective mechanism for disavowal: every look of "man at his exhibitionist like" is transformed into a scientific inquiry into the limits of human performance. The discourse on statistics and the vicissitudes of performance lend a mark of scientificity to sport; but it is competition itself and the record of wins which justify sport as a hermeneutic process, i.e., as a method for searching out, nurturing and displaying physical excellence.[7] The immediate question: Who will win? is but a part of this hermeneutic process which anchors the image of the body-in-motion. In a culture where the female image is proliferated and exchanged among and between both sexes, national spectator sports are *the* place where the male body image is central, if disavowed. The mechanism of carefully balancing the display of that image with play or contest as hermeneutic was outlined over two decades ago by urban sociologist Gregory P. Stone. He was sounding an alarm about a danger to sport from its commercialization.

Stone worried then that the "massification" of sport had done much to transform it into "ignoble" spectacle.[8] Stone's moral preference for primary sport participation led him to a global condemnation of the passive consumer-spectator or secondary participant:

> The game, inherently moral and ennobling of its players, seems to be giving way to the spectacle, inherently immoral and debasing. With the massification of sport, spectators begin to outnumber participants in overwhelming proportions, and the spectator, as the name implies, encourages the spectacular—the dis-play. In this regard the spectator may be viewed as an agent of destruction as far as the dignity of the sport is concerned.[9]

The surest sign of the degradation of sport into spectacle—as far as Stone was concerned—was the predominance of female spectators.[10]

In the 20 years or so since Stone sounded the alarm, spectatorship or vicarious enjoyment of sport has grown many times through the medium of television. The Super Bowl attracts 100 million viewers;[11] one study shows that 30 percent of Americans follow sport on television each day and another indicates that 50 percent of the American public listens to sport on the radio or watches sport on television each week. "Worldwide, the largest TV audiences have been attracted by sports events; audiences in excess of 800 million people watched the last Olympic Games and World Soccer Championship."[12] Considering this massive increase in spectatorship, has the "precarious balance" between play and display been affected? What is the place of the female spectator in this mass? Furthermore, beyond questions of quantity and gender, it is time to consider whether the experience of viewing sport has changed formally and psychically since the convergence of the two great sociocultural models, sport and television. Has television, itself a specular medium, enhanced the aspect of spectacle in sport through its mode of representation?

A related question concerns the image of the male body transmitted through sport on television. Over a decade ago, Norbert Elias asked whether television would have any impact on the lack of importance which "physical appearance and particularly bodily strength and beauty" had for the public esteem of a man.[13] Has televised sport had any effect on the perception and social importance of the male body image? If the balance has shifted toward display, then perhaps some significant changes have taken place both in the cultural model of sport and in the collective identifications or "social imaginary" which project and reinforce what it is to be a man. Perhaps males are on their way to becoming as dependent on "image" as females; perhaps the inhibitions which surround the gaze at maleness and the mechanism of disavowal which licenses it have diminished in importance.

Another possibility is that despite the increase in spectatorship and the enhancement of display in sport through television, the balance between play and display has been maintained, and the psychic experience connected with sport spectatorship may well have been enhanced rather than altered. Rather than being an endangered species, sport (on television) may have become the most powerful locus of collective identifications—both with locale and with masculinity—in modern society.

This article will explore three areas of inquiry as an opening contribution to the discourse on sport on television: first, what are the formal differences between sport in an arena and sport on television? Second, have these differences brought any significant changes in the spectator's psychic experience of sport or in the function of sport as a social imaginary? Third, what are the significant features of sport as a genre on television? Has the ideological or social function of sport changed through the convergence of two cultural models—sport and television? These questions are raised and discussed, but they are far too complex to be definitively answered. Football, often called the ideal television sport, has been chosen as the prime object of investigation. All televised sports share a common origin in industrial society and the "transfer of specific leisure occupations into sports";[14] all these sports share a common ethos of competition in an ideal realm apart from the public space of the division of labor;[15] and ultimately, whether an individual, dual or team sport, all these sports are "dual" or "imaginary" in the sense that it is a phantasmatic image of bodily perfection with which one competes, either imperfectly in the form of aggression against an opponent or in a more perfect approximation of an ideal performance embodied in statistics and records. These records function both as an element of scientificity, supported by the hermeneutic of the contest, i.e., play, and as an ideal projection or display. Out of this common ground, whatever can be said of football on television will have some implications for sports generally transformed by television.[16]

Transformations from Stadium to Screen

> "Well, there's a big game on tonight,
> And I know right where you'll be
> Watching that old T.V., drinking beer,
> ignoring me."
> —from "Play Me or Trade Me,"
> country song by Owen Davis

Both the stadium or arena and the television screen are set apart from the work place; but, aside from that, from the recording at a sports event to its appearance on television, "live" sport on television undergoes a considerable transformation. First, a stadium event is received by a spectator among a crowd from a fixed point of view (which is also an overview). The football game on television is received in privacy by an isolated, usually male viewer who must forego the pleasures of the crowd.

The choice to attend a stadium event is made out of many minor social, economic and emotional considerations;[17] but the event itself takes place in liminal space[18] and in the cyclic time of ritual, beginning from the common entrance of the spectators, jostling and touching,[19] and including the pledge of allegiance in unison, the common consumption of food and drink, the milling about and invasion of the field at halftime, until the common exit to isolation in separate vehicles. While the game on the field may have many of the attributes of drama or melodrama,[20] the participation of the crowd in the event is greater and the separation from the performers is far less complete than in the theater. The crowd itself is a mirror of the protagonists on the field, dual in allegiance and responding kinesthetically and vocally to each play in unison. The player-protagonists themselves are a small crowd, teams individuated only by color and number. But the primary identification of the sports spectator in the stadium is not with his team but with the crowd itself, the physical presence of a community which the team's local identity represents. The density of the crowd furthers mass identification through physical contact; the goal and ultimate release of density is the roar of the crowd, a discharge with one voice—Dionysian pleasures which the isolated television viewer must relinquish.

In contrast, television sport is one of those solitary pleasures like novel reading, cut to the measure of the individual and not the mass. The separation between viewer and event, despite its aura of immediacy, is absolute; the game on the field becomes a closed, diegetic world represented by switching video cameras and narrated by announcer-commentators. The hero of this novelistic world is the individual, not the team. Indeed, research into this question has long since shown that sport coverage focuses on the individual player,

> to the exclusion of other players as well as of the overall geometry of the game. . . . As a result of focusing on individuals, the medium event tended to present play-action in the form of individual performances rather than team efforts, and a particular game behavior was presented within a larger biographical and personalized perspective.[21]

Certainly the pre-game publicity has always made celebrities out of champions; but, now, within the game itself, the individual signified by a name added on the uniform, a body in close-up and an insert of a face and accompanying graphics of statistics is offered for specular identification.

Yet the possibility remains that some of the pleasures of the crowd have been retained through the evocation of a phantom crowd on the soundtrack. The solitary viewer "forgets himself," but his ejaculation of inarticulate sounds of approbation and dismay may seem quite strange to fellow occupants of the room who do not share his interest in sport.

> She: "Play me or trade me."
> He: "Well, I think they're gonna score."
> She: "There won't be no instant replay,
>   When I walk out the door."
> **—"Play Me or Trade Me"**

The second area of transformation in the passage from stadium to television screen is that of the visual and aural material of the game itself. What is at issue here are not differences in visual style, which may differ from network to network and from game to game, but major transformations in the signifying material of sport itself. Consider first the visual aspect of the representation of the game, including its temporal unfolding: the constant use of extremely long lenses both narrows the angle of view and flattens space; the convention of instant replay shows the same play two or three times from different angles and points of view. The game as represented undergoes considerable deformation, i.e., spatial compression and temporal elongation and repetition. The end effect of these distortions is to emphasize only points of action and body contact, to the detriment of the "overall geometry of the game." The ball-carrier is separated from his context within a team effort and much information about each play is lost.

At the same time there is a considerable gain in information about the movements of the ball-carrier and the men around him through the use of long-lens close-ups and slow motion, repeated from several points of view. The technique of slow motion allows the analysis and appreciation of body movements which are normally inaccessible to view; this capacity has justifiably lent slow motion an aura of scientificity. Slow motion replays are treated as part of a hermeneutic process of scientific discovery, which, among other things, allows the viewer to outguess the referee and see what "really" happened.

But, on the other hand, the frequent repetition of the same play in slow motion marks the game on television from the outset as no longer occurring in a world subject to the laws of ordinary linear and uni-directional time. Within the compressed space the body covers ground effortlessly, while the slowness of the motion seems to free it from the pull of gravity; slow motion also implies an increase in scale, for a large body needs more time to complete a movement. Finally, the slowness which we associate with dignity and grace transforms a world of speed and violent impact into one of dance-like beauty. The liminal space of ritual and masks is transformed into a "kaleidoscopic"[22] other scene of shifting appearances or phantoms which has its analog as much in the field of desire as in the football field. Slow motion sets apart sport on television in an oneiric world which can make few claims to "look like" quotidian reality; yet the scientificity of the techniques of slow motion and long-lens close-ups which create that other scene provides at the same time the means of its disavowal. Just as fast motion set the terms of the other world upon which silent comedy built its kinetic jokes, football on television is a world of representation which has abandoned Renaissance space and Newtonian physics—but not the claim to scientificity of sport.

Another change in the appearance of football on television has been often noted, i.e., the rapid shifts in point of view during a play through instant switching from one camera to another among the up-to-23 cameras taping the field. On closer inspection, however, this way of presenting an event is no different than the completely acculturated and typical approach of a Hollywood treatment of a real or fictional event. The rules of continuity editing are followed, in that all the cameras tape from one side of the field (except in those few instances when a "reverse-angle replay" on screen signals that the 180° rule has been broken and the opponents will have appeared to "change sides" on screen). The "natural" *mise-en-scène* of football, with its clearly marked directionality and end-zones, its color-contrasting opponents and its field neatly calibrated by ten-yard lines, seems tailor-made for continuity editing; so, as a transformation of the game experience, editing fades in importance. Long lenses and instant replay, however, lift football into another visual world, highly invested with desire and capital.[23]

Yet this oneiric world is received essentially as "documentary," due to the live coverage of the game, which excludes simulation. That no one knows the outcome for sure is essential to the hermeneutic appeal of the game, for it assures a real test of coordinated bodies and an answer not only to the question, "Who will win?" but also, "Who is best?' The violence associated with the game (and which is periodically addressed in the press[24] but almost never on television) may function as a guarantee of the "sincerity of effort" which "the spectacular-commercial game-form" and the emphasis on "entertainment value"[25] of televised sport might otherwise have put in question. This violence, however, is not emphasized in the visual representation—to the contrary, it is transformed into gracefulness. Other than simultaneity with the pro-filmic stadium event, and a sense that opponents are well-matched and sincere in their effort to win, football broadcasts make few appeals to realism. Instead, every aspect of the televised game openly "bares the device," allowing the enormous capital investment in sport itself and in broadcasting technology to gleam through the "live" event, exhibiting the highest production values in regularly scheduled television.

Examples of the high stylization typical of the football medium-event may be seen in the opening graphics, consisting of animated neon forms in saturated colors, choreographed in typical play postures. Then, throughout the game, graphics in similar bright contrasts are superimposed on the diegetic image of the game, keeping the viewer abreast of the record of an athlete or team. Sometimes a framed insert of a player's face or even of a part of the body is superimposed over the game, at times replacing the diegesis entirely. During the game, elaborate advancing and receding frames may set apart the instant replays; they may also appear unmarked. These colorful graphics and moving frames exert a visual fascination, but the statistics which are contained in them, elaborate in detail and supplied by computer, underline the scientificity of the game; thus, display *and* play are supported by the same graphic material added by television to the stadium event.

The *mise-en-scène* of football has been considerably enhanced for television. Stadium lighting gives an even luminosity. The stadium ceiling sometimes appears like the parting, light-penetrated clouds in a Baroque heaven. Star filters may elevate the scene even further. The colors of the turf and the uniforms are all saturated and bright; there is no mud to bring them down to earth. The football uniform itself inflates its already large bearers to gigantic proportions; it is a mask which not only serves the purpose of protection, but also of creating the phantasmatic body of a titan, which, when in slow motion, is uncannily like that of the first moon-walker. The most realistic aspect in the "look" of the game is the crowd with its motley colors and with its faces in close-up and reaction shots.[26]

The video photography, camera placement and editing do not strive for realism either. Not only are shots rapidly changing, but some are strikingly unusual; for example, there is the high-angle shot through the goal posts during the point-after kick, rendering space without depth and erasing the effort of the kick; or the arc trajectory of the camera as it tracks the ball at kickoff, while the ball itself remains virtually invisible against the crowd—reminding one how unimportant the role of the ball is in the televised game. The most memorable shots, however, are the ones shown in slow motion, where violent force and speed are electronically invested with grace and beauty. The emphasis on contact shots means tight framing, which cuts bodies into parts; the repetition of plays alternates between dispersion and heaping of bodies in aesthetic and erotic display. Finally, to show the ecstasy of victory, slow motion may spill beyond the end of the game itself into the crowd, unanchored by any hermeneutic process, to become pure spectacle. Yet the technological-scientific cachet of slow motion is enough to rescue it from recognition as display.

The American practice of high stylization is contrasted sharply with the British practice of televising soccer in a British Film Institute publication of the later 1970s.[27] Although soccer and football are not completely visually commensurable, soccer being a much faster, more unpredictable game and thus harder to keep on camera,[28] the British practice does provide an idea of possibilities in sport broadcasting which are unrealized in the United States. British television practice emphasizes realism through straight cuts, no split framing, and a "tendency to show a match from the perspective of a spectator actually present at a game."[29] *That* particular point of view is virtually absent from the multiple camera setups of U.S. network broadcasting. The American crowd is not the bearer of the gaze of the camera, but rather aware of itself on camera as an object to be looked at, gesturing and holding up its own graphics, at times dressed in outlandish costumes to attract the camera's gaze. Another perspective which is absent is that of the players themselves; i.e., we never see the game from the point of view of a lineman or quarterback. Both players *and* crowd are part of the diegetic world of the game established through regular alternation of video cameras as seen from a separate and omniscient consciousness, the shifting and distanced but intimate view through long lenses.

It is interesting that while one of the American networks is sending its stylized version of the game to home viewers, another version of the game is being filmed which is not for public consumption, but rather part of the "backstage" of football, for the internal use of professional, college and even high school coaches and players. This other film is commonly shot from the press box high above the 50-yard line using two cameras, one for offense and one for defense. These "game" films are aptly named since they take in the whole field and record virtually only "the geometry of the game." Coaches project these films in slow motion in order to assess players for future recruitment, to analyze the strategies of opponents by diagramming plays and to conduct postmortems.[30] Unlike network television, slow motion functions here to the maximum as an analytic-investigative tool in the work of producing the commodity, "sport."

Like the British soccer telecasts, the game film is seen after the game itself, when the issue is no longer who will win, but how the game was won or lost. Soccer coverage in Britain is rarely "live"; thus, shows consist of edited high points of the game followed by post-game inquests. Live American broadcasts, on the other hand, are preceded by pre-game buildup of speculation on the outcome (often including clips of high points of past games), interviews and wager talk. But this so-called "male soap opera"[31] is meant to underline the contest and to build personalities; there is seldom a post-game inquest, perhaps because the act of analyzing plays and assigning praise or blame is undertaken *during* the game itself by a team of commentators, generally a play-by-play man and a color-man. In regard to the image on screen, it would seem that the "liveness" of the U.S. media-event, its apparent "immediacy," is the overriding factor in its aura of realism. In semiotic terms, it is less the iconic than the indexical relation to the referent which is determining.

Turning to the aural material of the game, it is the commentary which dominates the U.S. network soundtrack, alternating between "play-by-play" and "color" functions. The play-by-play commentator is essentially in charge of game-time, anchoring the narrative of the game by calling out the proairetic code of football.[32] His job implies that the visual movements on screen are not sufficient to name each play but must be supplemented verbally. The color-man is in charge of the "dead-time" when the clock is stopped or the players are taking position, time now employed in instant replay analysis, ads or pre-game interviews, etc. Note that the visuals he comments on are neither narrative nor live. The color-man does, however, possess a hermeneutic function in using instant replay to judge individual performance, evaluating it as well as setting it in statistical and biographical perspective. But, as his name implies, the color-man is also responsible for the spectacle aspect of the game, for conveying the enthusiasms of the crowd vocally, inviting discharge. Aided by slow motion examinations of each play, his commentary often functions as a direct invitation to scopophilia:

> "Now there's a special football player. He looks like he's a lot stronger this year." . . . "It may look like you have him stopped, but he'll still make yardage." . . . "Look at the size of that foot!" . . . "He's not only big, he's strong and fast. Boy, what qualities he's got! Look at that block. And speed does the rest." . . . "Look at the strength of that body and those legs!" . . . "He's a great athlete."[33]

It is the dual nature of the slow-motion technique itself, scientific and dreamlike, which is reiterated in the commentary of the color-man, allowing the image of the male body to be displayed and the look at it to be disavowed.

But from whose point of view is this image offered verbally for display? And from where do these commentative voices emanate? Interestingly enough, unlike British "show" commentators, American network commentators are *invisible* except for brief pre-game appearances. Hampered by the loss of suspense at the outcome, the British commentators are in view, all the more driven to make "the anteroom the arena, the reaction the event, and the commentators the real agents."[34] The American play-by-play commentary is not often linked to a visual position in space; however, the *verbal* report replaces precisely the missing overview of the geometry of the game found in the game film. From where do the voices of the invisible commentators appear to come—aside from their obvious origin in a press box and their end point in a television speaker?

The voices would seem to emanate as part of a phantom crowd somewhere *close behind* and to the sides of the television viewer. It is as if the viewer were an eavesdropper on two magnificently informed experts and fellow fans, just outside his field of view. The roar of the crowd is transformed into background noise on television, aiding the process of eliding the difference between the stadium and the receiver's position in his living room. Sometimes another noise track is added to the aural material of the game when a microphone is placed on the field to capture the clash of plastic and the thump of bodies in contact. While such sounds are inaudible in a stadium, on television they add a note of realism. The soundtrack as a whole creates an imaginary stadium in which the commentators are fellow spectators, seeing the sports event unfold for the first time, in as much suspense as any other viewer. These odd narrators in the present historical tense are visually absent but aurally omnipresent, always "live," i.e., on the spot, and simultaneous to the "crowd" event. The commentators exist in a dual relation to the diegesis, both part of it and narrating it, but only the first function is emphasized through the phantom crowd effect. And it is precisely this "live" report from the crowd which lends the event aural realism and validates the unsimulated character of the game, freeing the image itself to become spectacle and object of desire.

In Britain, the temporal gap between the stadium event and the medium event apparently motivates both visual realism in game presentation and necessitates a show format with visible narrators which tends toward spectacle.[35] Only the "game" film escapes the charge of "display." Interestingly enough, the only network experiment with showing football on television without commentary—an NBC telecast in the fall of 1980—was generally considered a failure. A variety of factors could have contributed to this— perhaps display is as crucial to pleasure in sport as play. Perhaps also, the vital function of narration as commentary on television was underlined by the results—the *anchorage* of the visual material of the game.

The visuals alone, especially in the tight framing of the American networks, are scarcely enough to allow a viewer to identify what is happening in any one play. The visuals of one game bear such a strong resemblance to those of any other game and the sequence of movements and the plays themselves—even down to the miraculous interception, the tragic fumble and the spectacular touchdown—are so predictable, that one would not be amiss in concluding that the visuals of television sport enter history and are linked with particular opponents in a specific time and place only in the verbal commentary. It is also at that level that the epithets and metaphors in which sportcasters specialize—"Mean Joe Green"; "They're playing for blood after that nasty defeat in . . ."—lend specific personalities, characteristics and expectations to the game. In the stadium, the spectator knows what game he's come to see and why, before he enters the liminal space of ritual. The television spectator must be told what he is seeing, what kind of rivalry it is, and must be invited to identify with the specular image.

To summarize the considerable difference between the stadium event and the representation of the game on television, the stadium-goer is a participant in ritual, the television viewer looks at a phantasmatic realm never seen in any stadium; the visual and aural material of the game undergoes considerable additions and transformations; however, every increment in spectacle is accompanied by a hermeneutic principle which serves the game as scientific discovery. Finally, the "liveness" of the game, particularly as conveyed by invisible commentary from the crowd, anchors the game in history and the real. The electronic reshaping of the game appears to have maintained the delicate balance necessary to the game while increasing spectacle. The television event may indeed be a better vehicle to give form to the fantasies which animate the cultural model of sport. The process of transformation has begun to effect the stadium event as well. Not merely the requisites of television but television techniques have invaded the arena itself: an up-to-date stadium now possesses an instant replay screen and many spectators bring television sets with them as well, doubling the pleasures of the crowd with the novelistic pleasures of the screen. The next section will explore whether the psychic experience of viewing sport has been affected by these transformations, especially in relation to the male body image.

Television and the Imaginary of Sport

> The fact that man is able to construct from his own inventiveness what appears to be a "practically useless" activity may be a symbol of his own identity as a being who may build a "world" of his own and, because it is his own self-constructed "world," one in which he is comfortable rather than alien. And it is entering such a world that man may know himself symbolically as a powerful agent in being, since, in that world, he literally uses controlling necessities such as space, time and gravity to suit his own purposes which are, themselves, not controlled by necessities such as pursuit of food, clothing or shelter. Further, man in the sports world may modify that world at will.
>
> —Warren Fraleigh, "The Moving 'I' "[36]

The transformations made in sport by television have substituted a visual realm (with other laws of space, time and gravity) for the visual experience of sport in a stadium. It is possible that both the construction of such an other, utopian realm and the kind of world created through slow motion and long lenses are congruent with, are even the most fortuitous expression of what is already the imaginary of sport. Then television has not destroyed the game—it has given visual form to the "voluntary hallucination"[37] induced by sport, making phantoms of desire of what were once subjective and mental images.

Each of the most significant techniques in the transformation of stadium event to television image—the extremely long lens and slow motion—contributes its specific qualities to the creation of a separate scene, a fantasy having to do with the passage into manhood, a period of ambiguous sexual identity. The construction of a masculine image of power and beauty plays an important role in that passage. Laura Mulvey's analysis of the opposition between narrative and spectacle provides a framework for discovery of how a masculine image is constructed for the *male* gaze. Later, the question of the female gaze at that image will be raised.

Mulvey's article is concerned with the sexual difference in looking/being-looked-at in film; she shows that the male figure in film inhabits three-dimensional space and is the agent which drives the narrative. He is the bearer of the gaze at the female image within the diegesis. Attracting the narcissistic identification of the male viewer, he also functions as a relay of the look of mastery at the female figure; she is there to be punished or demystified, object of an erotic gaze with sadistic components. On the other hand, the female figure alone on screen becomes pure spectacle, an icon or cut-out, inhabiting a separate world of two dimensions. She is the object of the direct look of the camera and thus of the viewer. According to Mulvey, even in this system the image of woman as the possibility of an unmasterable otherness poses a threat to both the narrative and to male identity. In any case, women are not bearers of the gaze in return (except as castrating women).

Transposing these terms to the male body image in televised football, it would seem that the visual field has become primarily spectacle. Particularly during instant replay, the narrative *per se* ceases; but space is almost always flattened, and barely individuated male bodies are fragmented and regrouped by the frame, (slowly) shifting figures in a two-dimensional world. Furthermore, these male icons are direct objects of the gaze of the camera and thus of the television viewer, the mark of pure spectacle. But unlike the female figures in Mulvey's article, alone and frozen, these multiple, at times fragmented, male figures move. What is the significance of the slowness of their motion?

The use of slow motion (where fast motion is just as logically expressive, just as technically feasible, and also quite revealing, especially of choreography and geometry) would seem to have several psychic determinants. First, slow motion is an objective realization of a subjective experience in high performance sports. For instance, in motor racing "slow is fast" and

> ... what separates the great driver from the mediocre driver, is, among other things, the ability to "go slow" in a special way that ordinary mortals experience only in dream or drugged state, to slow down time, and thereby perceived event, by speeding up perception.[38]

As race car driver Jackie Stewart writes, ". . . you must have the mental faculty of slowing things down. . . . It is rather like a film where you reduce the speed of the frames in front of your eyes. . . ."[39]

Second, the figures in slow motion are as machine-like as if animated by some supernatural agency rather than human willpower and technology. They possess the deliberate slowness which is the attribute of perfect machines, automatons and robots which are doubles of and exchanged for the human body. This long-term cultural fantasy of the body as perfect machine is one shared by sports, where the goal is to attain instant automatic response through muscle memory, action "unimpeded by acts of the ego,"[40] flowing into the instinctual patterns of nature in a "harmonious oneness of being,"[41] enjoying a freedom beyond intellect or conscious willing. Not just athletes but also spectators of sport ritual participate vicariously in this "flow,"

> a state in which action follows action according to an inner logic which needs no intervention on our part; we experience it as a unified flowing from one moment to the next, in which we feel in control of our actions, and in which there is little distinction between self and environment, between stimulus and response, or between past, present and future.[42]

That flow is conceived of as slow and graceful can perhaps be understood with an example from an early 19th-century essay on the machinated body, "The Puppet Theater" of Heinrich von Kleist.[43] The marionette is the perfect machine and graceful because it is egoless, guided at its center by the hand of God. Motion flows through the reticulated limbs which respond by swinging in slow arcs. Kleist's point is that clumsiness and self-consciousness are the lot of man, for grace comes only from lack of consciousness or absolute knowledge. Sport, however, would be a ritual space where man can overcome his separateness from nature, God, other men and his own body, and achieve grace, signified by slow motion.

But those moments in sport when an athlete experiences oneness of body and intention are not only grace as "ease and refinement of movement" but also an instance of spiritual grace, "the divine influence which operates in men to regenerate and sanctify, to inspire virtuous impulses, and to impart strength to endure trial and resist temptation,"—words from the Oxford English Dictionary which summarize much of the ideology of sport.

Slow motion then realizes the fantasy of the body as perfect machine with an aura of the divine. In addition, slowness increases the scale of the bodies on screen to tremendous size and hence power. Where are the prototypes of such barely individuated giants with godlike powers seen other than in the adult world through the eyes of a child?

The television image of sport seems to reengage experiences of early childhood when the male child was betwixt and between being unsexed and taking a heterosexual position of identification with masculinity. That sport even before television had something to do with rites of passage into adulthood has long been surmised. Folklorist Alan Dundes declares in a controversial essay that American football is a male activity "belonging to the general range of male rituals around the world in which masculinity is defined and reaffirmed."[44] He points out that "in sport and in ritual, men play both male and female roles," and, after carefully demonstrating the homosexual connotations of football language ("deep penetration," "end zone," etc.), postures and body contact, he concludes, "American football is an adolescent masculinity ritual in which the winner gets into the loser's end zone more times than the loser gets in his!"[45] Because Dundes' essay brings out only the homosexual connotations of the rituals of the game, it does not do justice to the ambiguity of sexual orientation in the liminal state of love for *and* identification with the object of desire. This ambiguity of sexual orientation is repeated in the two kinds of gazes attracted by the spectacle of instant replay.

The male icon in slow motion is the object of two intertwining gazes; the commentary of the color-man articulates the oscillation between these two looks. The first is the scientific-investigative look of the will to know, the hermeneutic process which serves the contest even when the narrative has stopped. This scientific gaze in Freudian theory is a sublimation of the look which discovers sexual difference. Directed at the male image it is ultimately scopophilic and homoerotic. Paradoxically, it is the specular gaze which is free of uncomfortable homoeroticism, for it is the narcissistic and identificatory gaze at the mirror image before discovery of sexual difference. (There are other mirror effects in the play of football itself; the opposition of two teams enacting aggression and open affection are part of its global form.)

Instant replay exhibits another kind of psychic mechanism, the repetition associated with desire. The moment of narrative closure repeated two or three times in instant replay is but a micro-example of the cyclical repetition which is the nature of sport generally, from the seasonal reappearance of football to the ritual change of sports (i.e., football, basketball, baseball) from season to season. It is the scientificity of sport, its concern with records and progress, that lends it a history, and at the same time provides the means of disavowing that other need it serves, the constant reconstruction and display of the masculine image as object of desire. That no man can ever have or be such a phantasmatic image is another aspect of the need for the repetition of that moment of closure, when identification with it and love for it were intertwined.

What is the relation of the female gaze to this phantasm of male perfection? Within the present context of spectator sports, a woman is an outsider or third party. The most typical relation of women to sport is avoidance through lack of interest—but women are also unwelcome in the inner sanctum of sport.[46] The female gaze is that of an outsider, and, when erotically charged or scientifically motivated, is potentially threatening or degrading. Various strategies for deflecting that female gaze are part of the institution of football: e.g., women as spectators have little institutional access to learning about the game and are often ignorant of what is happening on the field; women can also function as a sign of potency for the accompanying male; cheerleaders invite rather than possess the gaze.

But has there been a shift in the sexual division of labor in looking since the advent of televised sport? The privacy of the television viewing situation as well as the increase in spectacle and simply the beauty of the game invite a female gaze which is not necessarily informed about the contest, but rather is attracted by kaleidoscopic pleasures and the eroticization of the male body. Does this mean that the female gaze is no longer regarded as castrating or degrading? Other areas of culture besides sport (such as fashion and politics) show an increasing tolerance of male display for an ambiguously sexed gaze, part of the growth of a commodity culture in which images function as currency. Even the sacred heroes of sport have begun to appear in such vehicles as *Playgirl*, self-proclaimed proponent of female sexual liberation. But the cover titles of the December 1981 issue ("A *very* sexy football player! Celebrity nude! He'll be catching more passes now.") and the photos inside are clear evidence of the dangers of beefcake—the proliferation of the male image in the same manner as that of the female image, a commodity exchange "fictioning" as liberation. Perhaps players of spectator sports are safe objects of the gaze, be it male or female, because they are surrogates of power. Football players are often of lower socioeconomic and minority ethnic or racial origin; sport is thought of as a place for the upwardly mobile and "hungry." While players may represent power within the game-fiction, what they enjoy is not so much power as the exchange value of their bodies and body-images. The actual positions of social and economic power lie elsewhere, invisible.

It might be interesting to compare the idea of the masculine image as commodity with the concept of the male body and its relation to power which governed another culture and time. The Greek ideal of *kalogagathon*, the good and the beautiful, linked male beauty to the *exercise* of power in the public realm; beauty was not only a sign of grace but also a political and social force. While sport today provides an imaginary which can unite the bonds of masculine and civic loyalty frayed by the division of labor, it is but a sign and perhaps a substitute for power rather than power itself. However, the mechanism of disavowal in sport tends to elide that difference.

The outsider status of the female gaze has one significant advantage when it comes to analysis and critique of the imaginary of sport: it is not included in the *same* specular reflections in which male identity is enclosed. Presumably at that particular point it has more access to the symbolic realm and little need for disavowal. But the specific relation of the female gaze to that phantasm of male perfection, not to mention the regime of looks in women's sports, remains to be analyzed.

American television practice has organized an array of techniques and means of presentation which have the greatest potential for fascination. If athletic bodies are the commodity of sport, the *look* at the image of male bodies in motion is what television has to offer the viewer. Because this image of masculine power and perfection is the commodity upon which television bases its exchange between sponsor and viewer, it is clearly in the interest of the medium to maximize spectacle while maintaining mechanisms of disavowal which maintain the sanctity of sport. Sport on television, then, functions to the maximum as a social imaginary, or *locus* of identifications set apart from the world of production and the division of labor; the critical function of just such a utopian realm has been minimized in the process. What function does such an imaginary serve when set into place in the programming of the television medium? Has the sociocultural function of sport shifted since it has become a genre on television?

Flow and Sports as a Genre on Television

Television is primarily oriented to using programming as a way of drawing viewers to commercial messages.

—**David L. Altheide and Robert P. Snow in "Sports Versus the Mass Media."**[47]

In essence, firms that sell automobiles, automobile-related products, and petroleum products, clothing retailers, toiletry producers, brewers, and firms that provide certain consumer travel-related service, as well as savings outlets—including securities, insurance, and banks—dominate the list of sponsors [of T.V. sports programs]. Most of these industries are oligopolistic and in each instance the sponsor is an industry leader.

—**Ira Horowitz in "Market Entrenchment and the Sports Broadcasting Act."**[48]

The term "flow" as the psychic experience of euphoric unity in ritual, encompassing both participant and viewer in sport, has taken on another meaning in relation to television since Raymond Williams' *Television: Technology and Cultural Form*, where it refers to the sequence of programs on a particular network day or, more specifically, to the sequence of audio-visual material presented to the viewer, including advertisements, trailers, bulletins, etc., as well as to the program itself. For Williams, flow has a larger sense as the "flow of meanings and values of a specific culture."[49] Sport on television, then, is not a discrete entity but offers itself first as a segment of time in the flow of a broadcasting week, i.e., weekend and *Monday Night Football*; it also appears on screen in unmarked alternation with ads and trailers for other shows. While the viewer is consciously aware of the difference between sport material and ad material, at another level the contiguity between these continuous and alternating images is an index of the flow of values between them. Note as well that advertisements present no strong visual contrast, for they, like sport, are another example of the abandonment of Renaissance space in television, rejecting any claim to "realism." Ads do not endanger the "live" framework of sport by offering a realistic contrast, but rather reinforce an atmosphere of otherworldliness.

If we examine the position of sport programming in terms of weekly flow, it is clearly targeted at a primarily male audience at leisure from the work week. (Even for working women, weekends do not necessarily mean leisure—on the contrary.) One can see also that sport broadcasts occupy a privileged position in comparison with other television genres, which must fit the procrustean beds of half-hour and hour slots. For sports, game time is also broadcast time, at least since the rage over the famous "Heidi" incident, when the last moments of an exciting game were dropped from the air in order to make way for a scheduled children's program.[50] Sport thus enjoys some of the privileges of instant-breaking major news stories as well as some of the authenticity of the news. Indeed, sports do make the news shows, after the political reports and before the weather. Thus the position of sport in television flow raises it, like the news, above genres which specialize in mere entertainment. The aura of scientificity of sport, its news-value, and its perceived realism protect its extraordinary status.

Sport is, however, not only a stadium event and an institution, but also a television genre, and, in the convergence of sport and television, it is clearly television which is the dominant partner. Once can list a large number of ways in which commercial considerations of the medium have intervened in the institution of sport itself, in terms of "finances, rule changes, scheduling and entertainment, the rise of the sportcaster, player salaries, and league standing."[51] Television even decides the future of sport on the basis of commercial criteria such as suitability for alternation with advertising and market potential. Altheide and Snow conclude that "the logic of the media has pervaded institutions such as sports and politics so that the form and logic of these institutions are media-based."[52]

While such an institutional transformation is of concern to those who deplore the commercialization of sport, this analysis has maintained that television has not destroyed but enhanced formal and psychic qualities inherent in sport as a cultural model. Furthermore, television has improved the functioning of sport as a social imaginary which embraces civic identities of all sizes (city, region, nation) as well as masculine identity *per se*. What is more important to consider here than the sanctity of sport as institution is the cultural function of sport *on television*.

Returning to the concept of flow, but at the micro-level of the sports segment, it is possible to see the alternation of plays and replays with advertising—another kind of display—as a significant addition to sport. Furthermore, the practice of rights-pooling, or "the monopoly right to telecast 'the only game in town' in every TV community"[53] has the significant quantitative effect of exposing the viewing public to not just any sport images, but to the *same* images of both sport and particular commodites. Rights-pooling not only creates "non-fractionated sports audiences for the sponsors' advertising messages,"[54] but it also centralizes and unifies the powerful social imaginary of civic masculine identity and restricts the object of discourse on sport. In turn, the unitary and powerful social imaginary of civic and masculine identity is linked to specific commodities, through contiguity with the ads of commercial sponsors.

Horowitz makes a strong economic argument against rights-pooling on free market grounds, for only a few large companies have access to these ad slots, and its effect is thus to further entrench oligopolies in the marketplace. However, there are consequences for the cultural function of sport as well. By implication, and through the flow of images on television, the acquisition of sexual and civic identity is linked with the acquisition of a very limited number and type of products. The masculine image itself becomes a commodity which can be acquired through a series of exchanges between sport and advertising images, the linked product and the consumer.[55] One could object first to the fact that sport is linked with such economic and symbolic exchange at all and that identities have become consumable. But in a market economy and consumer society such an objection is decidely utopian. Once the basic premises of consumerism are accepted, why indeed should not particular products function as signs in the rituals which construct and maintain male identity?

But there is another point of consideration within the assumptions which define consumer sport today, and that is the kind and quality of that construction of masculinity itself. Not only are the type and number of products linked with sport through ads limited (although beamed to the audience for sport as a whole) but these commodites are in turn associated with a limited and stereotypic view of masculinity. Television, then, in my view, brings with it a considerable impoverishment of the culturally-shared idea of what it means to be a man; at the same time it has enriched sport as the prime means of aesthetic and emotional gratification for millions of Americans, and has provided an image of the male body-in-motion as beautiful, graceful and powerful. That image could function as a goal and critique of the actual situation of powerlessness of viewing; however, I surmise that it functions primarily as substitute and compensation for lack of success and fortune in the work week. The enhancement of the imaginary of sport through television has brought with it an act of disavowal with greater cultural consequences than the alibi of science: identification with a team and with the male image of beauty and power can be supported only in that the spectator overlooks the distance between screen and armchair and the unbridgeable difference between himself and the phantasmatic image of male perfection in slow motion.

NOTES

1. Gregory P. Stone, "American Sports: Play and Display," in *The Sociology of Sport: A Selection of Readings,* ed. Eric Dunning (London: Frank Cass and Co., 1971), pp. 47-59; quotation p. 59.

2. Laura Mulvey, "Visual Pleasure and Narrative Cinema," *Screen* Vol. 16 No. 3 (Autumn 1975), pp. 6-18; quotation p. 12.

3. In the experience of Michael Oriard, reported in "Professional Football as Cultural Myth," (*Journal of American Culture* Vol. 4 No. 3 [Fall 1981], pp. 27-41), football players themselves are acutely aware of their own mortality and of their bodies as subject to risk. Haunted by the "shortness of careers, threat of injury, trade or waiver list" (p. 32), teammates divide the world into "insiders" who share the risk and an intense "male bond," and "outsiders," such as sportswriters and fans—by whom they are used as idols to be eventually used up and abandoned—and owners, who are allowed to depreciate the bodies of their players each year by the IRS (see p. 30ff.). Players are workers who sell not only their labor time, but even many of the natural rights over one's own body that we think of as inalienable.

4. The woman sportscaster, her value and her future, was a recurrent topic of discussion in *Sports Illustrated* from 1975 to 1978, with the advent and departure of Phyllis George from CBS Sports. The final word was Melissa Ludtke Lincoln's "Fancy Figures vs. Plain Facts," (*Sports Illustrated* [July 31, 1978], p. 53), in which the author asks, "Do they [the networks] want women sportscasters in the George mold—that is, beautiful, effervescent women who don't know zilch about sports—or do they want them to be as knowledgeable as the better men sportscasters?" According to George herself, "when a woman is too assertive or too knowledgeable, they don't want her." The article ends on a plaintive note by Houston sportscaster Andrea Martini: "Why can women talk about wars, riots and presidential trips and not be able to talk about sports? Why is there such a sacred bond between men and sports?"

5. Stone, p. 56.

6. Fran Tarkington, *ABC Monday Night Football* (October 5, 1981).

7. For a thorough treatment of the origin and function of record keeping and the scientific-experimental side of sport, see Allen Guttman, *From Ritual to Record: The Nature of Modern Sports* (New York: Columbia University Press, 1978).

8. Stone, p. 59.

9. Ibid., p. 60.

10. Ibid., p. 57ff.

11. William Oscar Johnson, "How Many Messages for This Medium?", *Sports Illustrated* (February 19, 1979), p. 38. The Super Bowl rating for 1978 was 104 million viewers.

12. Studies cited in George H. Sage, "Sport and the Social Sciences," *The Annals of the American Academy of Political and Social Science* Vol. 445 (September 1979), p. 3.

13. Norbert Elias, "The Genesis of Sport as a Sociological Problem," in *The Sociology of Sport*, p. 104.

14. Ibid., p. 92ff. See also R. Terry Furst, "Social Change and the Commercialization of Professional Sports," *International Review of Sports Sociology* Vol. 6 (1971), p. 156ff.

15. See C.E. Ashworth, "Sport as Symbolic Dialogue," in *The Sociology of Sport*, pp. 40-46. This utopian aspect of sport and its implications for the presentation of sport in film was developed in greater detail in an unpublished paper given at the Athens Ohio Film Conference in April 1981: "Slow Motion: An Analysis and Comparison of Sports Sequences in Vertov's *Man With a Movie Camera*, Brecht/Dudow's *Kuhle Wampe*, and Riefenstahl's *Olympia*."

16. Other major spectator sports such as baseball and basketball, plus the array of televised sports from tennis, golf, track and field to boxing, gymnastics and ice-skating each use space and time differently and project somewhat different images of bodily perfection; hence, each has different possibilities for the visual maximization of the ideal body-in-motion. Each, then, has different potential on television. Beyond that, the audience for each sport and the politics of the sport vis-à-vis the networks will differ. Furthermore, within each sport, especially one with a strong division of labor, variations in body image are important, i.e., a quarterback will differ from a tackle. Nonetheless, modern sports are variations on the same cultural model.

17. Barrett A. Lee and Carol A. Zeiss, "Behavioral Commitment to the Role of Sport Consumer: An Explanatory Analysis," *Sociology and Social Research* Vol. 64 No. 3 (April 1980), pp. 405-419. I would like to thank Barrett Lee for his help with current articles on the sociology of sport, as well as comments from the point of view of recent work in sociology.

18. The term liminality applied to rites of passage (into adulthood, for example) has been extended by Victor Turner to cultural institutions of performance such as carnival and public ritual. In his article, "Frame, Flow and Reflection: Ritual and Drama as Public Liminality," (in *Performance in Postmodern Culture*, ed. Michel Benamou and Charles Caramello [Madison, WI: Coda, 1977], pp. 33-55), Turner does mention sport, but does not develop the idea of liminality in sport.

19. According to Elias Canetti in *Crowds and Power* (New York: The Viking Press, 1973), it is only in a crowd that the fear of being touched turns into its opposite. Note also that sport is one of the few areas of public interaction which licenses touching between men.

20. There are many who see sport as drama, meant in a critical or positive sense—for example, Gregory Stone in the above article and Roland Barthes on "The World of Wrestling" in *Mythologies* (New York: Hill and Wang, 1972). Robert B. Heilman sees football as melodrama in "Football: An Addict's Memoirs and Observations," (*Journal of American Culture* Vol. 4 No. 3 [Fall 1981], p. 15): "an unmixed, straightforward fight, and it always simplifies itself into a battle of good against evil." Once on television, however, the event is narrated and the visual and aural representation of the game can be divided into the narrative itself and the diegetic world of the game invoked by the narrative.

21. Report on the research of Brien R. Williams, Indiana University Department of Telecommunications in "The Tube's Eye View of Football: Network Coverage Imposes Its Own Ideology," *Human Behavior* Vol. 7 No. 3 (March 1978), p. 34.

22. "Kaleidoscopic" is a term which occurs quite regularly in the discourse on sports events on television. It appropriately means "beautiful form" plus "look" (*Oxford English Dictionary*) applied to an optical instrument developed by Sir David Brewster in 1812, and by extension to "a constantly changing group of bright colours or coloured objects, anything which exhibits a succession of shifting phases." Raymond Williams, in *Television: Technology and Cultural Form* (New York: Schocken Books, 1975), p. 77, notes as one of the basic innovating forms of television "the experience of visual mobility, of contrast of angle, of variation of focus, which is often very beautiful." Televised sport seems organized to make the most of this aesthetic potential of television.

23. The capital investment in technology and media production capacity alone is enormous, aside from investment in the institution of sport itself as a commodity or the commercial investment in advertising and publicity connected to sport. While a regular Sunday afternoon sportscast on CBS or NBC runs with five to eight cameras and three to five videotape machines, the Super Bowl of 1981 used 23 cameras. In the struggle for dominance in sport which Ron

Powers labels "The Real Super Bowl War" (*TV Week* [January 24-30, 1982], p. 3), NBC has added a Louma camera (and crane, which can cross in front of the team bench for reaction shots) and CBS has installed a "Renfro" camera mounted above the 50-yard line.

24. See William Barry Furlong, "Football Violence," *The New York Times Magazine* (November 30, 1980), pp. 38-41, 122-134.

25. Furst, p. 167. He treats the negative impact of television on sport on pages 165-170.

26. Now these "all important reaction shots" (Powers) include the coaches and the bench with the advent of the Louma. Note that the bench functions as part of the crowd. I maintain that the crowd is part of the diegetic world of televised football. The look of the crowd in reaction shots is seldom well matched with the shot of the field. It seems more importantly to function as a visual identity for the phantom crowd invoked by the soundtrack.

27. Len Masterman, "Football on Television," in *Television Studies: Four Approaches* (British Film Institute Education Service Advisory Document, 1979), pp. 3-13. Masterman's paper builds on the work in BFI Television Monographs/No. 4, *Football on Television*.

28. The characteristics of soccer versus football are discussed in Joan M. Chandler, "TV and Sports: Wedded With a Golden Hoop," *Psychology Today* Vol. 10 No. 11 (April 1977), pp. 64-76.

29. Masterman, p. 17.

30. Unlike slow motion in film practice, slow motion sports are not shot at a higher-than-normal speed and then projected at normal speed, but *projected* at variable lower speed. The possibilities for variable and reverse projection of the 19th-century Praxinoscope are realized with the advent of the 1" videotape machine, which has replaced the "slow-mo" disc. On 1" machines all of a recorded event is retrievable and can be put in slow motion at 1/2 or 1/5 of normal or variable speed. (The fast foward capability of up to 10 times normal speed or the reverse capacity is never, to my knowledge, used for the version of the game which is broadcast.) See J.R. Young, "Producing with 1"," *Video Systems* (October 1980), pp. 16-21. The home viewer's video recorder gives him a similar capacity for temporal manipulation and repetition of a recorded game. These technological developments indicate that slow motion is no longer a cliché or a device, but the grounds upon which movement in sport is based: high speed has become signified by slow motion. Whether the minute differences between these methods in the visual realization is significant deserves investigation.

31. An apt label overheard in a conversation among local female football fans. Soaps and sport on television actually do not resemble each other in anything but their national importance for female and male fantasy, respectively. Sports interviews, however, come closest to the spatial and dramatic conventions of soap opera.

32. See "The Empiric Voice," in Roland Barthes' *S/Z* (New York: Hill and Wang, 1974), pp. 203-204, and "The Voice of Truth," pp. 209-210, for definitions of the proairetic and hermeneutic codes and their function in the narrative.

33. Garnered from two different color-men on *CBS Sunday Night Football* (October 4, 1981) , and *ABC Monday Night Football* (October 5, 1981).

34. Raymond Williams, "There's Always the Sport," *The Listener* (April 16, 1970), pp. 522-523; quoted in Masterman, p. 13.

35. Masterman, p. 17.

36. Warren Fraleigh, "The Moving 'I'," in *The Philosophy of Sport: A Collection of Original Essays,* ed. Robert G. Osterhoudt (Springfield, IL: Thomas, 1973), pp. 108-129; quotation on p. 114.

37. Stone, p. 54.

38. S.B. Purdy, "Of Time, Motion, and Motor Racing," *Journal of American Culture* Vol. 4 No. 3 (Fall 1981), p. 94. The San Francisco 49er quarterback John Brodie reported similar experiences on the football field: "At times, and with increasing frequency now, I experience a kind of clarity that I've never seen adequately described. Sometimes, for example, I have all the time in the world to watch the receivers run their patterns, and yet I know the defensive line is coming at me just as fast as ever. . . . The whole thing seems like a dance in slow motion." (Quoted in Ben Yagoda, "Getting Psyched," *Esquire* [April 1982], p. 34.)

39. Purdy, p. 94. Note that author Purdy and race car driver Jackie Stewart are describing two different slow motion effects, one obtained by perceiving faster, the other by projecting slower.

40. Roselyn E. Stone, "Assumptions About the Nature of Human Movement," in *The Philosophy of Sport*, p. 48.

41. Fraleigh, p. 117.

42. Victor Turner, "Frame, Flow and Reflection," p. 47. The concept is borrowed from cultural theorist Mihaly Csikszentmihalyi.

43. Heinrich von Kleist, "Ueber das Marionettentheater," (1801) in his collected works (Frankfurt: Insel-Verlag, n.d.). An excellent 20th-century analysis of this fascination with robots, mannequins and other types and orders of replication of the human body is Jean Baudrillard's *L'échange symbolique et la mort* (Paris: Gallimard, 1976). The relation of slow motion to death, and work as "slow death" adds another moment of psychological regression—the death drive—to the psychic significance of slow motion. Baudrillard describes another slow dance, the striptease (p. 165ff.) and claims it to be the only new dance invented in the 20th century. Perhaps we can add the male dance of sport in slow motion to the list. I consider its finest expression in film to be the opening sequence of *Raging Bull*, its definitive use in *Chariots of Fire*; but it occurs on television regularly and not only in the end-zone dance but in every instant replay.

44. Alan Dundes, "Into the End Zone for a Touchdown: A Psychoanalytic Consideration of American Football," in *Interpreting Folklore* (Bloomington, IN: Indiana University Press, 1980), p. 210.

45. Ibid.

46. Michael Oriard writes of the exclusion of women, even wives, from the discourse of the football player in his experience: "The sexual dimension of football is a complex subject that cannot be covered adequately in a few sentences, but the pressure on the football player to satisfy his public image as a masculine ideal and the drive to preserve the all-male nature of his experiences from feminine contamination contribute to this exclusion of women from the inner sanctum." ("Professional Football as Cultural Myth," p. 30ff.) Some women sportswriters have penetrated the locker room as well as entered the discourse on sport: Jane Gross, "A Woman Reporter in Yankee Country," *The New York Times Magazine* (October 25, 1981), pp. 32-46, 116-121.

47. David L. Altheide and Robert P. Snow, "Sports Versus the Mass Media," *Urban Life* Vol. 7 No. 2 (July 1978), pp. 189-204; quotation on p. 190.

48. Ira Horowitz, "Market Entrenchment and the Sports Broadcasting Act," *American Behavioral Scientist* Vol. 21 No. 3 (January-February 1978), pp. 415-430; quotation on p. 423ff.

49. Williams, *Television*, p. 118.

50. See William Johnson, "Towering Babble and (SOB) Heidi," *Sports Illustrated* (January 19, 1970), pp. 24-31. Part of a very informative history of sport on television in four parts beginning with the December 22, 1969 issue.

51. Altheide and Snow, p. 192.

52. Ibid., p. 204

53. Horowitz. p. 415.

54. Ibid.

55. See the analysis of advertising in print media of Judith Williamson, *Decoding Advertisements: Ideology and Meaning in Advertising* (London: Marion Boyars, 1978).

The Rhythms of Reception:
Daytime Television and Women's Work

Tania Modleski

In his book *Television: Technology and Cultural Form* Raymond Williams suggests that the shifts in television programming from one type of show to another and from part of a show to a commercial should be seen not as "interruptions"—of a mood, of a story—but as parts of a whole. What at first appear to be discrete programming units in fact interrelate in profound and complex ways. Williams uses the term "flow" to describe this interaction of various programs with each other and with commercials. "The fact of flow," he says, "defines the central television experience."[1]

Here I would like to examine the flow of daytime television, particularly the way soap operas, quiz shows, and commercials interrelate. More specifically, I want to look at how the flow of these programs connects to the work of women in the home. As the ladies' magazines never tire of telling us, this work involves a variety of tasks and requires a wide range of abilities. Moreover, this work tends to be very different from men's work. As Nancy Chodorow describes it:

> Women's activities in the home involve continuous connection to and concern about children and attunement to adult masculine needs, both of which require connection to, rather than separateness from, others. The work of maintenance and reproduction is...repetitive and routine ...and does not involve specified sequence or progression. By contrast, work in the labor force—"men's work"—is more likely to be contractual, to be more specifically delimited and to contain a notion of defined progression and product.[2]

Apparently, women's work itself is a kind of flow, so my task would seem to be especially pertinent.

One of the chief differences between daytime television and nighttime programming is that the former appears to be participatory in a way that the latter almost never is: it stresses, in other words, "connection to, rather than separateness from, others." This is obviously the case with quiz shows and talk shows like *Phil Donahue* and even the "Money Movie." But it is also true of soap operas. For example, on soap operas, action is less important than *rea*ction and *inter*action, which is one reason why fans keep insisting on soap opera's "realism," although critics continually delight in pointing out the absurdity of its content. Despite the numerous murders, kidnappings, blackmail attempts, emergency operations, amnesia attacks, etc., which are routine occurrences on soap operas, anyone who has followed one, for however brief a time, knows that these events are not important in themselves; they merely serve as occasions for characters to get together and have prolonged, involved, intensely emotional discussions with each other.

Furthermore, audiences are much more likely to become intimately involved with soap opera characters and to experience them as equals than they are with the characters on nighttime programs. A comparison with *Dallas*, the popular nighttime serial, is instructive. There the characters are highly glamorized, the difference between their world and that of the average viewer could not be greater, and the difference is continually emphasized. On soap operas, in contrast, glamor and wealth are played down. Characters are just attractive *enough* so that their looks are not distracting, well-off *enough* so that, as in a Henry James novel, they can worry about more exciting problems than inflation at the supermarket. But glamor and wealth are *not* preoccupations as they are on *Dallas*. Obviously, the soap opera world is in *reality* no more like the average spectator's than the world of *Dallas*; yet the characters and the settings all connote, to use a Barthesian neologism, "averageness." This accounts for the fans' frequent contention that soap opera characters are just like them—whereas no one is likely to make such a claim about the Ewing family. The consequent blurring of the boundaries between fantasy and life which sometimes occurs (for example, when fans write letters to the "characters," giving them advice about their problems) suggests that the psychological fusion which Chodorow says is experienced by the wife/mother applies in these instances to the *viewer's* experience of the characters.

This last observation would seem to lend support to Luce Irigaray's thesis that identification is an inadequate term for describing women's pleasure. As film critics have recently been pointing out: "Cinematic identification presupposes the security of the modality 'as if.' "[3] Soap operas tend, more than any other form, to break down the distance required for the proper working of identification. But rather than seeing these cases as pathological instances of *over*-identification (as in the case of the boy who stabbed a woman in the shower after seeing *Psycho*[4]), I would argue that they point to a different *kind* of relationship between spectator and characters, one which can be described in the words of Irigaray as "nearness"—"a nearness so close that any identification of one or the other is impossible."[5] The viewer does not *become* the characters (like the boy in the *Psycho* case), but rather relates to them as intimates, as extensions of her world. Speaking of woman's rediscovery of herself, Irigaray writes, "It is a sort of universe in expansion for which no limits could be fixed and which, for all that, would not be incoherent."[6] I need not belabor the similarities between this description and soap opera as a form. But I mention it because I believe it is crucial to understand how women's popular culture speaks to women's pleasure at the same time that it puts it in the service of patriarchy, keeps it working for the good of the family.

Television also plays on women's fears that they are not near enough to those around them. Consider the happy ending of a well-known television commercial: Wife: "Why didn't you *tell* me you like Stove-Top Stuffing with chicken?" Husband: "You never asked me." So, it seems, women must play guessing games, be mind readers. Is it then merely accidental that several popular television quiz shows emphasize mind reading over the possession of correct answers? I am referring to programs which have contestants guess the responses of a studio audience or a poll of people, programs like *The Match Game*, *Card Sharks* and *Family Feud*. In a perceptive article in *Screen Education*, John Tulloch argues that quiz shows on British television present a reified view of knowledge which is current in the culture at large.[7] Increasingly, daytime quiz shows on American television relate not so much to any particular view of knowledge as to a desire to overcome one's *exclusion* from knowledge, from the thoughts and feelings of others. Answers are no longer right or wrong in any "objective" sense; contestants are rewarded when they correctly guess what *other people* think.

Questions about what is on other people's minds provide many of the enigmas of soap operas as well as of other popular feminine narratives. In gothic romances, for example, the solution to the mystery lies less in the intellectual process of detection—following external clues to determine who provided the corpse, how, and with what motive—than guessing what the aloof, attractive, enigmatic male is thinking and feeling. In soap operas, characters spend an inordinate amount of time trying to find out what is "bothering" another character. Soap operas may be excessively wordy, as Horace Newcomb has pointed out, but this wordiness is built around deep silences.[8] Characters talk, speculate endlessly about why other characters are *not* talking.

Furthermore, not only are the characters on soap operas impelled to fathom the secrets of other people's minds; the constant, even claustrophobic use of close-up shots stimulates the audience to do likewise. Often *only* the audience is privileged to witness characters' expressions, which are complex and intricately coded, signifying triumph, bitterness, despair, confusion—the entire emotional register, in fact. Soap operas contrast sharply with other popular forms aimed at masculine visual pleasure, which is often centered on the fragmentation and fetishization of the female body. In the most popular feminine visual art, it is easy to forget that characters even have bodies, so insistently are close-ups of faces employed. One critic significantly remarks, "A face in close-up is what before the age of film only a lover or a mother ever saw."[9] Soap operas appear to be the one visual art which activates the gaze of the mother—but in order to provoke anxiety (an anxiety never allayed by narrative closure) about the welfare of others. Close-ups provide the spectator with training in "reading" other people, in being sensitive to their (unspoken) feelings at any given moment.

This openness to the needs and desires of others is, of course, one of the primary functions of the woman in the home. The wife and mother, who is excluded from participation in the larger world in which her husband and children move, must nevertheless be attuned to the effects of this world upon her family. Moreover, although her family cannot be bothered with the details of *her* world, with making such "trivial" decisions as whether to have stuffing or potatoes with dinner, such decisions nevertheless affect her family's attitudes and moods, and it is well for her to be able to anticipate desires which remain unuttered, perhaps even unthought. Thus, the enigmas of a significant number of commercials, as in the one quoted above, center around the wife's anxiety about what her husband or children will think of one of her little changes in the menu or the running of the household. She waits in suspense as her husband takes the first forkful of his meal, or breathlessly looks on as he selects a clean shirt, wondering if he will notice just how clean and fresh it is. Of course, he *does* notice, as she ecstatically exclaims. This last example seems to come very close to subverting its own project—the project of many commercials—of showing the immense rewards involved in being a housewife. To me, it announces a little too clearly how extraordinary it is when family members pay the least attention to all the work the woman in the home does for them. It is worth noting that in the many commercials in which a male tests a female (for example, gives her a new medicine to reduce tension) there is never any anxiety involved. He is absolutely certain what brand will please her. Men, it appears, don't have to try to "read" women; they already know them and fully understand their needs.

Not only is it the responsibility of the woman in the home to be sensitive to the feelings of her family, her job is further complicated by the fact that she must often deal with several people who have different, perhaps conflicting moods; and further, she must be prepared to drop what she is doing in order to cope with various conflicts and problems the moment they arise. Unlike most workers in the labor force, the housewife must beware of concentrating her energies exclusively on one task—otherwise the dinner could burn, or the baby could crack its skull (as happened once on a soap opera when a villainess became so absorbed in a love encounter that she forgot to keep an eye on her child). The housewife functions, as many creative women have sadly realized, by distraction. Tillie Olsen writes in *Silences*:

> More than in any other human relationship, overwhelmingly more, motherhood means being instantly interruptable, responsive, responsible.... It is distraction, not meditation, that becomes habitual; interruption, not continuity; spasmodic, not constant toil.[10]

Daytime television plays a part in habituating women to interruption, distraction, and spasmodic toil. Here I must take issue with Raymond Williams, who rejects the notion that television programs and commercials may be seen as interruptions. Indeed, I would argue that the flow of daytime television reinforces the very principle of interruptability crucial to the proper functioning of women in the home. In other words, what Williams calls "the central television experience" is a profoundly de-centering experience.

"The art of being off center," wrote Walter Benjamin in an essay on Baudelaire, "in which the little man could acquire training in places like the Fun Fair, flourished concomitantly with unemployment."[11] Daytime television programs, most obviously soap operas, also provide training in "the art of being off center" (and we should note in passing that it is probably no accident that the nighttime soap opera *Dallas* and its offshoots and imitators are flourishing in a period of economic crisis and rising unemployment). The housewife, of course, is, in one sense, like the little man at the fun fair, unemployed, but in another sense she is perpetually employed—her work, like a soap opera, is never done. Moreover, as I have said, her duties are split among a variety of domestic and familial tasks, and her television programs keep her from desiring a focused existence by involving her in the pleasures of a fragmented life.

The multiple plot lines of soap operas, for example, keep women interested in a number of characters and their various fates simultaneously. When one plot threatens to become too absorbing, it is interrupted, and another story line resumed, or a commercial is aired. Interruptions within the soap opera diegesis are both annoying and pleasurable: if we are torn away from one absorbing story, we at least have the relief of picking up the thread of an unfinished one. Commercials, of course, present the housewife with mini-problems and their resolutions, so after witnessing all the agonizingly hopeless dilemmas presented on soap operas, the spectator has the satisfaction of seeing *something* cleaned up, if only a stained shirt or a dirty floor.

Although daytime commercials and soap operas are set overwhelmingly within the home, the two views of the home seem antithetical, for the chief concerns of commercials are precisely the ones soap operas censor out. The soggy diapers, yellow wax buildup and carpet smells constituting the world of daytime television ads are rejected by soap operas in favor of Another World, as the very title of one soap opera announces, a world in which characters deal only with the "large" problems of human existence: crime, love, death and dying. But this antithesis embodies a deep truth about the way women function in (or, more accurately, around) culture: as both moral and spiritual guides and household drudges—now one, now the other, moving back and forth between the extremes, but obviously finding them difficult to reconcile.

Similarly, the violent mood swings the spectator undergoes in switching from quiz shows to soap operas also constitute a kind of interruption, just as the housewife is required not only to endure monotonous, repetitive work but also to be able to switch instantly and on demand from her role as a kind of bedmaking, dishwashing automaton to a large sympathizing consciousness. It must be stressed that while nighttime television certainly offers shifts in mood, notably from comedy to drama, these shifts are not nearly as extreme as in daytime programming. Quiz shows present the spectator with the same game, played and replayed frenetically day after day, with each game a self-contained unit, crowned by climactic success or failure. Soap operas, by contrast, endlessly defer resolutions and climaxes and undercut the very notion of success by continually demonstrating that happiness for all is an unattainable goal: one person's triumph is another person's bitter disappointment.

Not only this, but the pacing of these two types of programs are at opposite extremes. On quiz shows contestants invariably operate under severe time pressure. If the answer is not given in 30 seconds, a most unpleasant-sounding buzzer, rather like an alarm clock or an oven timer, forces the issue: "Time is up, your answer please." Whereas quiz shows operate on the speed-up principle, compressing time into tight limits, soap operas slow down the action and expand time to an extent never seen on nighttime television (not even on shows like *Dallas*). Soap opera time coincides with or is actually slower than "real" time, and, moreover, throughout the years, the lengths of the programs themselves have been expanding. If the two kinds of time embodied by these two types of programs reflect the fact that the housewife must both race *against* time (in completing her daily chores) and *make* time (to be receptive to the demands on her attention made by her family), on a deeper level they are not as divergent as they appear. Speaking of games of chance, in which "starting all over again is the regulative idea," Benjamin related the gambler's psychological experience of time to that of the man who works for wages. For both, it is "time in hell, the province of those who are not allowed to complete anything they have started."[12] The desire for instant gratification, says Benjamin, is the result of modern man's having been cheated out of his experience. But gratification instantaneously awarded (as in games of chance), or gratification infinitely postponed (as in soap operas) both suggest the deprivation of experience, a deprivation suffered not only by those who work for wages, but obviously also pertaining to those who work at repetitive tasks for *no* tangible rewards, but rather for the gratification of others.

The formal properties of daytime television thus accord closely with the rhythms of women's work in the home. Individual programs like soap operas as well as the flow of various programs and commercials tend to make repetition, interruption and distraction pleasurable. But we can go even further and note that for women viewers reception itself often takes place in a state of distraction. According to Benjamin, "reception in a state of distraction . . . finds in the film its true means of exercise."[13] But now that we have television we can see that it goes beyond film in this respect, or at least the daytime programs do. For the consumption of most films as well as nighttime programs in some ways recapitulates the work situation in the factory or office: the viewer is physically passive, immobilized, and all his or her attention is focused on the screen. Even the most allegedly "mindless" program requires a fairly strong degree of concentration if its plot is to make sense. But since the housewife's "leisure" time is not so strongly demarcated, her entertainment must often be consumed on the job. As the authors of *The Complete Soap Opera Book* tell us:

> The typical fan was assumed to be trotting about her daily chores with her mop in one hand, duster in the other, cooking, tending babies, answering telephones. Thus occupied, she might not be able to bring her full powers of concentration to bear on *Backstage Wife*.[14]

This accounts, in part, for the "realistic" feel of soap operas. The script writers, anticipating the housewife's distracted state, are careful to repeat important elements of the story several times. Thus, if two characters are involved in a confrontation which is supposed to mark a final break in their relationship, that same confrontation must be repeated, with minor variations, a few times in order to make sure the viewer gets the point. "Clean breaks"—surely a supreme fiction—are impossible on soap operas. Quiz shows, too, are obviously aimed at the distracted viewer, who, if she misses one game because she is cleaning out the bathroom sink, can easily pick up on the next one ten minutes later.

Benjamin, writing of film, invoked architecture as the traditional art most closely resembling the new one in the kinds of response they elicit. Both are mastered to some extent in a state of distraction; that is, both are appropriated "not so much by attention as by habit."[15] It is interesting to recall in this connection the Dadaist Eric Satie's concept of furniture music, which would be absorbed while people went about their business or chatted with each other. Television is the literalization of the metaphor of furniture art, but it must be stressed that this art is more than simply background noise in the way, for example, that muzak is; daytime programs, especially soap operas, are intensely meaningful to many women, as a conversation with any fan will immediately confirm. Moreover, as I have tried to show, their rhythms interact in complex ways with the rhythms of women's life and work in the home.

Ironically, critics of television untiringly accuse its viewers of indulging in escapism. In other words, both high art critics and politically oriented critics, though motivated by vastly different concerns, unite in condemning daytime television for *distracting* the housewife from her real situation. My point is that a distracted or distractable frame of mind is crucial to the housewife's efficient functioning *in* her real situation, and at *this* level television and its so-called distractions, along with the particular forms they take, are intimately bound up with women's work.

NOTES

1. Raymond Williams, *Television: Technology and Cultural Form* (New York: Schocken Books, 1975), p. 95.

2. Nancy Chodorow, *The Reproduction of Mothering: Psychoanalysis and the Sociology of Gender* (Berkeley, CA: University of California Press, 1978) p. 179.

3. Mary Ann Doane, "Misrecognition and Identity," *Ciné-Tracts* Vol. 3 No. 3 (Fall 1980), p. 25.

4. Doane refers to James Naremore's discussion of this incident in *Film Guide to Psycho* (Bloomington, IN: Indiana University Press, 1973), p. 72.

5. Luce Irigaray, "When the goods get together" (from *Ce sexe qui n'en est pas un* [Paris: Minuit, 1977]), in *New French Feminisms*, ed. Elaine Marks and Isabelle de Courtivron (Amherst, MA: University of Massachusetts Press, 1980), pp. 104-105.

6. Ibid., p. 104.

7. John Tulloch, "Gradgrind's Heirs: The Quiz and the Presentation of 'Knowledge' by British Television," *Screen Education* No. 19 (Summer 1976), pp. 3-13.

8. Horace Newcomb, *TV: The Most Popular Art* (New York: Doubleday/Anchor Books, 1974), pp. 168-169.

9. Dennis Porter, "Soap Time: Thoughts on a Commodity Art Form," *College English* Vol. 38 No. 8 (April 1977), p. 786.

10. Tillie Olsen, *Silences* (New York: Dell Publishing, 1979), pp. 18-19.

11. Walter Benjamin, "On Some Motifs in Baudelaire," in *Illuminations*, trans. Harry Zohn (New York: Schocken Books, 1969), p. 176.

12. Ibid., p. 179.

13. Benjamin, "The Work of Art in the Age of Mechanical Reproduction," in *Illuminations*, p. 240.

14. Madeleine Edmondson and David Rounds, *From Mary Noble to Mary Hartman: The Complete Soap Opera Book* (New York: Stein and Day, 1976), pp. 46-47.

15. Benjamin, "The Work of Art." pp. 239-240.

Crossroads:
Notes on Soap Opera

Charlotte Brunsdon

> Husband to wife weeping as she watches TV:
> "For heaven's sake, Emily!
> It's only a commercial for acid indigestion."
> —Joke on Bryant & May matchbox

Introduction: A gendered audience?

The audience for soap opera is usually assumed to be female.[1] In this paper I would like to examine this assumption, and to examine the extent to which the notion of a gendered audience can be useful to us in the understanding of a British soap opera, *Crossroads*.

I should like initially, following Willemen[2] and Morley,[3] to make a distinction between the subject positions that a text constructs, and the social subject who may or may not take up these positions. That is, we can usefully analyze the "you" and "yous" that the text as discourse constructs, but we cannot assume that any individual audience member will necessarily occupy these positions. With Neale[4] and Morley[5] we can argue that the relation of the audience to the text will not be determined solely by that text, but also by positions in relation to a whole range of other discourses,[6] such as those of motherhood, romance and sexuality. Thus it may well be, as Mulvey has argued,[7] that visual pleasure in narrative cinema is dependent on identification with male characters in their gaze at female characters, but it does not necessarily follow that any individual audience member will unproblematically occupy this masculine position. Indeed, feminist film criticism usefully deconstructs the gendering of this "you." As Winship has recently argued, "A feminist politics of representation...has then to engage with the social reader, as well as the social text."[8]

The interplay of social reader and social text can be usefully examined by looking at the extent to which program publicity, scheduling and ads imply a gendered audience. In its annual handbook, the Independent Broadcasting Authority (IBA) groups *Crossroads* with other Drama serials:

> TV drama serials have for many years been an essential ingredient in the programme diet of a large and devoted audience. Established favourites such as *Coronation Street* and *Crossroads* continue to develop themes and situations which often deal with the everyday problems and difficulties to which many viewers can relate. Occasionally the more adventurous type of serial is produced. . . .[9]

Apart from the structuring dietary metaphor, the opposition of "devoted" and "everyday" to "adventurous," I would suggest, specifies the femininity of the audience. There are a wide range of "spin-off" materials associated with *Crossroads*—novels, special souvenir supplements, interview material—and a *Crossroads* cookbook.[10]

Crossroads is broadcast at different times in different regions, and has been cut, since this research commenced, from four to three evenings a week. However, despite the varied times of broadcast, all transmissions take place within the 5:15-7:39 early evening slot. No soap operas—and this excludes "classic serials" and other melodramas such as *Dallas*—are broadcast after 8:00 pm, or during the weekend. Even *The Archers* only has an omnibus program of repeat episodes on Sundays. Richard Paterson has argued for the dominance of notions of "the family" and "the domestic" in the scheduling of British television.[11] If we accept this argument, it is quite clear that *Crossroads* is being scheduled for women—or more particularly, for wives and mothers. The program is broadcast in a slot when "fathers" are not expected to determine program choice. Paterson also suggests a relationship between scheduling and program structure:

> [*Crossroads'*] narrative is constructed of multiple short segments, with continual repetition of narrative information, but no overall dramatic coherence in any episode. In part this structure reflects its place in the schedule: continual viewing has to be ensured even though meal times and other domestic interruptions might make it impossible to follow a coherent narrative.[12]

I will take up later the question of the incoherence of *Crossroads* narratives.

If we use Raymond Williams' notion of television "flow," we find *Crossroads* surrounded by magazine news programs, panel games and other serials—all suitable for family, and interrupted, viewing. However, we can also consider the advertising that frames and erupts within the program. This is quite clearly addressed to a feminine consumer—beauty aids, breakfast cereals, instant "man-appeal" meals and cleaning products, i.e., the viewer as sexual, the viewer as mother, the viewer as wife, and the viewer as housewife. (This is in contrast to the ads for lawn mowers, car gadgets, DIY [Do-It-Yourself] equipment or large family purchases that dominate from 8:30 p.m.

on.) These ads often seem also to assume an older viewer, in that there is usually at least one ad for products associated with dentures.

These extra-textual factors can be understood to indicate that women are a target audience for *Crossroads*. I would like now to consider selected aspects of the textual strategies of the program.[13]

A discontinuous text

The ideological problematic of soap opera—the frame or field in which meanings are made, in which significance is constructed narratively—is that of "personal life"; more particularly, personal life in its everyday realization through personal relationships. This can be understood to be constituted primarily through the representations of romances, families and the attend-ant rituals—births, engagements, marriages, divorces and deaths. In Marxist terms, this is the sphere of the individual outside waged labor. In feminist terms, it is the sphere of women's "intimate oppression." In recent history, society has recognized feminine competence only within this realm of the domestic, the personal, the private.[14] However, the action of soap opera is not restricted to familial, or quasi-familial institutions, but as it were *colonizes* the public masculine sphere, representing it from the point of view of the personal. It is through the concerns and values of the personal sphere that the public sphere is represented in soap opera.

Thus in *Crossroads* we have a family-run business, the Crossroads motel, with an attached garage. The motel is near a village, Kings Oak, which at various times has included a market-garden, a doctor's surgery, a post office, an antique shop, etc. Regular characters are members of one of three groups—the Crossroads family, the motel/garage workforce, or the village. The fictional community (its hierarchy made clear through *mise-en-scène* and dialogue) is kept interacting through a series of interlocking economic relationships, but this business interaction is only of diegetic importance as the site of personal relationships. It is always emotionally significant per-sonal interaction, often reported in dialogue, which is narratively fore-grounded. This can be seen most clearly through the narrative construction of time and place.

There is no single linear time flow; the minimum three concurrent narratives proceed through a succession of short segments (rarely exceeding 2½ minutes). In contrast with classical narrative cinema,[15] the temporal relationship between segments is rarely encoded. There is no standard tem-poral relationship between segments, although it is possible to say that time in general moves forward, with some repetition. Relationships between segments can be read as sequential or simultaneous in most cases. One continuous scene can be broken into several segments—notoriously over commercial breaks and between episodes, but this is a standard intra-episode suspense device. Tania Modleski has pointed to the centrality of "interruption" in soap opera narratives.[16] This lack of any overarching time scheme allows the rise and fall of different narrative threads. As each narrative has only its time of exposition, there is no loss of "real" or referential time if narrative lapses. Similarly, the very simplicity of the use of "interruption" as the major form of narrative delay, fabulously extending dramatic action, also works against the construction of coherent referential time. The different narratives co-exist in a simultaneous present.

Space in *Crossroads* is also organized in a way which is quite distinct from the conventions of classical narrative cinema. These conventions are utilized in some other forms of television drama, such as crime series. The shoestring budgets mean very restricted sets (all internal, usually no more than five in one episode) and few available camera positions.[17] Generally, sets have two distinct spaces arranged laterally to each other—that is, there are two distinct camera fields, and it is the articulation of these fields which constructs the space.[18] Some sets allow only one camera position. These camera setups are not variable, and camera movement is limited. Most scenes are shot in mid-shot or medium close-up, opening with either a close-up or a longer shot. The narrative does not mobilize space within any particular set, nor is there any attempt to make the different spaces of the different sets cohere. We are instead presented with a series of tableau-like views, more theatrical than cinematic. The sets thus function very literally as setting or background, seen always from the same points of view, as familiar as the room in which the viewer has the television.

I am thus arguing that the diegetic world of *Crossroads* is temporally and spatially fragmented, and that this fragmentation, accompanied by repetitious spatial orientation, foregrounds that dialogue of emotional and moral dilemmas which make up the action. The coherence of the serial does not come from the subordination of space and time to linear narrativity, as it does in classical narrative cinema, but from the continuities of moral and ideological frameworks which inform the dialogue. It is these frameworks that are explored, rehearsed and made explicit for the viewer in the repeated mulling over of actions and possibilities. *Crossroads* is in the business not of creating narrative excitement, suspense, delay and resolution, but of constructing moral consensus about the conduct of personal life. There is an endless unsettling, discussion and resettling of acceptable modes of behavior within the sphere of personal relationships.

There are two key elements in this. First, structurally, there is the plurality of story lines, which allows the use of the narrative strategy of interruption, and second, diegetically, there is the plot importance accorded to forms of lying and deceit. Structurally, although the different physical spaces of narratives do not cohere, except in the meeting place of the motel lobby, the same set of events, or the same dilemma, will be discussed by different characters in "their own" environment. A range of different opinions and understandings of any one situation will thus be voiced. At the same time, the use within this of interruption, the consistent holding-off of dénouement and knowledge, arguably invites the viewer to engage in exactly the same type of speculation and judgement. The viewer can, as it were, practice possible outcomes; he/she can join in the debate about how a particular event is to be understood.[19]

The use of deceit in the narrative works slightly differently. By deceit, I mean the development of a narrative line in which the audience knows that one character is consciously lying or misleading other characters. Here, the viewer is in a position of privileged knowledge in relation to the protagonists, and can see clearly what and who is "right." The drama of morality is here produced by the tension between the fact that "good" characters must continue to be trusting, to remain "good," and the fact that they will suffer unless they "find out" about X's true nature.

In both cases, what is being set in play are repertoires of understandings and assumptions about personal and familial relationships, in which the notion of individual character is central. Thus, although soap opera narrative may seem to ask "What will happen next?" as its dominant question, the terrain on which this question is posed is determined by a prior question: "What kind of person is this?" And in the ineluctable posing of this question, of all characters, whatever their social position, soap opera poses a potential moral equality of all individuals.

A gendered audience

Recently, Tania Modleski has very suggestively argued for the inscription of the female (maternal) subject. She has suggested that the multiple narrative structure of soap opera demands multiple identification on the part of the viewer, and thus constitutes the viewer as a type of ideal mother, "a person who possesses greater wisdom than all her children, whose sympathy is large enough to encompass the claims of all her family . . . and who has no demands of her own." I would like to consider the related question of the type of cultural competence that *Crossroads* as soap opera narrative(s) demands of its social reader. Just as a Godard film requires the possession of certain forms of cultural capital on the part of its audience for it to "make sense"—an extra-textual familiarity with certain artistic, linguistic, political and cinematic discourses—so, too, does *Crossroads*/soap opera. The particular competences demanded by soap opera fall into three categories:

   1. Generic knowledge—familiarity with the conventions of soap opera as a genre;[20] for example, expecting discontinuous and cliff-hanging narrative structures.
   2. Program-specific knowledge—knowledge of past narratives and of characters (in particular, who belongs to whom).
   3. Cultural knowledge of the socially acceptable codes and conventions for the conduct of personal life.

I intend only to try to expand on the third category here. My argument is that the narrative strategies and concerns of *Crossroads* call on the traditionally feminine competencies associated with the responsibility for "managing" the sphere of personal life. It is the culturally constructed skills of femininity— sensitivity, perception, intuition and the necessary privileging of the concerns of personal life—which are both called on and practiced in the genre. The fact that these skills and competencies—this type of cultural capital—is ideologically constructed as natural does not mean, as many feminists have shown, that they *are* the natural attributes of femininity. However, under present cultural and political arrangements, it is more likely that female viewers will possess this repertoire of both sexual and maternal femininities which is precisely called on to fill out the range of narrative possibilities. That is, when Jill is talking to her mother about her marriage (January 17, 1979) and the phone rings, the viewer needs to know not only that it is likely to be Stan (her nearly ex-husband) calling about custody of their daughter Sarah-Jane (serial-specific knowledge) and that we are unlikely to hear the content of the phone call in that segment (generic knowledge) but also that the mother's "right" to her children is no longer automatically assumed. These knowledges only have narrative resonance in relation to discourses of maternal femininity which are elaborated elsewhere, already in circulation and brought to the program by the viewer. In the enigma that is then posed— will Jill or Stan get Sarah-Jane?—questions are also raised about who, generally and particularly, *should* get custody. The question of what *should* happen is rarely posed "openly"—in this instance it was quite clear that "right" lay with Jill. But it is precisely the terms of the question, the way in which it relates to other already circulating discourses, if you like, the degree of its closure, which form the site of the construction of moral consensus, a construction which "demands," seeks to implicate, a skilled viewer.

Against critics who complain of the redundancy of soap opera, I would suggest that the radical discontinuities of the text require extensive, albeit interrupted, engagement on the part of the audience, before the text becomes pleasurable. I am thus arguing that *Crossroads* textually implies a feminine viewer to the extent that its textual discontinuities, in order to make sense, require a viewer competent within the ideological and moral frameworks (the rules) of romance, marriage and family life.

Acknowledgements:

To Ann and Brett Kaplan for help and hospitality, and to Dave Morley and Janice Winship for discussion and support. Love and thanks.

NOTES

1. For example, early research on American radio soaps either assumes a female audience, or only investigates one. (See Rudolf Arnheim, "The World of the Daytime Serial"; Herta Herzog, "On Borrowed Experience"; and Helen Kauffmann,"The Appeal of Specific Daytime Serials," in *Radio Research: 1942-1943*, ed. Paul F. Lazarsfeld [New York: Arno Press, 1944; rev. ed. 1979]). Similarly, Raymond William Stedman's *The Serials: Suspense and Drama by Installment* (Norman, OK: University of Oklahoma Press, 1971) uses the familiar profile of partially attentive housewives. It is of course precisely the perceived "feminine" appeal of the genre which has fueled the recent feminist interest—for example, Richard Dyer, Terry Lovell and Jean McCrindle, "Soap-Opera and Women," *Edinburgh International Television Festival Programme*, 1977; the work of the Women and Film Study Group in London; and Ellen Seiter, "The Role of the Woman Reader: Eco's Narrative Theory and Soap Operas," *Tabloid* No. 6 (1981).

2. Paul Willemen, "Notes on Subjectivity: On Reading Edward Branigan's 'Subjectivity Under Siege,' " *Screen* Vol. 19 No. 1 (Spring 1978), pp. 41-69.

3. David Morley, "Texts, Readers, Subjects," in *Culture, Media, Language*, ed. S. Hall, D. Hobson, A. Lowe, P. Willis (London: Hutchinson, 1980).

4. Steve Neale, "Propaganda," *Screen* Vol. 18 No. 3 (Autumn 1977), pp. 9-40.

5. David Morley, *The 'Nationwide' Audience: Structure and Decoding*, BFI Television Monographs/No. 11 (London: British Film Institute, 1980).

6. Richard Dyer's *"Victim: Hermeneutic Project"* (*Film Form* Vol. 1 No. 2 [Autumn 1977], pp. 3-22) provides an early attempt to hypothesize "differential decoding."

7. Laura Mulvey, "Visual Pleasure and Narrative Cinema," *Screen* Vol. 16 No. 3 (Autumn 1975), pp. 6-18.

8. Janice Winship, "Handling Sex," *Media, Culture and Society* Vol. 3 No. 1 (1981), pp. 25-41.

9. *Television and Radio 1979*, IBA Handbook (London: Independent Broadcasting Authority, 1979), p. 92.

10. I do not have space to examine the "intertextuality" of *Crossroads*. Material includes: *Crossroads* novels by Malcolm Hulke; *My Life at Crossroads* by Noele Gordon (Foreword by Mary Wilson); *The Crossroads Cookbook*, by Hazel Adair and Peter Ling; and the *Crossroads Special Souvenir Issue* from ATV Publications (1978). Philip Drummond discusses a similar proliferation of texts in relation to *The Sweeney* in "Structural and Narrative Constraints and Strategies in *The Sweeney*," *Screen Education* No. 20 (Autumn 1976), pp. 15-33.

11. Richard Paterson, "Planning the Family: The Art of the Television Schedule," *Screen Education* No. 35 (Summer 1980), pp. 79-85.

12. Ibid., p. 82. See also Charlotte Brunsdon and David Morley, *Everyday Television: 'Nationwide,'* BFI Television Monographs/No. 10 (London: British Film Institute, 1978) for discussion both of the slot and the alternative viewing to *Crossroads*.

13. The formalism of my analysis in this paper is circumstantial rather than a theoretical commitment—I recognize that this makes much of the paper very assertive, and hope to add to these notes shortly.

14. Leonore Davidoff, Jean L'Esperance and Howard Newby, "Landscape With Figures," in *Rights and Wrongs of Women,* ed. Juliet Mitchell and Ann Oakley (Harmondsworth, U.K.: Penguin, 1976) gives one account of the elements of this process. Richard Sennett in *The Fall of Public Man* (New York: Alfred A. Knopf, 1979) provides a rather different discussion of the imperialism of the "personal."

15. Recognizing that there is no monolithic "classical narrative cinema," some generalization about conventions of the narrative fiction film in the West seems useful at this point. David Bordwell and Kristin Thompson, *Film Art: An Introduction* (Reading, MA: Addison-Wesley Publishing Co., 1979) gives a lucid account of these conventions.

16. Tania Modleski, "The Search for Tomorrow in Today's Soap Operas: Notes on a Feminine Narrative Form," *Film Quarterly* Vol. 33 No. 1 (Fall 1979), pp. 12-21.

17. Geoff Brown, "I'm Worried about Chalet Nine," *Time Out* (November 24-30, 1978), and Rosalind Miles, "Everyday Stories, Everyday Folk," MA Dissertation (University of Leicester, 1980) both examine the production constraints of *Crossroads.*

18. I am indebted to Andy Lowe, who originally raised related questions about the articulation of space in *Coronation Street* in an unpublished paper at the Centre for Contemporary Cultural Studies (University of Birmingham, 1977).

19. Medvedkin's first film, *Scouts* (1927), which was a training film, apparently had a break, after the scouts of the narrative had got into a sticky corner, in which the audience could discuss possible solutions.

20. Tom Ryall usefully discusses genre and audience in *The Gangster Film,* Teachers Study Guide/No. 2 (London: British Film Institute, 1979).

The *Real* Soap Operas: TV Commercials

Sandy Flitterman

> Television condemns us to the Family, whose household
> utensil it has become just as the hearth once was, flanked
> by its predictable communal stewing pot in times past.
>
> —Roland Barthes[1]

"Who speaks?" *Six Times Two, or On and Under Communications,* and
France Tour Detour Two Children—Jean-Luc Godard's series of tapes about
television—reiterate this fundamental question. The ideological issues which
the series raises for television are crucial. Who speaks? Who is being spoken
to? And how is the spectator addressed in such a way that he or she is made to
participate vicariously, is brought *into* the situation, whether it is a daily news
item, a narrative fiction, or . . . a commercial? The television commercial can
be a privileged *locus* for the analysis of cultural meanings, condensing as it
does questions of narrative and address in a single instantaneous representation. This is especially true for feminist analysis when the commercial
happens to be among the 30-odd "messages" ("We will continue after these
messages") that transect any hour-long daily episode of a soap opera.

Daytime vs. Prime Time

A first, superficial comparison between daytime and evening prime-
time programming yields some immediate—and obvious—generalities
about television advertising. The number of commercials for a daytime hour
is almost twice that of a prime-time show, roughly 31 as opposed to 17. For an
afternoon soap opera, that comes out to about one commercial for every two

minutes of narrative drama. One can conclude that soap operas are geared to a more staccato, ruptured attention span than evening programs, which allow a more developed "narrative" flow between commercial breaks.

But more important than the viewing-rhythm which this plethora of commercials creates is the economic advantage produced by daytime advertising. Indeed, a brief glimpse at the revenues indicates that afternoon television dramas are selling much more than soap. It is worth quoting from a *Newsweek* feature article about *General Hospital:*

> With advertising rates that average $26,000 for a 30-second-spot—and production costs that are a fraction of prime-time levels—"GH" earns something on the order of $1 million a week in profit for ABC. By comparison, even as big a prime-time hit as "Dallas" brings the network only about half as much in weekly profit. Indeed, for all the networks no other single programming arena is more important than the afternoon serials. The thirteen regular soaps broadcast daily by ABC, CBS and NBC bring in upwards of $700 million a year in advertising revenue—roughly one-sixth of the networks' total ad income.[2]

Concomitant with this is the distribution of commercial time within the soap opera itself. Using *General Hospital* as an example, we find a fairly consistent pattern of alternation between advertising and melodrama. (These are approximate estimations based on viewing and logging commercials, and are intended to provide an overall picture of the general structure; they do not pretend to scientific accuracy.) The program usually opens with a four-minute segment, comprised of perhaps three distinct episodes (most often conversations) which pick up the various narrative threads from preceding programs. Then the opening theme music inaugurates a two-minute series of four commercials. After a return to a seven- or eight-minute segment of dramatic action, another two-minute commercial segment intervenes.

This alternating pattern of two-minute advertising breaks with roughly seven-minute segments of soap opera continues throughout the hour, with the exception of an enlarged commercial break of four minutes (that is, eight commercials), usually at the midpoint of the program, itself divided by a brief interlude of theme music. The final narrative segment of the soap opera lasts about five minutes and its corresponding commercial break has only three commercials instead of four. I will return to this process of segmentation and integration in a moment.

Let us switch from the quantity of daytime commercials to their content. As can be expected, the products advertised on daytime television differ widely from those on prime-time commercials. A plethora of household items, defining and delimiting the role of good mother, wife and homemaker, predominate in soap opera advertising. After all, the term "soap opera," coined by the entertainment trade paper *Variety*, refers specifically to these melodramas (first on commercial radio in the '30s, then on television in the early '50s) which were created primarily to "sell soap." In fact, Procter & Gamble, the largest television advertiser in the world,[3] holds the copyright on a number of daytime dramas.

The standard fare of soap opera advertising ranges from laundry detergents and other wash products, floor and furniture polishes, household cleansers, through diapers, children's toys, vitamins and medications, various food products (such as cake mixes, side dishes, cereals, snacks and pet foods), to a whole range of feminine products from cosmetics and shampoos to hygiene products, skin treatments and bath oils. The commodities one *never* sees advertised in daytime commercials are, predictably, those products involving major economic decisions, traditionally designated as part of society's masculine prerogative: automobiles, business machines, major appliances, car repair services, realtors, banks, credit card companies, investment firms, stockbrokers, etc.

One can generalize still further by determining the reservoir of social meanings and prescriptions for women's behavior to be found within the contrasting daytime and prime-time commercials themselves. Daytime commercials affirm the centrality of the family and the important function of the woman as nurturing support system. Feminine needs and desires are often defined in terms of maternal imperatives. Two random examples, one for a fruit drink and one for a cold medication, demonstrate this by their slogans, succinct crystallizations of the woman's familial role: "Moms depend on Kool-Aid like kids depend on moms," and "Give them Comtrex and a hug."

In contrast, the majority of prime-time commercials appeal to a business sense traditionally connoted as masculine. In an article entitled "It Helps If You Look Like a Chicken,"[4] the recent trend of having corporate executives appear in their own commercials is discussed. This approach is intended to improve both the corporate image and the sales of the product. Some examples are Lee Iacocca for Chrysler, Frank Borman for Eastern Airlines, and Frank Perdue, of course, for Perdue chicken. Characteristically, these ads almost always appear only on prime time. Likewise, slogans like "Smith-Barney makes money the old-fashioned way: they *earn* it," and "Federal Express: when it absolutely positively has to be there overnight," employ a practical, corporate approach which emphasizes the business and economic attributes of the product. In short, it might be said that while the prime-time commercial promotes goods, the daytime ad promotes services, with this important distinction—in the former the qualities are attributed to the commodity, while in the latter, in an interesting reversal, they are attributed to the consumer.

One final point, in terms of contrasting daytime and prime-time commercials, concerns sexuality. While the evening program ads for such products as perfume and alcoholic beverages (like wine or cream sherry) offer an image of the liberated, sexually sophisticated and glamorous woman, the dicta for female beauty provided by daytime ads emphasize quite another thing. Concentrating on the housewife's need to appear younger and more attractive than she might feel, many commercials on daytime television advertise diet plans (particularly in the springtime), various creams for younger-looking skin, and hair color to hide signs of aging. The focus is on cosmetic *improvements*, with the implication that the housewife should be as concerned about her own youthful, healthy looks as she is about the cleanliness and order of her household. Contrary to this, prime-time ads emphasize a kind of female beauty which is independent of domestic surroundings.

Analysis and Description

Content analysis, however, can only take us so far. For a more nuanced understanding of the *effects* television commercials can have on a viewing— and consuming—public, we must turn to an analysis of the specific mode of meaning production of these commercials: television commercials analyzed as *texts*. For this purpose, I have selected four fairly typical commercials which are representative (both in their methods of presentation and in the kinds of products they offer) of those found during daytime soap opera viewing. They advertise a laundry product (Final Touch Fabric Softener), two cake mixes (Pillsbury Bundt Cake and Pillsbury Streusel Swirl) and a pain reliever (Bufferin). The analysis will demonstrate that they offer a system of values and a specific form of narrative pleasure as well. I'll start with a brief description of each commercial.

FINAL TOUCH AD

Visuals	Sound
Alternation of CU of Mrs. Kidwell and bottle of final Touch (in CU). Mrs. Kidwell has baby girl on the table at her right. Some (hovering) camera movement, especially on CU's of bottle.	Total continuity on soundtrack, alternating between male announcer's voice-over and Mrs. Kidwell's direct address to (invisible) announcer, and thus to spectator.
	Mrs. Kidwell: I'll stop using it. Point blank.
	Announcer: We're teasing Mrs. Kidwell. We told her we're taking the whitener *out of* Final Touch Fabric Softener. Listen...
MCU Mrs. Kidwell (& baby).	*Mrs. Kidwell: Please* leave it in. She likes things soft. She doesn't want her clothes (baby gurgles) to be scratchy.
CU Bottle.	And I care about the whitening.
CU Mrs. Kidwell.	I think that's very important.
CU Bottle (Only fingers of man appear	*Announcer:* Don't worry, Mrs. Kid-

with "Don't worry" to add the "with bluing for whiteness" part of the label.).

CU Mrs. Kidwell.

well. Final Touch will keep softening *and* whitening. Without our whitener, we'd be just another fabric softener.

Mrs. Kidwell: When the baby's grown and gone, I'll still be using Final Touch.

PILLSBURY BUNDT CAKE AD

Visuals	Sound
Elderly woman bringing cake to guy; three shots.	*Chorus:* If you wanna say thank you but don't know how, Let a Bundt Cake do the talkin'
Little girl w/broken doll; cut to:	If you wanna say I'm sorry but you can't somehow, Let a Bundt Cake do the talkin'.
CU of cake, baking; another of cake.	*Man:* Pillsbury Bundt Cakes, with their own special fillings that bake right inside. *Always* make a loving surprise.
Girl brings cake to Dad; one shot.	*Chorus:* Yes, more than any other thing, a Bundt Cake says I love you. Let a Bundt Cake do the talkin'!

Musical chorus—mostly female voice. Man's voice intervenes, over instrumental continuation of chorus, the bridge. Then, picking up, singing continues.

PILLSBURY STREUSEL SWIRL AD

Visuals	Sound
Cake, box in background.	Pillsbury Streusel Swirl, the sensational six-meal cake
Cake, closer, rotating.	with a special swirl of flavor and light glaze that's *perfect* for any meal.
Two couples (Cake on rotating cake-plate).	Meal One: An impressive dessert for company.
Boy eating (Cake).	Meal Two: A yummy treat for kids.
Breakfast, man in suit (Cake).	Meal Three: A delicious breakfast cake.
Hands wrapping school lunch (Cake).	Meal Four: A light lunchbox cake.
Two women (Cake).	Meal Five: The best break your coffee ever had.

Couple by fireplace (Cake).	Meal Six: Dessert the second night.
Box of cake-mix.	Pillsbury Streusel Swirl: The sensational six-meal cake

Fourteen shots: each "episode" is one shot, "punctuated" by shots of ever-smaller cake on (rotating) cake plate. Male announcer, light musical background.

BUFFERIN AD

Visuals	Sound
Elderly woman gets out of bed (Some camera movement pan right)	
Puts on bathrobe	*Female Voice-Over:* Mom's incredible. She insists on making the family breakfast
Walks down hall (Frontal Ams)	even when her arthritis is acting up.
Into bathroom (from back, CMS, opens cabinet)	In the past, when she got up (. . .) she'd take aspirin.
CU pills	But she's more careful to use Bufferin now.
Downstairs, side view	Aspirin sometimes upset her stomach.
CU feet downstairs (slippers)	But Bufferin adds protection ingredients
Frontal downstairs	that Bayer and Anacin don't . . .
High angle (LS, going into kitchen)	So Bufferin relieves her minor pain and stiffness fast.
She turns (CU low angle)	*Child's Voice:* Mornin' Grandma! *Female Voice-Over:* And it works for hours.
Bottle next to folded towels	I'm glad Mom's more careful to use Bufferin now.

All lap dissolves (combined with motion—either "Mom's" or camera's, very fluid).

Syntagmatics

All of these commercials partake of a narrative process which organizes their meanings around some form of fictional representation. But each commercial orders the spatial and temporal relationships within it differently, resulting in the fact that each commercial can be seen as a specific *type* of narrative sequence. Christian Metz' Large Syntagmatic Category[5] can be useful at this point, for it systematically describes, on the level of the organization of images, the different ways in which space and time can be ordered through montage. By establishing that there is a fixed number of patterns according to which individual shots can be grouped into units, Metz created a typology of these combinations. The units are autonomous segments, or "syntagmas," and the Large Syntagmatic Category consists of eight distinct syntagmatic types.

Metz first divides the Large Syntagmatic Category into two types of autonomous segments: those made up of only one shot, and those consisting of more than one shot. Television commercials, even those appearing the most neutral or simple, almost always consist of more than one shot. Autonomous segments of more than one shot can either be chronological (that is, narrative) or non-chronological (that is, descriptive). There are four types of chronological syntagma, and each of the four commercials under analysis corresponds to one of these narrative types. It is important to note the preponderance of *narrative* syntagmas in daytime television ads; this is essential to the kind of fictive flow specific to the soap opera viewing situation, as will be shown shortly. For the moment, I would simply like to mention that the non-narrative syntagma—particularly the type which organizes shots in which there is neither spatial continuity nor chronology, but in which there is a *thematic* relation of the shots—appears quite frequently on prime-time television. (Two recent examples are the ad for Lincoln Mercury which depicts shots of portions of the car, a bobcat and surrealistic desert-scapes, and the ad for Chanel No. 5 which depicts fragmentary images of glass, liquid and silk.)

The Final Touch commercial gives the impression of being the most direct, the least constructed, and hence the most "truthful." Our analysis will demonstrate, however, that a complex series of manipulations was necessary in order to achieve this well-calculated aura of truth. The syntagmatic type to which this ad corresponds is the "scene." The shots are organized in such a way as to show a chronological, consecutive progression from shot to shot. The lack of spatial or temporal ellipses augments the impression of "simple recording" characteristic of the "scene." In some sense, the "scene" can be said to be the least cinematic type of syntagma because it signifies a unified and continuous time and space despite the fact that it is composed of several shots.

Consequently, the Final Touch commercial represents an attempt to appear as spontaneous and naturalistic as possible; it takes an unmediated, documentary approach toward its commodity. In addition to the images, the soundtrack provides us with several other powerful guarantees of authenticity. The disembodied voice of the male announcer, hovering godlike over the images of the housewife and the product, identifies the voice of truth and authority with the masculine position. Alternately playful and consoling, the voice confirms the importance of laundry brightness to well-being and to product quality. This is similar to the textual voice of an omniscient narrator, or the "objective" voice of historical discourse; all are meant to guarantee the veracity of the facts presented, and to obviate doubt or critical judgement.

The second guarantee of authenticity is related to the ideology of the personal testimonial and comes from the housewife's on-screen voice. Her direct address to the spectator is meant both to elicit identification on the part of the female spectator and to speak with the authority of common wisdom about the importance of whiteness. Thus the personal testimonial convention, used as an assurance of experiential truth, and gender-identified as female, is combined with the omniscient power of the "being-beyond-the-screen," the male announcer. The real subject of enunciation of the ad, the principle which selects and organizes the images and sounds with the aim of motivating purchase of the product, is successfully masked by an overlay of apparently natural images and sounds.

The Pillsbury Bundt Cake commercial uses a snappy jingle as the sound-track accompaniment to images; this places it within the conventions of the musical comedy genre. In fact, this mini-musical sequence corresponds to the type of syntagma frequently used for musical numbers in film, the "episodic syntagma." In an "episodic syntagma," the ordering of the images is chronological but discontinuous. Each shot (or small grouping of shots) comprises an episode, and these are generally connected by some form of cinematic punctuation, such as a fade or a dissolve. When music is used, it binds the sequence of disconnected "episodes" into a coherent whole. In Vincente Minnelli's *Gigi,* for example, the sequence of Gigi's lessons or the string of Gaston's parties at Maxim's are illustrations of this type of sequence organization.

The musical chorus of female voices in the Bundt cake ad, with its linguistic message of warmth and caring, provides such a binding function. The episodes on the image track illustrate variations on the musical theme, while the repetition of the chorus line punctuates each stanza. Each episode (the elderly woman bringing a cake to her young friend, the mother consoling her little girl, the daughter surprising her father) is thus taken not as a separate instance, but as a partial illustration of the total meaning—"Let a Bundt cake do the talkin'." Narrative material is condensed into a few exemplary shots, and the musical accompaniment unifies the ad into an overall whole. When the masculine voice-over intervenes, it is to give additional information about the cake mix itself; the music and the mini-narrative episodes carry the supplementary—ideological—message.

The "alternate syntagma," in which two discrete spaces are linked together in a sequential arrangement of shots, is represented by the Pillsbury Streusel Swirl commercial. In terms of narrative material, this cake-mix commercial evokes the light domestic situation comedy of television. However, its structure goes all the way back to the early forms of cinematic storytelling systematized and best represented by the rescue sequences of D.W. Griffith. In the "alternate syntagma," the ordering of shots is chronological and consecutive, but the temporal relationship between its two (or more) series of intercutting images denotes simultaneity.

With the Streusel Swirl commercial, the chronological time of a full day is marked out, from evening to evening, by the pieces of cake corresponding to different meals or snacks. Two series of images, one of cutting the cake, one of eating it, are alternated as a masculine voice-over narrates the progression. Within each series, the temporal relationships are consecutive—meals 1, 2, 3, 4, etc., and dessert, treat, breakfast, lunch, etc. But taken as a whole, the relationship of alternating images in this narrative sequence is one of simultaneity: meal 1 = dessert, meal 2 = treat, and so forth. This denoted simultaneity thus marks the consecutive daily progression of "meals."

Through this structure of narrative expansion a lesson in economy is generated: one single box of cake-mix produces a seemingly bountiful array of nourishment. In addition to this, each "meal" designates a tiny ideological lesson in middle-class manners and values, and each prescribes a specific function for the woman. The actual labor process involved, the baking of the cake, is abstracted. (In the Bundt cake commercial this was indicated, if only minimally, by a time-lapse shot of the cake rising.) What *is* revealed, in almost emblematic clarity, is the series of functions befitting a good wife and mother: entertainer, practical meal-planner, friend, etc. The light musical background which accompanies the voice-over narration both unifies the commercial into a compact whole and adds a note of levity ("whistle while you work") to the interminable round of food-preparation chores.

The Bufferin commercial can be said to be the most cinematic, and, not surprisingly, it corresponds to the "ordinary sequence," the narrative syntagma which Metz has called the most filmic. In the "ordinary sequence," there are elements of discontinuity in the consecutive ordering of the shots. In other words, while the action depicted is continuous and chronological, its *representation* is broken up by small ellipses in space and time. For example, rather than simply producing a change in camera distance or angle, a shot-change might pick up the action after a moment or two, creating an effect of condensation.

As a standard narrative type, the Bufferin commercial most readily resembles a melodrama, a small tale of suffering and triumph over pain, related in a chronological sequence which moves toward resolution. In this case, the "story" is told by a female voice-over which designates itself from the start as a character in the fiction. This unseen narrator, daughter to the elderly woman depicted on the image-track, describes her mother's struggle with arthritic pain and the assuaging powers of Bufferin. The narrative situation is simple: eleven shots illustrate, in slow and painful detail, the mother's process of arising from bed, taking the Bufferin out of the medicine cabinet, walking downstairs and going into the kitchen to prepare the "family breakfast" mentioned at the beginning of the commercial. The other characters are invisible, indicated only by their voices on the soundtrack: the aforementioned narrator, whose monologue is continuous throughout the commercial, and the grandchild (presumably the narrator's son) who greets his grandmother.

The small discontinuities inherent in the "ordinary sequence" are somewhat masked in this commercial by several procedures. A sense of continued and continuous motion is created by the constant cuts on movement, either of the camera or of the character. In addition, every transition between shots is made fluid by a lap dissolve. This apparent homogeneity of continuous movement smoothes over the great but not-so-apparent variety of shots and angles in the ad. Shot types range from close-up to long shot; angles range from frontal to high angle; the figure is shown from profile to back as well as from the front. Although the action depicted is chronological, its denotation is elliptical, each shot representing one of the unskipped moments of the action. The result is a complex narrative process designed to communicate the *experience* of pain, the desire for its relief and the belief in the power of the product. The residual message of self-sacrifice for women is no less important or emphatic.

Flow vs. Interruption

The preceding syntagmatic analysis of these four commercials leads to some interesting generalizations about the function of television ads in daytime soap operas. Metz' Large Syntagmatic Category was devised to aid in the analysis of a film by focusing on the structure of the *sequence;* semiology contends that the sequence, and not the shot, is the basic unit of filmic construction. Films (and soap operas) are composed of any number of syntagmas, but, in general, commercials correspond to one syntagma per ad. From this perspective, far from *disrupting* the narrative flow of the daytime soap opera, commercials can be seen to *continue* it.

Often music is used to ease the transition from a commercial "break" into the continuing soap opera. For example, *General Hospital* employs a five-note theme, a minor scale, or a percussive roll in many of its reentry segments. Sometimes an announcement will make it appear as if the commercial is an interruption by providing a statement which promises continuity ("We'll return in a moment," or "Our program will continue . . ."). But such references to disruption are misleading. The micro-narrative *form* of the commercials in fact ensures that while the content (the denoted material) might be changed, the narrative form of fictional representation is continuous.

In her seminal article entitled "The Search for Tomorrow in Today's Soap Operas," Tania Modleski characterized the narrative movement of soap operas in the following way: "(T)he narrative, by placing ever more complex obstacles between desire and its fulfillment, makes anticipation of an end an end in itself."[6] This creates a rather interesting place for the daytime commercial. Although the soap opera thrives on a process of anticipation and frustrated desire, the self-enclosed micro-narratives of television commercials, these discrete syntagmas, offer a kind of containment and fulfillment by their very form.

Far from interrupting the narrative flow of stimulated yearning for a just conclusion and perpetual indication of its impossibility, commercials are small oases of narrative closure, homogeneous and systematic units of unproblematized meaning. They do not function as interruptions because rather than frustrating the overall impulse for narrative, they prolong and maintain it.

To extend this a little in terms of formal composition and structure, the television commercial is comparatively rich in syntagmatic forms and their technical execution, while the soap opera tends toward relative poverty. The television commercial exploits almost every type of syntagmatic organization, while the soap opera generally relies on the syntagmatic "scene." The soap opera episode is almost always a dialogue, shot in the standard reverse-angle figure. There is little reliance on fancy camera technique, optical devices, camera movement or music, although some recent attempts on *General Hospital* have demonstrated an interest in stylistic variation through transitional devices like match-cutting.

Commercials, on the other hand, almost always use some form of camera movement, even in those ads which appear static or devoid of technique. Optical devices, such as dissolves and punctuating fades and wipes, appear frequently, as do rapid montage sequences. In addition, commercials often use music, either as background accompaniment or as the organizing jingle. This use of music increases the homogeneity and containment of the commercials, isolating them as specific narrative units in the programming flow.

There is a clear demarcation of good against evil in the television commercial. With the condensation characteristic of the television ad comes a reduction of life's ambiguity into "characteristic situations," emblematic representations of a much greater time span in a housewife's life. In the commercial, good inevitably triumphs in its 30-second struggle against the forces of evil as symbolized by dirt, pain, hunger and the economy. Conflict, which is the very substance of the soap opera, thus becomes hypostatized. Where its perpetual irresolution generates the textual work of the soap opera, the *resolution* of conflict is posed even before the commercial begins: it is the condition of its existence. In other words, the establishment of a clear demarcation between good and evil—household dirt and soiled laundry are not met with ambivalence—precedes the commercial, which is merely the demonstration of the triumph of the good.

Along with narrative closure, commercials offer idealized images of the family. For example, to the soap opera's conventional and consistent fare of illegitimacy, rivalry, false parentage, adultery, secrecy and betrayal, the commercial offers the happy family, the good mother, the affectionate companion and the conscientious housewife. In terms of both form and content, then, commercials provide an interesting kind of foil. The result is a dialectical alternation between the vision in the soaps and that in the ads. What I wish to emphasize is the *interactive* function of commercials and drama in daytime programming.

Homogeneous and continuous units that they are, commercials are never presented singly in their "intervals." Even when discussing the suspenseful intercutting of narrative threads in daytime drama, it is important to understand that the commercial break always consists of several ads. The ruptured, episodic, impeded and deferred movement of the soap opera is thus continued across the commercial break, with an important exception: each commercial "narrative" is self-contained, isolated and independent of its surrounding context. Taken as a whole, then, the soap opera with its commercials included is an astonishing multiple form. If the number of commercial breaks is broken down into its individual units, and each segment of a soap opera narrative is considered in terms of its compositions (a number of short episodes with different characters, conveying multiple points of view and shifting identifications, not to mention diverse story threads), the result becomes a plural dispersion, a veritable explosion of narrated meanings.

Conclusion

The condensation of values and aspirations with commodities and consumer needs prevalent in commercials makes them emblematic nuggets of social meanings. Embedded as they are in the fantastic yet quotidian tales of daytime soap operas, commercials can have an important function in shaping society's values. Rising levels of expectation that people have about their lives in relation to what they see, a paradoxical view of desire as finite yet capable of being infinitely prolonged, and an equation of material consumption with well-being are among the many examples one could cite. In a recent televised interview, Jean-Luc Godard stated, "Television doesn't make programs—it makes viewers: *télé-spectateurs*."[7] This is of utmost importance to anyone interested in social change, for it means that not only *what* we see on television, but *how* we see it, has important ideological consequences. Understanding the process of meaning-production in television commercials— processes of narrative and address that mobilize our participation as viewers—is another way of establishing the construction of our contract with television as spectators and consumers—and the degree to which these two roles are intimately related.

NOTES

1. Roland Barthes, "Upon Leaving the Movie Theater," in *Apparatus,* ed. Theresa Hak Kyung Cha (New York: Tanam Press, 1981).

2. "Television's Hottest Show," *Newsweek* (September 28, 1981), p. 60.

3. Max Gunther, "Testing Commercials for Impact: To Burke or Not to Burke," *TV Guide* (February 7, 1981), p. 4. According to *Time* magazine (Gerald Clarke, "Sanitizing the Small Screen," [June 29, 1981], p. 83), Procter & Gamble spent $486.3 million on tv advertising in 1980; the company owns and sponsors at least six afternoon soap operas.

4. Don Kowet, "It Helps If You Look Like a Chicken: Executives Who Peddle Their Wares on TV," *TV Guide* (February 21, 1981), pp. 20-23.

5. Christian Metz, *Film Language,* trans. Michael Taylor (New York: Oxford University Press, 1974). See especially chapter five, "Problems of Denotation in the Fiction Film," and chapter six, "Outline of the Autonomous Segments in Jacques Rozier's film *Adieu Philippine.*"

6. Tania Modleski, "The Search for Tomorrow in Today's Soap Operas: Notes on a Feminine Narrative Form," *Film Quarterly* Vol. 33 No. 1 (Fall 1979), p. 12.

7. *The Dick Cavett Show* (PBS, October 28, 1980).

On Reading Soaps:
A Semiotic Primer

Robert C. Allen

Until very recently the analysis of soap operas has been the domain of elitist aesthetic criticism and mass media "content analysis." To the elitist critic, conducting an analysis of soap operas constitutes a contradiction in terms. Art works are the products of individual artistic genius; they are self-contained and autonomous; they make intellectual demands on the spectator. Soap operas, on the other hand, are assembly-line products, comicbook-like in their lack of closure, and (it is supposed) formally transparent. At most, soap operas are sources of puzzlement for elitist critics. How, they implicitly ask, can anyone with an I.Q. exceeding that of a turnip subject herself (female viewership is presumed) to a daily diet of what Renata Adler has called "sustained morbidity and dread"?[1]

Content analysts, at least, take soap operas seriously enough as a social phenomenon to go beyond simply dismissing them as garbage. To them, soap operas are pseudo-realities that present curiously distorted reflections of empirical social reality—the "world" of the soap opera is more violent than the real world, is more concerned with sex and parentage, suffers more from amnesia, mental illness, and coma-producing maladies. Content analysts assume that *what* a soap opera means can be separated from *how* a soap opera means, that the production of meaning in soap operas is simple and unproblematic.

This paper argues first, that the lack of serious aesthetic attention given soap operas has less to do with their simplemindedness than with the inability of many critics to read them as texts; and second, that soap operas should be studied as social phenomena (any media product that is consumed by 14 million persons daily and generates $700 million for its producers annually is an important social phenomenon), but that the analysis of social and cultural aspects of soap operas and soap opera viewing must be predicated upon a better understanding of how soaps work as producers of meaning and pleasure.

The Soap Opera As Text

The first problem the soap opera presents the textual analyst is one of defining his/her object of study. The analyst examining *Ulysses* or *Strangers on a Train* or *Love Story* has no difficulty in specifying the text under scrutiny, since each of these works is, in narrative terms, self-contained, autonomous, and closed-off. What, however, constitutes the soap opera as aesthetic object? A single episode? Surely not, since the meaning of any one episode is clearly dependent upon those which have preceded it. A week's worth of episodes? Why a week? Why not a month? A year's worth?

A central aesthetic characteristic of the soap opera is its absolute resistance to narrative closure. While subplots are regularly resolved, the "story" of the soap itself is never completed and never can be. Even when soaps have been cancelled (as was *Love of Life* in 1980), their final episodes have not tied all the narrative threads together—they were not closed down so much as they expired defiantly *in media res*.

The soap opera's open-endedness makes it resistant to many types of narrative textual analysis in that the textual models from which these analyses work presume narrative closure. They assume that one of the chief operations of the text is the solving of the enigma/s posed at the beginning of the work (in Barthes' terminology, the operation of the hermeneutic code),[2] bringing the text to resolution, audience satisfaction and closure. How, then, to deal with a form in which audience satisfaction cannot possibly be derived from the telos at the end of the work (since there is none), a form in which the operation of the hermeneutic code is perpetually retarded?[3]

I would argue that the soap opera as text can be specified only as the sum of all its episodes broadcast since it began. Hence what we are dealing with is a huge meta-text which has, in some cases, taken shape over the course of 30—or more—years, a saga which, if all its episodes to the present were broadcast sequentially, would take 780 hours (or 32.5 days) to run (assuming an average episode length of one-half hour). But even at the end of this marathon screening, the critic could still not claim to have "read" the entire text of the soap, since during the 32.5 days of continuous viewing, 16 additional hours of textual material would have been produced.

Hence, to approach the soap narratively is to push oneself into the embarrassing corner of not being able to specify the text one is studying and to be forced to admit that the narrative under scrutiny lacks closure—one of the defining characteristics of narrative.

If we turn to the broader field of semiotics, we find an analytical framework better able to deal with the peculiar problems presented by the soap opera. Such a shift allows us to consider narrative as but one of several aspects of the soap opera as text. In "The Role of the Woman Reader: Eco's Narrative Theory and Soap Operas," Ellen Seiter has proposed Umberto Eco's *The Role of the Reader* as the basis for a possible feminist reading of popular culture, particularly the soap opera. I should like to use Seiter's and Eco's works to open up the soap opera to textual analysis, while at the same time diverging somewhat from their interpretations of the soap opera's semiotic operation.[4]

Seiter's feminist consideration of the soap opera is based upon Eco's distinction between open and closed texts. For Eco, soap operas are closed texts in that the reader's response has been carefully and precisely governed by the text's author. Closed texts, says Eco:

> apparently aim at pulling the reader along a predetermined path, care-fully displaying their effects so as to arouse pity or fear, excitement or depression at the due place and at the right moment. Every step of the "story" elicits just the expectation that its further course will satisfy. They seem to be structured according to an inflexible project.[5]

The open text, on the other hand, has built into it multiple levels of interpretation. Whereas the closed text is a straightforward linear pathway of stimulus and anticipated response, the open text is a "structural maze" of possible readings. Because of the one-dimensionality of the closed work, because it aims at an "average" reader,

> it is enough for these texts to be interpreted by readers referring to other conventions or oriented by other presuppositions ["other" than those of the author] and the result is incredibly disappointing (or exciting—it depends on the point of view).

In other words, ironically, the "closed" text is open to all sorts of aberrant readings—its textual "path," to use Eco's metaphor, is so narrow that the reader for whom the text was not intended finds it easy to stray. In the open work, while the possibility of pluri-signification is built in, so is the notion of the model reader—the person with sufficient knowledge of codes at work in the text to be able to read it competently.

The open work is not entirely open to any interpretation. The reader, says Eco, is "strictly defined by the lexical and syntaxical organization of the text." So while the possible aberrant interpretations of the closed text remain always open, the multiple interpretations of the open text have been foreseen by the author and are hence to some extent closed off. "You cannot use the [open] text as you want, but only as the text wants you to use it."[6]

Seiter accepts Eco's inclusion of the soap opera in the category of closed texts and in her own work suggests "possible ways that women can read soap operas subversively—ways which do not exclude or negate the widespread negative interpretation of soap opera viewing as escapist fantasy for women working in the home."[7]

But to see reader response to soap operas in terms of a single anticipated response and the possibility of a number of alternative, even subversive, readings is to sell short the semiological complexity of the soap opera. A careful examination of the semiological operation of the soap opera shows that it shares much more with Eco's model of the open text than it does with that of the closed texts of Superman or James Bond. Further, the openness of the soap opera is supported by empirical audience analysis and helps to explain the wide appeal and longevity of the soap opera form.

Reading the Soap Opera

What is involved in reading a soap opera? Commentators and television critics have long made soap opera viewing the *sine qua non* of a mindless mass media passivity requiring little more thought than the act of munching all the bonbons we are told "housewives" consume while being consumed by their "stories." In fact, what occurs is a complex exchange between viewer and text, in which a number of distinct codes engage the reader in the interpretive process.

A full description of the semiotic structure of soap operas is not possible here. However, in order to suggest the complexity of that structure, let me at least mention the codes by which meaning in soap operas is achieved.

1. *Video-Cinematic Code*

This is the complex of codes television has borrowed from the classical Hollywood narrative cinema, which the soap opera shares with most other narrative television forms. Indeed, it might well be that in the soap opera the "zero-degree" style of Hollywood films (as Noël Burch has called it), has reached its apex. A device such as an unmotivated camera movement, which would probably go unnoticed in the average Hollywood film, is such a departure from the norm in soap opera style that its use immediately privileges the content of the shot for the audience—the viewer "reads" this device as "something important is about to happen."

2. *Codes of the Soap Opera Form*

There is another set of codes derived in large measure from the soap opera form itself—although, obviously, some of them overlap with other forms of narrative as well. Included in this category would be the soap opera's use of time and space: the prolongation of events (rather than their compression as in most other narrative forms), and the construction of a world that is for the most part an interior one. Also included would be codes of soap opera acting (a style in which facial expression carries as much semiotic weight as dialogue), the use of multiple, intersecting narratives, the use of a certain type of non-diegetic music, the use of commercials as a structuring device in each episode (a large and very important topic in itself), and a very high degree of both inter-episode and intra-episode narrative redundancy. There are certainly other soap opera codes which could be enumerated as well as these, and any one of the above could be explored much further.

3. Textual Codes

There are currently 13 soap operas being broadcast on network commercial television. While they all share the above codes, each is different. To know that these differences are significant to their respective audiences, all one need do is ask a soap opera viewer about his/her preference. You will find that far from being indiscriminate, most soap opera viewers express strong likes and dislikes for certain soaps. They can also tell you immediately when they feel something is "wrong" with their soap—a plot line is headed in the wrong direction, a character is behaving in an uncharacteristic manner, etc. In other words, each soap sets up its own set of expectations, its own parameters in terms of content and style recognized by the audience and used by them to derive meaning from each episode. An important aspect of this textual coding is the network of interpersonal relationships among characters in a given soap. The longtime soap viewer can recognize not only appropriate and inappropriate behavior in a given character, but appropriate responses of a given character to another, based on the two characters' often varied relationships in the show's past. The knowing wink that Joe gives Mary might escape the novice viewer, but it would carry great signification to the experienced viewer. Such a viewer would know Mary once carried on a secret love affair, which resulted in Mary giving birth to a child who everyone thought was really fathered by her then husband Frank, etc., etc., even though the "baby" might now be grown and involved in clandestine affairs himself.

4. Intertextual Codes

All cultural products exist within networks of other texts to which they inevitably in some way refer. Soap operas are no exceptions. The reader is constantly comparing the text under consideration with the encyclopedia of other texts he/she has experienced. Intertextuality is sometimes used quite explicitly by soap opera writers in their never-ending search for new plot twists. Soap opera subplots have been based on the Mafia, the occult, the kidnapping of a wealthy heiress by a fringe political group, messianic religious figures, another television show (Dallas), the movie Jaws, etc. Sometimes intertextual reference will take the form of the appearance in the soap of a television or movie star as him/herself. In each case, a level of meaning is produced by reference to another text or set of texts.

5. Ideological Codes

Quite often in making sense of an action in a soap opera, the viewer will rely upon his/her own experience of the world, sense of right and wrong, truth and realism. Eco calls this set of codes "common frames."[8] The viewer constantly compares soap opera actions with "what should" happen in such a situation—what is plausible, veristic, morally correct, etc., not in terms of the world of the soap but in terms of the viewer's own world of experience and values.

The Semiotic Operation of the Soap Opera Text

Having listed the codes involved in the reading of soap operas, I want to suggest that the operation of the soap opera text opens up multiple levels of meanings, making of the soap if not an open text, at least not a closed one.

I first realized the possible openness of soaps because I was puzzled by the universal use of redundancy. What we might call inter-episodic redundancy—that is the reiteration on Tuesday of plot developments on Monday—is to a large degree explicable as a device to keep non-daily viewers "up" on narrative developments. Soaps always walk a thin line between moving the narrative along too quickly, and thus "using it up" too soon, and stretching subplots out for too long, and thereby risking boring the audience. But I was also struck by the great deal of intra-episodic redundancy—that is, the repetition of information from character to character within each daily episode. The latter can hardly be explained in the same way as the former. For example: Judy is having an affair with Alan. In scene one, Judy confides to her friend Sylvia that she is having the affair. In scene three, Sylvia through a verbal slip hints of the affair to Fred. In scene five, Fred, a friend of Alan, warns him (Alan) of becoming too involved with Judy. Such reference to the affair might continue for days or weeks, without anything "happening" to alter the state of affairs—the same information is passed along from character to character to character. In terms of the syntagmatic (in this case narrative) dimension of the soap, such exchanges *are* redundant, since the audience already knows that Judy is having an affair with Alan, and since such redundant dialogue scenes do not move the plot forward. Paradigmatically, however, such exchanges are far from redundant, and are, in fact, quite meaningful to the experienced viewer. As such a viewer knows, Sylvia was once married to Alan—their marriage breaking up because of Alan's impotence. Furthermore, the reader knows that Sylvia still loves Alan, although she has kept this hidden for many years, and, in fact, refuses offers of marriage from Jack because of her romantic nostalgia. The reader also knows that it was Fred who paid for Judy's abortion, the result of a one-night fling with Dr. Bates, and who further believes her to be self-destructive, etc., etc.

In discussing the musical film, Charles Altman and Jane Feuer have pointed out that when regarded syntagmatically the musical is a particularly uninteresting genre—95 percent of its plots can be summarized as "boy meets girl; boy loses girl; boy gets girl back." Their paradigmatic structures, however, often turn out to be surprisingly complex—the oppositional structure of characters and the values they represent providing a source of meaning much richer than that of the "plot."[9] Similarly, if regarded as a series of episodes of unmitigated suffering or an interminable rehashing of hackneyed subplots, then the soap opera must also seem extremely one-dimensional. But the soaps' elaborate paradigmatic structure of character relationships opens up whole new avenues of possible meaning. Not only do soap operas contain 30 or more characters, most of whom are related to each other in various ways, but this network of relationships has a history. Soap operas, unlike prime-time series, have memories, and, in fact, frequently encourage the viewer's recognition of that memory through references to departed characters or past relationships. Several characters on *As The World Turns*— Penny, in particular—have not been seen on the screen for years (their parts were written out long ago) but are still fondly remembered.

One of the reasons critics treat soap operas with such disdain is that, as naive viewers, they are unable to decode this paradigmatic textual code. To them the reiteration of the fact of Judy's affair is redundant, because they can read along the syntagmatic axis only. They are, in fact, incompetent readers of soaps just as much as the lexically and literarily impoverished high school student is an incompetent reader of *Ulysses*. The complex paradigmatic structure of the soap opera outlines its model reader "as a component of its structural strategy"—even though "model reader" is a term Eco reserves for open works; it is just that the model reader of *The Guiding Light* is more apt to be a 50-year-old woman than a male semiotician.

I would further argue that soap operas are "over-coded"—that is, their visual and auditory signifiers are coded not just as narrative elements, but in a number of other ways, allowing for multiple audience appeal. It is this over-coding that helps to account for the increasing diversity of the soap opera viewing audience. Since the days of Herzog's study of radio serial listeners, researchers have presumed that the soap opera audience consisted of lower middle class married women between the ages of 18 and 49. While this group still constitutes a large part of the audience, the past five years have seen a steady broadening of the demographics of soap opera viewing. A study conducted in March 1981 at the University of North Carolina, using a randomly selected sample of nearly 800 undergraduate and graduate students, found that nearly half (47 percent) considered themselves to be soap opera viewers, with another 17 percent stating that they would watch if they had the time. Twenty-one percent of the college soap viewers were male.[10] It has also been noted in the general press that pre-college age individuals constitute a significant portion of the audience for soaps such as *General Hospital,* which are aired in most markets in the late afternoon.

Just as interesting as this broadening of the audience for soaps is the diversity of functions soap opera viewing provides for its audience. A comparison of college soap opera viewers with a random sample of urban non-college viewers conducted in the spring of 1980 found that for members of both groups soap opera viewing served a number of functions: it acted as a time-filler; served as the basis for social intercourse; compensated for a lack of social intercourse in the everyday lives of some viewers; provided a source of information on the outside world (information on law, medicine, clothing styles, dealing with social situations, etc.); and enabled some viewers to escape into a fantasy world and thus be temporarily diverted from problems in their own lives. In other words, soap operas were decoded and used in a variety of sometimes seemingly contradictory ways (reality counseling/fantasy; social facilitating/social compensatory).[11]

Over-coding helps to account for both the diversity of the soap opera audience and the concomitant variety of functions viewing serves. To give but a very simple example: the character Noah Drake in *General Hospital* is "read" by adolescent girls in the audience as teen-idol rock star Rick Springfield ("I've Done Everything For You," "Jesse's Girl,") playing Noah Drake; to others he is read as the person having the relationship with Bobbie; to still others as a character with a particular function in one or more subplots; to another as a set of behaviors which correspond to a "real-life" situation, etc., etc. And, of course, none of these readings of Springfield/Drake is mutually exclusive. Indeed, the model reader is able to decode him as all of these, and possibly more.

In 1975, Sari Thomas conducted extensive interviews with a sample of 40 soap opera viewers. Working from a theoretical distinction made by Worth and Gross, Thomas found that soap opera viewers seemed to make sense of soap operas by decoding them according to two frames of reference or orientations: what Worth and Gross have called "attributional" and "inferential" and which we might call "fictive" and "realistic." According to this model, when the reader encounters what he/she believes to be a fictional text, he/she decodes it by attempting to assign the patterns of signification (the "message") found in the text to its author. When the reader encounters what seems to be a non-authored text (a natural phenomenon, a piece of unedited new film, etc.), he/she decodes it by inferring meaning from it by reference to "real life," or, more accurately his/her experience of real life.[12] Thomas does *not* suggest that soap opera viewers with an attributional frame of reference regard soaps as "reality," but that they tend to rely more on what I have called "ideological" codes in their decoding; that is, soap opera characters and situations are "made sense of" by integrating them into the viewer's own field of knowledge, values and experience. For example, Thomas asked her respondents to predict what would happen in a given plotline in the soap opera *All My Children*. One woman responded:

> I think Chuck and Tara will stay together for the sake of the baby. Even if it is Phil's child, Chuck has really acted as the father. I don't go for that. I mean irregardless of who actually made the baby, it's the parents who raise the child that counts.

Other viewers tended to project the plotline according to non-ideological codes: those of narrative expectation, acting conventions, inter-textual codes, etc.:

> Chuck and Tara will stay together because this way there's always room for complication later on. If Tara and Phil actually did stay together, the whole story there would be kaput.

Thomas concludes:

> It is clear that in the first case, the viewer only takes real-life stereotypes into consideration when formulating her prediction (attribution). In the second case, the respondent bases her judgment on her explicit familiarity with soap opera story-telling conventions.[13]

Integrating Thomas's finding into the critical framework of this paper, I would argue that attributional/inferential orientations of soap opera readers do not represent correct/aberrant decoding practices applied to a closed work. Rather, the semiotic operation of the soap opera text not only allows for but actually encourages both these orientations, or, more accurately, the soap opera text is encoded in such a way that there is considerable slippage among codes, particularly between the ideological and others. The narrative openness, episodic structure, and the nature of the plot situations themselves (many of which overlap into the daily experience of the viewer herself) all encourage a reading of the soap within a common frame of reference, whereas the rigidity of some soap opera conventions encourages a different sort of decoding operation.

The soap opera consciously walks the line between texts that can be read as fiction and those which, for various reasons, constantly spill over into the experiential world of the viewer as few, if any, other fictions do. Eco remarks that fiction is marked by a distance from the reader; the author uses certain devices by which "the reader is invited not to wonder whether the reported facts are true."[14] The soaps, however, use devices which both distance the world of the soap from that of the viewer and make quite explicit connections with it.

Conclusion

Many critics like to talk of the "world of the soap opera" in comparison to that of the "real world," or at least that of the viewer, as if the social significance of the soap lay in the comparison between the two. But rather than offering a simple message, soaps offer amazingly complex fields of semiotic possibilities which a variety of audience members can use in a variety of ways. It is precisely this openness that makes the soap opera historically unique as a form of television programming, but which also makes the "message" or "ideology" of the soap very difficult to specify. It seems less important to argue that the soap is a closed or open text, in Eco's scheme, than to recognize that in soaps we are dealing with extremely significant economic, aesthetic and cultural products of a complexity just now, after nearly half a century, being recognized by mass communications scholars.

NOTES

1. Renata Adler, "Afternoon Television: Unhappiness Enough, and Time," in *Television: The Critical View,* ed. Horace Newcomb (New York: Oxford University Press, 1979), p. 76.

2. Roland Barthes, *S/Z* (New York: Hill and Wang, 1974).

3. To give but one further example of the problems soap operas present to narratological analysis, in his book *Story and Discourse: Narrative Structure in Fiction and Film* (Ithaca, NY: Cornell University Press, 1978), Seymour Chatman makes a useful distinction between essential and non-essential narrative events. A "kernel," he says, is an event crucial to the narrative, one without knowledge of which the discourse would cease to be meaningful to the reader. By constructing a chain of kernels we can reduce the discourse to its bare-bones, but still narratively meaningful, set of events. What fleshes out the text are "satellites"—events that might add color, dimension, flavor to the narrative, but which could be removed from the discourse without disturbing the basic causal chain of events constituting the narrative. This distinction, useful as it is in discussing traditional narratives, is nevertheless dependent upon narrative closure to give it meaning, since the significance of any event in a narrative is dependent upon its relationship to narrative resolution. While kernels and satellites might be specified in a given soap opera subplot, determining which events are essential or non-essential in terms of the soap's meta-narrative is much more problematic, since there is no ultimate closure to generate criteria by which they can be judged.

4. Ellen Seiter, "The Role of the Woman Reader: Eco's Narrative Theory and Soap Operas," *Tabloid* No. 6 (1981), (I am grateful to Ms. Seiter for making her work available to me prior to publication); Umberto Eco, *The Role of the Reader: Explorations in the Semiotics of Texts* (Bloomington, IN: Indiana University Press, 1979).

5. Eco, p. 8.

6. Ibid., p. 9.

7. Seiter, p. 3.

8. Eco notes that "common frames come to the reader from his storage of encyclopedic knowledge and are mainly rules for practical life." (pp. 20-21.)

9. Charles F. Altman, "The American Film Musical: Paradigmatic Structure and Mediatory Function," *Wide Angle* Vol. 2 No. 2 (November 1978), pp. 10-17; Jane Feuer, "The Self-Reflective Musical and the Myth of Entertainment," *Quarterly Review of Film Studies* Vol. 2 No. 3 (August 1977), pp. 313-326.

10. Robert C. Allen, et al., "The College Student Soap Opera Viewer," unpublished paper (University of North Carolina, April 1981).

11. Sally M. Johnstone and Robert C. Allen, "The Audience for Soaps: A Comparison of Two Populations," paper presented at the 1981 Conference on Communication and Culture (University of Pennsylvania, April 1981).

12. Sol Worth and Larry Gross, "Symbolic Strategies," *Journal of Communication* Vol. 24 No. 4 (Autumn 1974), pp. 27-39.

13. Sari Thomas, "The Relationship between Daytime Serials and their Viewers," (Ph.D. Dissertation, University of Pennsylvania, 1977).

14. Eco, p. 12.

The Social Matrix of Television:
Invention in the United States

Jeanne Allen

One of the familiar aphorisms about 20th-century technological development is that the pace of scientific invention far outstrips the ability of
societies to prepare for and adjust to it. This suggests not only the idea of
"cultural lag" but also a technological determinism which argues that societies adapt to inventions emerging from an autonomous realm of human
imagination. The development of television in the United States challenges
this notion. From the invention of Nipkow's scanning eye mechanism in
1884 until the entry of television into the American home at the end of World
War II, television was heralded, even given numerous premature "births," in
mass-circulated periodicals from the mid-1920s through 1940s.

Yet the degree of public debate about the functions and form television
was to assume does not even approximate that for radio during the rapid
diffusion of the 1920s. Following the 1932 government investigation of
concentration in the radio industry,[1] some critical voices argued for different
terms of ownership and social function for television. Gilbert Seldes heralded
"television as the utility of the future,"[2] and the trade journal *Electrician*
advocated "invention in relation to national welfare and its legislative control."[3] But these voices were few and far between, and did not, for the most
part, find their way into the business and popular magazines of the era. This
paper will explore both the terms of discussion of television and its possible
uses in the two decades before it was marketed, for what this can reveal about
the relation of technological change to social and economic developments and
their political implications.

Particular attention will be paid to the possibilities of two-way television and the constraints on its development, since two-way or interactive television represented perhaps one of the most explicit challenges or oppositions to the centralized and centralizing structures of commerce, government and the military which Raymond Williams has cited as basic to broadcasting's development.[4] Television's development in the United States does suggest the historical pattern of new technologies fitting into the terms of the previous ones and the socioeconomic practices that previous technologies have established and reinforced. And the discussion of television in various business, engineering and science journals as well as mass circulation magazines allows us to trace the influence and power of various sectors of society. We can then get a sense of the collective and staggered development of television rather than its uniform and linear emergence as a staple of American life.

The matrix of social functions into which television was introduced by the early 1930s was a combination of the following: television as a channel of movies through radio giving way to public showings of large-screen television in theaters; television as an advertising promotional tool as well as a demonstrator/educator for both consumer and sales personnel; television observation in work or factory settings; television surveillance and reconnaissance in a military setting or confrontation; and television as a new avenue of interpersonal communication for radio amateurs.

Despite a few late 1920s announcements in *Scientific American* and *Popular Mechanics* of radio movies entering the home, television's entertainment setting was initially the public theater. Announcements of its arrival read like echoes of film exhibition history: "Television advances from peephole to screen," or "Television hits Broadway." Indeed, on October 24, 1931 the Sanabria apparatus, a scanning and projecting mechanism, went on stage at the B.S. Moss Broadway Theater (a 2000-seat theater), among comedians, dancers and movies, and began its regular vaudeville roadshow tour. Its inventor, Ulysses A. Sanabria, travelled with it to maintain its working order. Although reviewers claimed it offered negligible entertainment value, they recommended it be seen for its technical features in a manner not unlike that which greeted the Lumière Cinématographe.[5] In fact, theatrical exhibition of television proceeded on a scale sufficient to warrant warning articles to Hollywood that they needed to woo this infant industry.[6] Although film and television were certainly tied to each other through Hollywood's conversion to sound (General Electric, AT&T, Westinghouse, RCA), the relationship was not one of subsidiaries using the one to promote the other. As early as 1941 *The Society of Motion Picture Engineers Journal* offered regular reports on television development and its relation to the film industry. Clearly the public image of competition between film and television belied the business and professional collaboration that characterized them.

At the time that television was entering the entertainment picture, home movies, innovated by Kodak in the early 1920s, provided another reference point for television's reception. What seems critical in this instance was the expectation set by home movies for the quality of the visual image of television, a factor which we will discuss later as crucial to the setting of industrial standards for television development and the repercussions that this had on the squeezing out of two-way television. A 1933 article titled "What Constitutes Perfect Detail in Television?" adopts a criterion based on the convergence of lines relative to the viewer's distance from the screen, and the author concludes: "Given the same conditions as obtain in a home movie showing...180-line television not only welcomes comparison with home movies, it seeks it!"[7] By 1936 *Radio News* claimed the quality of the television image had attained that of home movies.[8] Since television's public exhibition was primarily through theater in the 1930s, it seems curious that its image quality would be compared with that of home rather than theatrical commercial movies, especially since the public was much more familiar with theatrical film than it was with home movies. The association of television with radio as broadcasting must have been very powerful to have so emphasized privatized home consumption as the primary dimension of television.

That association in the public mind with radio accounts for much of the eager anticipation of television's selling abilities. Radio had accepted commercial sponsorship by 1924, in a decade marked by the spread of mass production and distribution into consumer goods and by the growth of the chain store, chain broadcasting in 1924 and film theater chains. Radio's ability to offer intimate contact with consumers in the home was crucial during a world-wide Depression for the movement of goods through a sluggish economy. Radio, like film, boomed in the wake of financial disaster. As film companies were lending their promotional services to American businesses in both the Hollywood theatrical film and the industrial narrative film,[9] business trade journals as early as 1930 were anticipating a new weapon in their selling arsenal.[10] Perhaps T.H. Thompson put it most poetically in a 1935 article in *Advertising and Selling* when he referred to television as a "pearl of great prevision."[11]

Published scripts of advertisements were available in 1939 in trade journals and the samples suggest a well-honed blend of the techniques of the Kliquot Eskimo days of radio and the pressbook product promotion of Hollywood. The early predecessor for Jack Klugman modeling Botany 500 clothes on *Quincy* was the Botany Wrinkle-Proof Tie lamb who forecast the weather every night at 9:00 pm on NBC's WNBT (1941). The creation of David Leigh "who has 16 spectaculars currently on Broadway," the lamb appeared in 14 different one-minute 16mm films dramatizing different weather conditions and, simultaneously, attributes of Botany Wrinkle-Proof Ties. The ads open with the Botany lamb scanning the skies with a telescope until the end of the instrument swings toward the televiewer and the lamb begins to recite. Each adventure predicts the next day's weather and the charms of the tie: the lamb tossed across a windy sea uses the tie for a danger flag when marooned, although the rescuer snatches the tie and leaves the lamb; or rain drenches the tie on the clothes-line but, despite rain and a tug of war between two dogs, the tie emerges wrinkle-proof.[12]

But business was not merely interested in contracting producers to make ad playlets for television. According to *Printer's Ink*, Selfridge's in London innovated a television studio in the late 1930s to stimulate customer attendance in the same way as it had used film.[13] In 1939 Bloomingdale's and Abraham and Straus applied to the FCC for a television station license through their subsidiary, Metropolitan Television Inc., just as Westinghouse had started KDKA in the 1920s. Confirming the ties with film techniques, trade journals pointed out the value of technicolor shorts (the color fashion sequence in the 1928 film *Fig Leaves*, by Howard Hawks and fashion designer Adrian) and of borrowing directly from movie promotion:

> Go to the movies; analyze everything you see in the picture, every product, be it dress, real estate, transportation; think of it then as if you were trying to sell it. Study your reactions to the picture of automobiles, food, women's fashions, or men's fishing rods. Does the picture show them persuasively—with sales appeal? If it does, then memorize the particular technique as far as you can.[14]

By 1944 the trades were suggesting the potential in television for using trademarks like Aunt Jemima, Quaker Oats, Psyche, the White Rock girl—by beginning with a still that would "come to life" as the Kirkman Flakes woman does, particularly her legs. George S. Kaufman was writing comedy skits for Procter Electric and advertisers looked forward to television's smaller, but more attentive, audience. Consider the darkened room, the one television for the whole family, and the attention made more critical by virtue of listening *and* watching. Department stores' use of television for demos in stores and sales personnel training (Wanamaker's, GE demos for department stores) encouraged predictions that television, when it arrived at long last for mass consumption, would go commercial overnight. DuMont's, who listed Bloomingdale's among its other department store clients, was helping to make predictions reality by offering its facilities free of charge to provide a meeting ground for advertisers to formulate sponsorship programs for television.[15] As the ultimate blend of radio and film, television promised an open door to advertisers rather than the restrictions of the film industry, while the latter provided a virtual handbook on visual and dramatic promotion and persuasion.

A second tie between television and industry emerged in the early 1940s with the suggestion that television function as a monitoring device for factory production. The extent to which wartime innovations in television technology played a key role in this proposed use is not yet clear. But it seems no coincidence that Ralph R. Beal, assistant to the vice-president in charge of RCA Laboratories (the same company that produced the Orthicon miniaturized television camera for guiding missiles and providing nighttime reconnaissance information) began promoting television for industry surveillance and control at engineering societies in 1944. Beal declared it a likely area of expansion in postwar America, another dimension of war production adapted for business use.[16] Citing the significance of television's emergence from centralized structures as one-way communication, Fina Bathrick has pointed out to me that the term "television monitor" is more than a coincidental coupling of concepts; it correctly labels a social function that implies control and a non-reciprocal power relation.

Article titles in *Scientific American* and *Electronics* offer revealing glimpses of the concepts articulated by Beal: "Industrial television can serve to improve process control," and "Electronic eyes for the works manager."[17] Although Beal does not refer specifically to the surveillance of workers but of "hazardous operations," "monitoring factory operations from a centralized fixed point allowing the foreman to save time" is presented as an attractive goal in achieving plant control. The use of film for Taylor-oriented time-motion efficiency studies in the first two decades of the century and the contemporary use of computers for word processing machines as well as assembly-line work amplify a picture of electronic media as monitoring devices for maximizing management control and profits. Marketing techniques for electronic software which maximizes so-called "consumer control" (see advertisements for video tape recorders and playback consoles as examples of this appeal) make explicit the role of entertainment media in reconciling and compensating for workplace media applications.

Like film, television's surveillance potential was quickly associated with aircraft intelligence gathering. Where film had been instrumental in this area during World War I, television's application to wartime surveillance came during its formative developmental period. In addition, aircraft provided television with a substitute for high towers to boost transmission of broadcast signals. Aircraft use of television was a category of television literature from early in the 1930s, so that it hardly came as a surprise to see television converted to war uses such as detecting enemy aircraft, guiding bombs and missiles through television camera installation close to gun sights, and spying on enemy lines. Although *Advertising and Selling* asked "Is television a war casualty?", referring to the freeze on commercial television development,[18] television came out of the war with mobile television equipment, the RCA Image Orthicon, and the Mimo-Miniature Image Orthicon. (The size and portability of these innovations made them readily adaptable to the industrial factory.) The Utiliscope, a remote viewer, was in use by 1947. Documenting the wartime incentive for television development, *Radio News* published consecutive articles analyzing recent patents in electronics, including those filed through the Alien Property Custodian, a government agency that allowed for the nationalization of foreign patents considered necessary to domestic wartime production.[19]

With these factors favoring the development of one-way television communication as performance or monitoring, it may not seem likely that the patterns set by film and radio could be significantly altered. Yet two groups had an interest in interactive or two-way television. In the late 1920s AT&T experimented with two-way television to replace the two-way telephone, thus fulfilling the implications of the name "television." AT&T in conjunction with Bell Laboratories had been actively researching television since 1927, when their demonstration established its scientific practicability. By 1930-31 *Electrical World, Scientific American,* and *Smithsonian Report* carried news of the experiment between 195 Broadway and 463 West Street. The quality of the image did not depend on distance, since the signal was relayed by wire rather than being broadcast (which would require a relay system).[20] Despite the publicity, the complexity and cost of the system made immediate commercial exploitation prohibitive. The explanation for the lack of further research to lower costs or to explore the market which might compensate for these costs is not readily available. A number of engineers, among them most prominently H.E. Ives, published results of their research in the *Journal of the American Institute of Electrical Engineers* and the *Bell System Technical Journal* in this two-year period. But then discussion of two-way television ended, at least in print, for this sector of the society.

The sector that picked up the development of two-way television after 1930 was amateur producers, that group of radio users so significant for the development of radio.[21] Serviced by such journals as *Scientific American, Popular Mechanics* and *Popular Science Monthly* in this country, and *Hobbies* and *Practical Radio* in England, the marginal status of amateurs and amateur production is signalled by these very titles. Although some of these journals presented simplified explanations of mechanical and electronic processes in a manner that emphasized the wonders of science and technology with adventurous-looking graphics and emphasis on dramatic narrative, both *Radio News* and *Practical Radio* offered explicit "how to" information about the construction of television transmitters and receivers. After Hollis Semple Baird presented a demonstration of television reception and transmission in 1926, the London-based company of J.L. Baird started to manufacture equipment which was distributed in the U.S. by the Shortwave and Television Corporation in Boston. *Radio News* listed the parts and kits necessary at the end of its articles on "how to," and by 1931 a complete kit, minus tubes and cabinet, was listed for $56.25.[22] Such equipment seemed to rely on transmission of signals from experimental stations. As of December,

1934, 28 stations had been established in states ranging from New York, Massachusetts and Pennsylvania to California and including Iowa, Michigan, Missouri, Wisconsin and Illinois.[23] It was not until 1940 that a series of articles on two-way television included a camera "eye" tube or iconoscope, costing slightly less than $25, which provided 120-line pictures. Combined with transmitting and receiving station equipment, the entire operation could be purchased and assembled for less than $300.[24]

Although *Scientific American* hastened to add in its article "Ham Television" that the 120-line image is inferior to the 441 lines broadcast in New York, we may remember that the journal announced that 180 lines provided detail comparable to home movies in 1934, and that in 1941 the representation afforded by 120 lines offered the equivalent of newspaper halftone engraving. Recalling that department stores were already applying for licenses by 1939, it is important to understand how quickly amateurs sensed they were being squeezed out. In October, 1936, *Radio News* was alerting its readership to the "mad scramble" for television frequencies that "threatens amateurs." They were in danger of losing the five meter band (which was not much good for 441 lines but which they had discovered and developed). The lack of open discussion about television's development in the United States, they argued, would result in the same two-corporation concentration that marked the radio industry.[25]

The amateurs did not have long to wait for the opening-up of information about television development. It came in the form of a conference of the Radio Manufacturers Association, whose acting chairman of the Television Committee published the standards for television equipment in *Electronics* in July, 1938. Hailed by *Electronics'* editor as an "outstanding example of cooperation in a highly complex technical and commercial field," these television standards laid down the ground rules for television transmission and reception.[26]

Trade associations like the Radio Manufacturers Association (RMA) had developed as early as the mid-19th century, largely out of a response to unionization. Like the National Association of Broadcasters, formed later largely in response to labor union organization and strikes, trade associations generally provided for management's collective action within a single industry to share information, lobby government and counter organized labor. The movement towards standardization which emerged from 19th-century mass production and distribution and which was advanced by trade associations, gained its greatest momentum in the 1920s, when the U.S. Department of Commerce served as a clearinghouse for industries to avoid "wasteful, cutthroat [read 'free market'] competition" by establishing product specifications they would all adhere to. This business/government cooperation which went under the title "national standardization movement" developed connotations with the public of criteria for *excellence,* for *consumer* protection, dependability and interchangeability for maximum *consumer* flexibility.

Rarely, if ever, even in the business trade journals, did the setting of standards indicate how this movement protected the most established manufacturers. RMA's Albert Murray described the agreed-upon television standards as "best from a practical operating viewpoint." But, as is frequently the case with criteria for judging commodities and services, Murray was not explicit about whom these standards benefited and for what social function of television as defined by what sectors of the society.

This essay has attempted to make explicit what groups in American society defined social function and under what conditions. The article in *Electronics* reported that the standards were "unanimously agreed upon" and indeed this is probably the case among the business community represented by the Radio Manufacturers Association. But what, if any, input did other sectors of American society contribute to this consensus? The importance of radio and film in moving goods during the Depression years and the warnings about postwar recession unless markets expanded rapidly, coupled with the surveillance or monitoring uses of television, were powerful forces which a marginalized group of "amateurs" could do little to counter, given the lack of public and governmental debate about the emergence of television.

The standards which the RMA unanimously agreed upon provide a point of reference for the way in which a "new" medium conforms to the aspects of previous media and their socially defined functions: 441 lines (necessary to approach current home movie quality); frame frequency of 30 per second (to eliminate flicker completely); a scan aspect ratio of 4:3 (to conform with existing motion picture practice); and television service channels limited in width to allow for the maximum number of channels to provide information and programming (an image of diversity belied almost immediately by practice and patterns already existing in radio network concentration).

Setting such standards effectively solidifed the marginal position of amateurs and their two-way operations. Amateurs were positioned as dedicated assistants for both government (the Amateur Radio League was organized into an emergency communications force by the U.S. Army Signal Corps in case of emergency disaster or military confrontation) and business (RCA in cooperation with the Amateur Radio League supplied an inexpensive operating unit with a limited market). Amateur engineers in electronics, furthermore, were not a sector that would be likely to press for a counter-cultural development of television as a widely diffused grass-roots egalitarian form of communication rather than as a concentrated professionalized and generally restricted means of diffusing economic and governmental informa-tion using entertainment as a means of gaining audience attention. Amateurs were generally middle-class employees who saw their avocation as a diversion and a possible avenue to upward mobility in electronics employment for business or government. But they do present historians with a moment in the development of television in the United States when an emergent possibility of relatively decentralized high participative communication existed for television.

NOTES

1. Frank C. Waldrop and Joseph Borkin, *Television: A Struggle for Power* (New York: William Morrow, 1938).

2. Gilbert Seldes, "Television as the Utility of the Future," *Public Utility* 20 (August 19, 1937), pp. 239-241.

3. "Invention in Relation to National Welfare and Its Legislative Control," *Electrician* 112 (March 23, 1934), p. 406.

4. Raymond Williams, *Television: Technology and Cultural Form* (New York: Schocken Books, 1974).

5. E.H. Felix, "Television Advances From Peephole to Screen," *Radio News* 11 (September 1930), pp. 228-230; "Television on the Theatre Screen," *Literary Digest* 106 (July 5, 1930), p. 24; Robert Hertzberg, "Television Hits Broadway," *Radio News* 13 (February 1932), pp. 654-655, 712.

6. F. Daugherty, "Movies Woo Television," *Christian Science Monitor Weekly Magazine* (December 22, 1937), p. 3; W.D. Hurd, "Hollywood's Opportunity," *Christian Science Monitor Weekly Magazine* (July 1, 1939), p. 8.

7. W.H. Peck, "What Constitutes Perfect Detail in Television?", *Scientific American* Vol. 149 (December 1933), p. 273.

8. "Television as Good as Home Movies," *Radio News* 18 (November 1936), pp. 265-266.

9. Jeanne Allen, "The Film Viewer as Consumer," *Quarterly Review of Film Studies* Vol. 5 No. 4 (Fall 1980), pp. 481-499.

10. John Black, "What Television Offers as a Selling Medium," *Printer's Ink* 186 (March 30, 1939), pp. 63-68.

11. T.H. Thompson, "Pearl of Great Prevision," *Advertising and Selling* 25 (July 18, 1935), p. 24.

12. "Animated Films in Television," *Advertising and Selling* 34 (November 1941), p. 19.

13. "Retail Stores to Use Television," *Printer's Ink* 188 (August 11, 1939), p. 22.

14. Black, pp. 63-68.

15. George H. Plagens, "How Will Television Audition Programs for Sponsors?", *Printer's Ink* 212 (July 20, 1945), p. 89.

16. Ralph Beal, "Radio Relays Promise Far Flung Television Networks After the War," *Scientific American* Vol. 170 (March 1944), p. 128; "Remote Viewer Represents Television's Entry Into Industry," *Scientific American* Vol. 176 (March 1947), p. 126.

17. Ralph Beal, "Electronic Eyes For the Works Manager," *Electronics* 17 (July 1944), p. 278; "Industrial Television Can Serve to Improve Process Control," *Scientific American* Vol. 171 (July 1944), p. 36.

18. The federal government could ration celluloid while they outproduced Hollywood in film footage, but they did not even try to ration the airwaves. (Sydney Head with Christopher Sterling, *Broadcasting in America* [Boston, MA: Houghton Mifflin Co., 4th. ed., 1982]).

19. Robert Eichberg, "Wartime Progress in Electronics: Analysis of Recent Patents," *Radio News* 28 (December 1942), pp. 20-21, 70; and *Radio News* 29 (February 1943), pp. 24-25, 62-65.

20. "AT&T Demonstrates Two-Way Television," *Electrical World* 95 (April 19, 1930), p. 772. "Two-way Television Demonstrated," *Scientific American* Vol. 142 (June 1930), p. 467. H.E. Ives, "Two-way Television," *Smithsonian Report* (1931), pp. 297-301.

21. Captain David Talley, "The Army's Amateur Radio System," *Radio News* 12 (April 1931), pp. 892-894, 925-931 (the story of television in World War II has not been as thoroughly researched by historians as that concerning World War I has by Head, Barnouw and Kittross); Austin C. Lescarboura, "Blitzkrieg Television," *Radio News* 24 (December 1940), pp. 6-7, 51.

22. "Baird Television," *Radio News* 12 (June 1931). Joseph Calcaterra, "The Boston Television Party," *Radio News* 12 (May 1931), pp. 986-988, 1028.

23. Calcaterra, p. 988.

24. C.L. Ragsdale, "Do Your Own Televising," *Radio News* 21 (May 1939), pp. 6-8, 54.

25. "The Mad Scramble for Television Privilege Threatens Amateurs," *Radio News* 18 (October 1936), pp. 201-202.

26. H.M. Lewis, "Standards in Television," *Electronics* 11 (July 1939), pp. 10-13. Albert F. Murray, "RMA Completes Television Standards," *Electronics* 10 (July 1938), pp. 28-29, 55.

Television, Hollywood, and the Development of Movies Made-for-Television

Douglas Gomery

All television viewers in the United States are familiar with the "Late Show," the "Early Show," the various "Nights at the Movies," and other series which have turned homes using television into archives exhibiting the best and worst of Hollywood's creations. Nearly everyone in the current "film generation" first encountered the magic of Hollywood's past through television. Indeed, it is not surprising to learn that by the late 1960s the television industry had "run out" of theatrical fare, and therefore started to commission its own films. Today, television movies outnumber theatrical films in prime time. Looking toward the future, movies of all types will continue to represent a popular, staple entertainment attraction on television. In fact, they should be so attractive that they will constitute a cornerstone of the emerging cable, pay subscription and direct broadcast satellite television industries.

Like other forms of U.S. television, the presentation of theatrical and made-for-TV movies has gone through a 20-year period of innovation and diffusion. Throughout that transformation one fundamental factor seems to stand out: the driving force for any programming change has come from a desire for more profit. For television, with its sophisticated ratings estimates and limited advertising slots, executives have listed only those offerings which produced the highest profits. Consequently, a history of this genre (feature-length narrative films shown on U.S. television) must begin as a business history. We need to examine the history of two industries—

television and motion pictures. Since we have precious little that qualifies as analytical history in this area, we should, as a first step, begin to integrate a business history of the coming of movies to television into a literature so well synthesized by Alfred Chandler in *The Visible Hand*.[1]

Early Interaction

At first glance, understanding initial relations between the film and television industries in the United States seems simple enough. We read that from 1945 to 1955 the heads of the film industry resisted any interchange with the television industry, and that only after the movies had lost their mass audience did the moguls reluctantly consent to open negotiations with their counterparts in television. I posit that such an argument is far too simple. The movie studios did, correctly, withhold their catalogues of features and shorts, for then even NBC and CBS could not ante up fees competitive with short-run box office revenue. No incentives existed to push movie executives to forfeit their strong card in inter-industry media competition. In all other areas, however, Hollywood not only dealt with the television business, it tried to take it over. Unfortunately, two decades too early, the dominant concerns of the chief executives of the motion picture industry included the then viable options of subscription and large-screen television.

The motion picture industry also tried to acquire extensive holdings of television stations. For example, Paramount Pictures secured a share of the DuMont network and its owned-and-operated stations, and KTLA in Los Angeles. From the exhibition side the United Paramount Theatre Chain gained control of the American Broadcasting Corporation. Yet the motion picture industry failed to obtain a significant, lasting foothold. Why? The reasons were complex. In part the movie producers unwisely invested vast sums in subscription and theater television. Also, radio stations and newspapers acquired television licenses in America's larger cities and hooked up with NBC or CBS. The movie companies lacked the necessary community involvement and political muscle to win FCC approval. In addition, that governmental regulatory body frowned on movie producer applications because of recent convictions in the Paramount anti-trust case (1949). That same case forced producers to truncate their theater holdings precisely when they needed the security of that vertical integration. The owners of the old theater chains generally turned to other investments, and the United/Paramount Theatre/ABC merger proved an exception to the rule.[2]

The smaller Hollywood producers, however, saw television as a market into which they could expand. They gladly offered their vacant studio lots for the production of programs especially made for television. Until 1955 no major studio (Fox, Warners, Paramount, RKO or MGM) stepped forward to provide such facilities. But in 1951 a minor studio, Columbia, did; in that year it established Screen Gems as a wholly owned subsidiary for television series production. By mid-1955 the success of Screen Gems and others, plus the continued decline of revenues from the rental of features, provided a sufficient incentive for the majors to plunge headfirst into television series production. Warners, together with ABC, pioneered such programs as *Cheyenne, 77 Sunset Strip* and *Maverick*. Soon this type of relationship proved so profitable for both sides that Hollywood was transformed into the center of television production in the United States, replacing New York City.[3]

As this jockeying for market position was taking place, feature film material was being shown by local television stations. Initially features were imported from Europe, in particular by the Ealing, Rank and Korda corporations of Great Britain, who perceived television as a method by which to break into the American market so long dominated by Fox, Warner Brothers, RKO, MGM and Paramount. Specialized producers such as Monogram and Republic also offered their backlists to local stations for precisely the same reason. More than 4,000 titles came forth from these sources. But their cheap production values only served to remind early television viewers of the storehouse of treasures still resting in the vaults of the five majors.[4]

Coalescence

By 1955 the film industry in the United States had survived its most tumultuous decade. Attendance and revenues had declined by one-third to one-half, depending on the measurement one used. There seemed to be three causes for this drop. First, the aforementioned Paramount case had disrupted the process of distribution. Second, the urban audiences, so long the staple of the film-going public, were migrating to the suburbs—no longer did they live near neighborhood theaters, or close to public transportation which would get them downtown. Third, network television, complete with its own oligopolistic structure and conduct, reached full strength. Audiences were sizable, advertising dollars were plentiful—viewers had journeyed from their radio sets to the "tube." Only the more recalcitrant movie executives wanted to stand firm; newcomers to the movie business held no illusions and sought change.[5]

In 1948 Howard Hughes purchased control of RKO, and in five short years he increased debts to $20 million and reduced production by 50 percent. In 1954, to appease minority stockholders, he took over their shares (writing a check for $23,489,478.16 to cover the amount). One year later he sold the company to General Tire & Rubber for $25 million. (At the time General Tire owned WOR-TV in New York City and sought RKO's features for its *Million Dollar Movie* series.) But General Tire did not want to enter film production and distribution so it quickly tendered all non-filmic physical property to others: the studio facilities, for example, went to former RKO star, then America's number one television attraction, Lucille Ball, for her Desilu

Corporation. General Tire also peddled rights to RKO's 704 features and 1100 shorts to television stations in markets where General Tire did not own a station. This alone turned up $15 million. In sum, *Variety* estimated that General Tire realized a profit of nearly $10 million in one year from its RKO investment, a return in excess of 60 percent.[6]

Such figures impressed even the most recalcitrant movie mogul. Within the space of 24 months all the remaining major Hollywood corporations released their pre-1948 titles to local television stations. (Only these titles were tendered because they required no residuals to creators.) For the first time in American film history a sizable audience could re-view a broad cross section of Hollywood sound film production. Few silent motion pictures proved popular enough to warrant frequent showing. We must date this as the beginning of a new cinematic age.

From sale or lease to television the dominant Hollywood film companies were able to tap a significant source of needed revenue precisely at the low point of their adjustment to the post-World War II world. Columbia, which had been the first Hollywood company involved in telefilm production, also moved first in this arena. In January, 1956 it announced that Screen Gems, its subsidiary for television, would rent packages of Columbia films to local television stations. One hundred and four features constituted the first package. Three more of 195 features were out by mid-1957, and profits soared. In fiscal 1955, Columbia achieved a $5 million profit—a minor studio had instantly become a major.[7]

On March 1, 1956, Warner Brothers sold its pre-1948 group of 850 features and 1500 shorts to Associated Artists Productions, a television distributor working in conjunction with PRM, a Canadian-American investment company. This $21 million deal included all rights for television presentation as well as the right for film remakes and 16mm distribution. Suddenly Warners could announce its best year in a decade: for the fiscal year ending August, 1956, Warners recorded a profit of $15 million. (In 1957 United Artists acquired controlling interest in Associated Artists Productions and with it the Warner package.)[8]

Twentieth Century-Fox took in even more money. In May, 1956 it licensed its pre-1948 features to National Telefilm Associates (NTA) for cash, a percentage of television rentals, and a block of NTA stock. Monies totalling $32 million eventually changed hands; total features released reached 500 titles. In turn, this library was divided into five packages delivered over the next five years. NTA bicycled films in exchange for a minimum of 90 commercial minutes a week which NTA in turn sold to national advertisers.[9]

In August, 1956 MGM completed separate contracts for 725 of its back titles. The buyers were three CBS owned-and-operated stations, two King stations, four Triangle stations and KTTV in Los Angeles (in which MGM acquired an interest). The return for these deals totalled $20 million, the largest single day's business in MGM's history. In 1957 MGM-TV peddled additional packages of its 750 features and 1500 shorts to other stations for $34 million.[10]

Paramount held out the longest because it had invested the most in subscription television. In February, 1958 it sold, rather than leased, its pre-1948 library to MCA, then a talent agency—this sale was worth $50 million. But because Paramount, like Warners, *sold* rather than leased its titles, the buyer made out far better in the long run. By 1964 MCA had grossed more than $70 million and had not even tapped into the network market. The excess profits MCA generated from this investment enabled it to purchase Universal, Inc., and join the ranks of the major Hollywood studios.[11]

Network Movie Nights

From 1955 on, pre-1948 feature films functioned as a mainstay of local television programming practice. Infrequently, the networks would present a feature film as special, but not regular programming. Thus, for example, during the 1956-57 season, CBS began its annual ritual of airing *The Wizard of Oz*. But, with the high ratings for pre-1948 features, NBC, CBS and ABC reasoned that *post*-1948 Hollywood products should generate sizable audiences if offered in prime time. Before the networks could begin this process, however, the Hollywood studios had to negotiate with craft unions concerning residuals. In a precedent-setting action, the Screen Actors Guild, led by its president, Ronald Reagan, walked out and successfully won guaranteed compensation. Consequently, on September 23, 1961, NBC initiated *Saturday Night at the Movies* with *How to Marry a Millionaire*. NBC had worked out a deal with Twentieth Century-Fox for all 31 titles in this first series. All titles were made after 1949; fifteen were in color. (At the time NBC had a monopoly on color presentations; then, as now, RCA owned NBC and RCA was in the process of innovating colorcasting in the United States.) In addition, feature-length movies enabled NBC to effectively counter-program proven hits on CBS (*Have Gun, Will Travel; Gunsmoke*), and ABC (*Lawrence Welk*). As was generally the case during the 1960s, ABC quickly imitated NBC's success, and began a mid-season replacement in April, 1962—*Sunday Night at the Movies*. CBS, the long-time ratings leader, felt no compulsion to join the battle until September, 1965.[12]

Complete diffusion of theatrical movie fare as a prime-time genre was accomplished in less than six years. By the fall of 1968, ABC, NBC and CBS were presenting Hollywood feature films seven nights a week. By the early 1970s, overlapping permitted ten separate "Movie Nights" each week. Programming innovator NBC retained the greatest commitment to this particular form because of continued corporate interest in colorcasting, but this lead was temporary. As the ratings numbers poured in, all three networks realized that recent Hollywood productions provided one of the strongest weapons in their programming arsenal. All employed motion pictures as a tool to boost local station ratings during selected measuring periods each year (the so-called sweep weeks), and so bid competitively on the more popular theatrical products.

This push for network presentation of feature films significantly affected local station practice. Since 1955 sizable quantities of classic Hollywood movie material had consistently appeared on local stations. For example, the number of features televised in the New York market increased from three per week in 1948 to a zenith of 130 per week during the early 1960s. Network movie casting forced this rate down to about 100 per week. As expected, stations not affiliated with one of the three major networks scheduled more hours of movies. So, on average, during the early 1970s these independent stations allocated about one-quarter of their broadcast day to feature films. Network affiliates, in contrast, counted on movies for only one-sixteenth of total broadcast time.[13]

Movies Made-for-Television

The vast display of movie programming presented during the 1960s quickly depleted the available stock. Although the total number of usable features had grown from 300 in 1952 to over 10,000 a decade later, increases after that were negligible. Station managers and network programmers began to wonder just how often they could repeat certain titles. NBC, CBS and ABC had established a formula for scheduling post-1948 movies—show it twice in prime time and then let local stations run it in off-network hours. The movie studios seized the moment and began to demand higher and higher fees for the more popular product. Escalating prices came to a head in September, 1966 for a broadcast of *The Bridge on the River Kwai*; the Ford Motor Company paid $1.8 million for the right to be the sole sponsor of this three-hour extravaganza. Presented on a Sunday night (September 25), this screening bested two proven hits—*The Ed Sullivan Show* on CBS and *Bonanza* on NBC—and drew an estimated 60 million viewers. The trade press soon began to speculate on $50 to $100 million dollar price tags for multiple screenings of recent MGM, Fox and Paramount product.

Network executives realized that costs had reached the point where profits would soon disappear. NBC again took the lead—it commissioned Universal to create a package of two-hour films for first-run presentation in prime time. Costs varied between $300,000 and $1,000,000 per feature; NBC would hold exclusive rights for U.S. network presentation, and, after network screening, the films would revert back to Universal for possible U.S. theatrical release, and foreign theatrical and television sales. Such a practice helped NBC reduce costs and provided a method for making pilot programs for projected series. Since at this time the three networks normally paid for part or all of the development of pilots, significant savings could be effected. Made-for-TV movies enabled NBC to efficiently test the drawing power of proposed series.[14]

The first movie made-for-television offered as part of a regular series, not as a special, was presented on Saturday, November 26, 1966, by NBC— *Fame is the Name of the Game*.[15] The American television viewing public took to television movies in less than five seasons. By 1972 all three networks had, for the first time, scheduled in prime time more made-for-TV motion pictures than theatrical fare. Again, lowly ABC quickly followed NBC's lead. In 1967 ABC reached agreement with MGM for the production of 90-minute made-for-TV features. Ratings leader CBS did not come aboard until the following season.[16]

The rapid transformation to made-for-TV movie presentation took place because profits grew larger than anyone had anticipated. On the supply side a movie made-for-television cost one-half to one-third the price of the average theatrical feature. On the demand side, television movies quickly proved they could attract sizable audiences, at times even surpassing blockbuster theatrical features. We would expect to learn that the top network rating choices for movie showings on television would include *Gone With the Wind, Love Story, The Godfather* and *Ben Hur*. More surprising is the fact that *Little Ladies of the Night* (ABC, January 16, 1977) places 15th on the list for movie presentations of any type. The top 100 list also includes such topical hits as *Helter Skelter, A Case of Rape, Women in Chains* and *Jesus of Nazareth*. In general, ABC has produced the best ratings results for television movies. In 1971-72, for example, ABC garnered 13 of the top 15 made-for-TV movie ratings. And, as if to signal that the transformation to television movies was complete, Barry Diller, the head of ABC's movie programming for that season, moved to become chairman of Paramount Pictures in 1974.[17]

Conclusion

In 20 years movie presentation on television gradually became a staple of prime-time programming practice. At first the Hollywood studios withheld their more popular films and explored station ownership, and subscription and theater television. By the mid-1950s, with profits down significantly, the dominant corporations in the motion picture industry agreed to sell or lease their *pre-1948* features (and shorts) to local television stations. In 1961 the networks began to broadcast *post-1948* features in prime time. Costs quickly escalated as available inventories approached zero. Consequently, during the late 1960s, NBC, ABC and CBS commissioned their own films. These made-for-TV features proved so popular that they sometimes surpassed the ratings of even the most expensive theatrical products. The movie made-for-television was established as a force on network television in the United States by 1972, completing two decades of innovation and diffusion.

Change did not stop in 1972. During the mid-1970s the television networks and their Hollywood suppliers created miniseries, novels for television and docudramas. These forms differed from feature films in their far greater length. In the 1980s, Twentieth Century-Fox has begun to produce movies made-for-pay-cable-television. At about one-third the cost of theatrical product, these features would first appear on pay cable networks, then in video discs and cassettes, and would then go to overseas markets. Home Box Office has also begun to create movies for pay cable television. Economic theory and industrial history would suggest that miniseries and novels for pay cable television ought to arrive sometime in the mid to late 1980s.[18]

Movies presented on television, either theatrical or made-for-television, have created sizable profits for both the television industry (stations and networks), and the motion picture industry (the Hollywood producers). The availability of these profits thrust movie-viewers into a new age of film exhibition. It became possible to see a film several times, to draw pleasure from multiple viewings. This major shift constitutes what business historian Alfred Chandler has labeled the 20th century's revolution in production and distribution.[19] Innovators sought speed, volume and regularity in production and distribution. Corporations could then process larger numbers (i.e., viewers) and generate substantial revenues (i.e., advertising dollars) while controlling costs through regularized, routine operation. Television is a far more cost-effective way to reach potential movie-viewers than was the neighborhood movie house. It simply took 20 years for the transformation to take place. Certainly the advent of satellite distribution of movies (HBO, Showtime, The Movie Channel—all on cable television) will surely create more changes in who presents movies, who watches them, and who profits from their showing.

NOTES

1. Alfred D. Chandler, *The Visible Hand* (Cambridge, MA: Harvard University Press, 1977).

2. Robert Pepper, "The Pre-Freeze Television Stations," in *American Broadcasting,* ed. Lawrence W. Lichty and Malachi C. Topping (New York: Hastings House, 1976), pp. 139-147; Douglas Gomery, "Review—*The Movie Brats,*" *Screen* Vol. 21 No. 1 (Spring 1980), pp. 15-17.

3. Orton Hicks and Haven Falconer, *MGM Television Survey: Interim Report* (Madison, WI: Dore Schary Collection, Wisconsin Center for Film and Theatre Research, April 29, 1955), pp. 1-8; Charles Higham, *Hollywood at Sunset* (New York: Saturday Review Press, 1972), pp. 145-150; Harvey J. Levin, *Broadcast Regulation and Joint Ownership of the Media* (New York: New York University Press, 1960), pp. 62-63; Michael Conant, *Antitrust in the Motion Picture Industry* (Berkeley, CA: University of California Press, 1960), pp. 108-110.

4. Hicks and Falconer, pp. 8-11; *Broadcasting* (January 17, 1955), pp. 50-51; Opinion in *Autry v. Republic Productions,* 213 F 2d 667 (1954); Christopher H. Sterling and John M. Kittross, *Stay Tuned* (Belmont, CA: Wadsworth, 1978), pp. 345-346.

5. Gomery, "Review," pp. 16-17.

6. Hicks and Falconer, pp. 14-25; *Broadcasting* (April 23, 1956), p. 96; Richard Austin Smith, *Corporation in Crisis* (Garden City, NY: Doubleday, 1966), pp. 64-66; *Broadcasting* (March 15, 1954), p. 35; *Broadcasting* (December 19, 1955), p. 40; *Variety* (May 1, 1957), p. 50; Gertrude Jobs, *Motion Picture Empire* (Hamden, CT: Anchor Books, 1966), pp. 368-369; Donald Barlett and James B. Steele, *Empire* (New York: W.W. Norton, 1978), pp. 165-170, 210.

7. *Variety* (May 1, 1957), p. 50; Bob Thomas, *King Cohn* (New York: G.P. Putnam, 1967), pp. 262, 347.

8. *Broadcasting* (March 5, 1956), p. 42; *Broadcasting* (April 23, 1956), p. 98; *Broadcasting* (August 30, 1954), p. 58; *Broadcasting* (August 27, 1956), p. 68.

9. *Broadcasting* (May 21, 1956), p. 52; *Broadcasting* (November 5, 1956), p. 48; *Broadcasting* (October 15, 1956), p. 58; *Broadcasting* (July 2, 1956), p. 56; *Variety* (June 5, 1957), p. 27.

10. *Broadcasting* (June 25, 1956), p. 48; *Variety* (March 6, 1957), p. 25; "Stock of Aged MGM Movies Released to TV for $20 Million," *Business Week* (September 1, 1956), pp. 62-64.

11. *Broadcasting* (June 10, 1956), pp. 50-53; "MCA: Putting the Business in Show Biz," *Forbes* (November 15, 1965), pp. 24-27; Stanley Brown, "That Old Villain TV Comes to the Rescue and Hollywood Rides Again," *Fortune* (November 1966), pp. 270-273.

12. Robert Rich, "Post '48 Features," *Radio-Television Daily* (July 29, 1960), p. 27; John B. Burns, "Feature Films on TV," *Radio-Television Daily* (July 30, 1962), p. 32; *Variety* (June 21, 1972), p. 34; *Variety* (September 20, 1978), pp. 48, 66; Hollis Alpert, "Now the Earlier, Earlier Show," *The New York Times Magazine* (August 11, 1963), pp. 22-24; Cobbett Steinberg, *Reel Facts* (New York: Random House, 1978), pp. 355-357; Harry Castelman and Walter J. Podrazik, *Watching TV* (New York: McGraw Hill, 1982), pp. 148-149.

13. Amy Schnapper, "The Distribution of Theatrical Feature Film to Television," (unpublished Ph.D. Dissertation, University of Wisconsin-Madison, 1975, pp. 135-142).

14. Neil Hickey, "The Day the Movies Run Out," *TV Guide* (October 23, 1965), pp. 6-9; *TV Feature Film Source Book,* ed. Avra Fliegelman, Vol. 13 No. 3 (Autumn 1972), pp. 10-15; Martin Quigley, Jr., "11,325 Features for TV," *Motion Picture Herald* (January 18, 1967), p. 1; Walt Spencer, "Now Playing at Your Neighborhood Movie House: The Networks," *Television* Vol. 25 No. 1 (January 1968), p. 49.

15. The first TV movie, run as a special, was *See How They Run,* aired on October 7, 1964. See Alvin H. Marill, *Movies Made for Television* (Westport, CT: Arlington House, 1980) for a list of TV movies through 1980.

16. Marill, pp. 11-24; Henry Erlich, "Every Night at the Movies," *Look* (September 7, 1971), p. 63; Jack E. Nolan, "Films on TV," *Films in Review* Vol. 17 No. 10 (December 1966), pp. 655-657; *Variety* (August 18, 1971), p. 30; *Variety* (June 14, 1972), p. 29; *Broadcasting* (January 15, 1973), p. 37; Don Shirley, "Made for TV Movie: Its Coming of Age," *The Washington Post* (October 6, 1974), pp. E1-E2; Douglas Stone, "TV Movies and How They Get That Way," *Journal of Popular Film and Television* Vol. 7 No. 2 (1979), pp. 147-149.

17. Caroline Meyer, "The Rating Power of Network Movies," *Television* Vol. 25 No. 3 (March 1968), pp. 56, 84; Jack E. Nolan, "Films on TV," *Films in Review* Vol. 24 No. 6 (June-July 1973), p. 359; Herbert Gold, "Television's Little Dramas: First the Verdict, Then the Show," *Harpers* (March 1977), pp. 88-89; *Broadcasting* (September 25, 1972), p. 61; Dick Adler and Joseph Finnigan, "The Year America Stayed Home for the Movies: How Films Have Burgeoned on Television and Why," *TV Guide* (May 20, 1972), pp. 6-10.

18. *Broadcasting* (October 19, 1981), p. 61.

19. Chandler, pp. 207-209.

Video Art: Theory for a Future

Maureen Turim

"Video art"—the very term opens a contentious debate. From many different sectors come elaborate disclaimers of video's possible ascension to the realm of art forms. Film artists and theorists despair about image quality in video. They are worried about the possibility that video display will become more economically desirable than projected film, and that film production will end. This fear usually stops them from considering the specificities of the video image. They fail to consider how video's qualities and spatial-temporal configurations can be used for different effects than are available to film.

Some art historians who might write with interest about parallel imagery in photography or graphic art still balk at awarding the television set legitimacy; this tendency to limit the media considered proper to artistic expression is a reactionary stance seen numerous times before. Such distinctions or prejudices merely take time to break down. Other art theorists have examined a group of early video works by artists from other media whose interest in video was centered on the artist performing for the mirroring instantaneous replay of the image in the closed-circuit system. Applying psychoanalytic theory, they reject video as an inherently narcissistic art form, incapable of carrying other messages or displaying other concepts.

Some Marxists, whose critique of commercial television focuses on its manipulation of the audience, only see video art in that context. It becomes another subsidiary tool of alienated fascination, substituting formal techniques "devoid" of meaning for the ideologically-charged plentitude of soap operas or quiz shows. This position is reinforced by the recent use of the electronic imaging techniques developed by video artists in the most inane of television commercials. This ideological concern is quite real, and leads us to ask how video art can remain in its primary position of opposition to commercial broadcast television. Most video that attempts to be directly critical of television has trouble constituting an effective level of meta-criticism and successful irony.

Re-edited sequences of broadcast television or mild satires of television style remain closely linked to the concerns and forms of commercial televi-sion. Though they accelerate or interrupt the flow of broadcast imagery, although they poke fun at its forms, it is ultimately unclear what sort of commentary on television such works propose. Any formal innovation in the image can be used to create promos for rock stars or sell products as "scien-tific," or the "latest in technology." Exaggerations, acceleration, technical exploitation of television as a video art form too often gesture in a manner that is less critical than mimicking.

So how can video attain a self-definition, a theoretical stance? In many ways, video represents an overdetermined step along a path taken by those exploring the implications of science and technology for contemporary cre-ative cultural expression. Just as the shadow play, the magic lantern and the zoetrope have been described as the prehistory of cinema, the entire history of photography and cinema, serial and electronic music, and computer lan-guages can be considered the prehistory of video. Video then becomes the logical outcome of the structural experimentation of the avant-garde in film and music.

Perhaps the artist-theorist who best envisioned the development of a medium such as video was Lazlo Moholy-Nagy, a member of the Bauhaus School of artistic innovation in Germany during the 1920s. His light display devices, so crucial to his theories of painting, sculpture, architecture and film, were primitive models of the color light displays possible with the video apparatus. The apparatus he built was a metal deflector whose sculptural form bent light aimed at it into shifting projected and reflected patterns as the apparatus itself rotated. But as early as 1936 he saw not only film, but also television as an apparatus for presenting abstract light composition. In a section of a letter to Fra Kalivoda he enumerated his concepts of "indoor light display":

    a) The film, with its unexplored possibilities of projection, with color, plasticity and simultaneous displays, either by means of an increased number of projectors concentrated on a single screen, or in the form of simultaneous image sequences covering all the walls of the room.

    b) Reflected light displays of pattern sequences produced by such color projectors as Lazlo's color organ. Such displays may be of an open isolated nature or they may be multiplied by means of television.

    c) The color piano, whose keyboard is connected with a series of graduated lamp units, illuminates objects of special materials and reflectors.

d) The light fresco that will animate vast architectural units, such as buildings, parts of buildings or single walls, by means of artificial light focused and manipulated according to a definite plan. (In all probability a special place will be reserved in the dwellings of the future for the receiving set of these light frescoes, just as it is today for a wireless set.)[1]

In many ways video fulfills the conceptual dream Moholy-Nagy programmed for the future. Technological developments have combined analog synthesizers and computers with television display to create an apparatus that can "process" images, an apparatus that is an elaborate electronic stylus for a new kind of "writing."

This type of processing system allows the artist to rearrange elements of the image, altering codes of iconic representation and temporal-spatial order. It allows for representational imagery to be modified by or alternated with non-representational visual structures. As such it is a tool capable of reinscribing all the issues and explorations of late 19th- and 20th-century art. Video processing systems can spin through the visual modes of cubism, fauvism, orphism, sequential imagery and photo collage. We now have a magic box (that isn't magic at all, but logical, scientific, mathematical) that can conjure all the redefinitions of image that artists struggled to achieve through their craft and imagination.

This, too, Moholy-Nagy foresaw. His theory sees the "isms," the various modern artistic movements, as searching for new optical principles of compositional order, clearing the ground for a construction of an autonomous optical concept of composition, one free of representational constraints.[2] He suggests that new mechanisms, new "tools" will carry further this redefinition of the image and of art:

"...It is safe to predict even today that the optical creation of the future will not be a mere translation of our present forms of optical expression, for the new implements and the hitherto neglected medium of light must necessarily yield results in conformity with their own inherent properties."[3]

Yet we must ask, in the face of the negative responses to video art discussed in the opening of this article, what has gone awry in Moholy-Nagy's prophecy? What needs to be amended in his theoretical plan for a "dynamic-constructive energy system"?

One factor that Moholy-Nagy did not consider is the automatic aspect of the "tool." Video processing systems, once constructed, interlaced through electronic "patches" and programmed, generate images mechanistically. Take the example of a digital computer program: once an image or a sequence of images is fed into a given program, the system will endlessly perform a series of variations. There may be an optical concept involved, one that is continually changing in a quite elaborately detailed manner. But this processing is not necessarily "dynamic" in the full sense of the word. For a predictable, repetitive change, an exhaustive repertoire of variations is finally just another stasis. Video art demands that an artist interact with a mechanical apparatus. An artist must use a tool rather than merely run a machine. Otherwise the risk is the production of images whose function is decorative but not profound, flashy but not provocative. As I see it, there are three major obstacles to be overcome in the production of art using a video apparatus:

1. The artist must avoid the use of the apparatus to merely produce "special effects." The industry calls much of the transformative video technology "special effects generators," indicating the use commercial television wishes to make of such machinery. It sees these video apparati as producing images whose colors are tampered with for a "special effect"; images whose rapid sequencing provides for a special "montage effect"; a cheaper means than film editing to attain fancy wipes, dissolves, "glows," "sparkles," image rotations, etc. The artist must use these techniques not as flashy additions of images that otherwise are mundane; the rule should be, not added to as special, but intrinsic, integrated to the substance and signification of the image.

2. The artist must get past the seductive lure of simply "exploring the capabilities of the technology," because the result is to produce a mere catalogue of possible imaging techniques. There certainly is a great value in the production of video "samplers," which, like their needlework antecedents, are a display and mastery of techniques. Perhaps some day these video samplers will be revered as folk art, but the problem is how they are mistakenly misconstrued at the present as being all the video systems are capable of producing: decorative patterns and their variations that ultimately signify "this is what this experiment can do."

3. The artist must move beyond video versions of image redefinition that have already been accomplished by artists working with non-electronic craft. It is intriguing to know that multiple cameras put through a sequencer (a video device that arranges simultaneously transmitted images into patterns of superimposition and sequential order) can "simulate" cubism. But the added factor of temporality is not enough to justify reworking cubism *per se*, especially when the subject matter of the representational images used to create the cubist video vision are still lifes, portraits, landscapes. Painters have already done this. The same is true of futurism, impressionism, etc. The risk here is that video art will limit itself to kitsch citation, with no new imagination.

If much of the video work that has been done to date stumbles over one or more of these obstacles, we should remember that we are seeing the first sketches, the preliminary exercises, of a new art form. The economics of video is such that artists have limited access to the advanced production equipment. They cannot sketch and practice on a daily basis, nor can they afford to retain their early experiments as private notebooks. They need to show this work to obtain the grants and recognition necessary to continue their explorations. And they serve each other by sharing their technical discoveries as well as their more complete works.

Yet it is the purpose of video theory and criticism to point out these obstacles and to suggest a more meaningful use of video's capabilities. Video is a form with important image qualities, transformational qualities, that make it ideal for three areas of artistic exploration: visual perception; the imaginary; and the density of discursive presentation. Each of these areas places the artist in contact with major issues of contemporary theory: psychophysiology of perception; psychoanalysis; and semiotics. And each of these areas bears a more or less direct relationship to theories of ideology.

The most abstract use of video is that which explores the perceptual properties of the image. An initial approach to video's relationship to psychoperceptual studies is the overlap in terminology: scanning, circuit, processing, units of information, selective registration. While these terms refer to different concepts in video production than they do in the scientific study of perception, there is an intriguing, if imperfect, analogy to be drawn between how video systems process visual information and how the human perceptual system processes that information.

In human perception our eyes scan space (or images) to acquire information that is encoded as discrete contrasts, comparisons, presences and absences, so that it can be transmitted to brain centers that decode this information as a perceived image. A video camera electronically scans the inverted image of a camera obscura, transmitting that information as a series of impulses that other equipment can decode as various grey levels (or in the case of color, as color values). This encoding of the image can be submitted to various processes that "tamper with" the pattern as originally coded. When the revised image is displayed, it registers as an image whose own contrasts, presences and absences, and dual signals are already encoded information. Take the simple process of "dropping out" grey levels—reducing the displayed image to only four shades of grey instead of the graduated tones that comprise a saturated "normal" image (one that gives us the customary range of analogous representation). The result is a highly contrasted image, not unlike a woodblock, German Expressionism, the film noir image, or high contrast photography.

What is special about video is its ability to move between different image registrations, to perform these shifts in coding. By splitting the image or superimposing images, video can present different views or temporal instances simultaneously. Each of these views may already be a "processed" image, that is, an image transformed by a process of shifting graphic values and codes of representation as I described earlier. The results are images that challenge and train human perception. They demand what scientists call "dual attention": perceptual searching and registration of two sets of visual information simultaneously. They create new perceptual problems in distinguishing depth cues, relative size, motion and velocity. Instead of reproducing a visual field as analogous to normal human perception, these video images challenge our capability to perceive extraordinary circumstances.

Temporal changes can occur in video at a variable rate within what we perceive as a single video "image" (unlike film, whose individual frames are fixed so that the rate of change is uniform over all the frame field and limited to a rate of 1/24th of a second). This means that not only the rate of perception, but the density or quality of visual change in video is different from film. Temporality is perceived in relationship to the properties of spatial and iconic representation discussed above. Therefore video can add a unique temporality to the ways in which it transforms the other image codes.

Another property of video of interest in perceptual theory is that of easily schematizing, as visual diagram, various properties of mathematics, energy wave forms and computer languages. Video allows us to perceive as representations what would otherwise be abstract formulas. It draws out the correlations between geometry, mathematics, cybernetics and physics. While this has practical application in science, for the artist it means providing the public with a new visualization of what for us has never been cognitively understood through a visual charting. Digital imagery ceases to be a fairground amusement when we see it as its own symbolic realm, a means of representing information.

An artist can seriously delve into this perception of the visually unknown, and the other perceptual challenges of video display, without getting lost in the obstacle course of simplistic technological adventurism I discussed earlier. But in order to do that, he or she will have to be sensitive to the issues of perceptual theory. The artist will also have to think through the ideological issues of perception and the representation of scientific process. We have lived through one wave of "cybernetic serendipity," the naive embrace of a computer realm as a utopian fantasy solution. We hardly need any more of that style of mystification through art of the properties of technology. But seeing video as a link between human perception (as a complex, developmental historical process) and technological development is a very creative area for artists to seriously explore.

The relationship of video to the unconscious is also a rich area of exploration. Like any image, video can be used to explore and comment on mechanisms of fascination and desire. What is specific about the psychoanalytic dimensions of video is how "trace-like" the video image can seem to be. The elements of a "solid" representation can be transformed into specter-like, shifting, transformable, energized versions of a "real scene." Alternations between inside and outside, presence and absence, solid volume and schematized outline can be charged with a force of the psyche, its associations and remembrances. The play with perceptual thresholds can also be explored for its psychological implications. Repetitions and variations can urge us to ask, "Have I seen this before, or am I only imagining that?" The viewer is placed in a position of uncertainty, of trying to sort out perception from memory, real from imaginary, forms from their transformations into abstractions or other forms.

The artist, in exploring this "imaginary" aspect of video, will find the hard edges, the mechanistic aspects of the technologically-produced images softening, melting, blending with imagination. It is ironic that a system so based on measurable quantities being encoded and transmitted as other measurable quantities so lends itself to a field of exploration—the unconscious of the human mind—in which everything that is transferred is irregularly transformed. Dreamwork and the unconscious have certain distinct processes of transformation, but the result of their operation is always somewhat unexpected and, therefore, functions as concealment. The artist can evoke this same irregularity through intervening in video's regulatory processes of transformation. By inserting the creative gesture into the controlled process, by combining, timing, selecting and composing, the video artist can wrest from the measurable that which is most illusive.

As for narrative and discursive presentation, video, like film, can present the essay or story as a visual, aural and verbal form, an interweaving of language, music, sounds and images. Unfortunately, most works done in narrative or essay form in video fail to distinguish themselves as video works—they borrow so heavily from the techniques of film that most viewers can't distinguish a film transmitted by television from a work that originated as a videotape. While there are economic justifications for shooting "films" using videotape, that does not make works done in this way video art. But video can be a narrative art, integrating its own technical properties, not as special effects but as elements of narration, as components of narrative voice and mode. In fact, video processes could have as profound an effect on narrative technique as film has had over the last 80 years. Video could change narrative rather than being made to play the impostor of cinema.

Although video has been used as a documentary media, once again it has served as social and historical document by employing the coding processes of film. I can think of nothing less appealing than a colorized image in a documentary on poverty; video techniques could be elements of bad taste for many documentary subjects. And it is in the realm of documentary that video techniques run the greatest risk of being perceived as separate from the content of the film, an obtrusive element of form that stands apart from the signification processes of the work. However, there is something else that video can do, discursively, that is derived from the type of filmic essay Jean-Luc Godard developed out of narrative film. Increasingly, in Godard's films, the story has receded, and image, sound, music, voice and text have been woven into a new essay form. Not photojournalism, nor pictorial essay, but a weave of signifying material—ironic disjunctive, highly edited along principles of recombination. Artists could conceive of composing video as a writing, a tracing out of a text in various signifying matters including written language, which is easily displayed in video by means of a character generator. It is no coincidence that video has captured the imagination of Godard and a fellow traveller from the New Wave, Chris Marker. For more than film, it is the medium of text combined with flat image, of voice in an intimate context rather than pompous, detached voice-overs, of image presented as coded, as artifact, rather than transparently real.

Video is an art of our future—it is only as narcissistic as we let ourselves be, only as inherently commercial as our minds become. Video can be a site where the artist faces science and technology, inspired by their energy. It can be the site where human perception and imagination creatively express themselves in a system whose mechanics alternately resist and yield, differ from and defer to human aesthetic impulses. We have to learn how to play/work with video, how to see the video apparatus not as an entity whose inherent properties determine its limitations but as a tool for diverse art-making projects.

NOTES

1. Richard Kostelanetz, (ed.), *Moholy-Nagy* (New York: Praeger, 1970), pp. 34-41.
2. Ibid., pp. 34-36.
3. Ibid., p. 33.

SELECTED BIBLIOGRAPHY

E. Ann Kaplan

Adler, Dick, and Joseph Finnigan. "The Year America Stayed Home for the Movies: How Films have Burgeoned on Television and Why." *TV Guide*, 20 May 1971, pp. 6-10.

Adler, Renata. "Afternoon Television: Unhappiness Enough, and Time." In *Television: The Critical View*, ed. Horace Newcomb.

Adorno, Theodor W. "Culture Industry: Enlightenment as Mass Deception," (1944). In *Dialectic of Enlightenment*, ed. Theodor W. Adorno and Max Horkheimer. New York: Seabury Press, 1972.

Allen, Jeanne. "The Film Viewer as Consumer." *Quarterly Review of Film Studies*, vol. 5, no. 4 (1980), pp. 481-499.

Allen, Robert C., *et al.* "The College Student Soap Opera Viewer." Unpublished paper, University of North Carolina, 1981.

Alpert, Hollis. "Now the Earlier, Earlier Show." *The New York Times Magazine*, 11 August 1963, pp. 22-24.

Altheide, David L., and Robert P. Snow. "Sports Versus the Mass Media." *Urban Life*, vol. 7, no. 2 (1978), pp. 189-204.

Althusser, Louis. *Lenin and Philosophy*. New York and London: Monthly Review Press, 1971.

Altman, Charles F. "The American Film Musical: Paradigmatic Structure and Mediatory Function." *Wide Angle*, vol. 2, no. 2 (1978), pp. 10-17.

Arnheim, Rudolph. "The World of the Daytime Serial." In *Radio Research, 1942-1943*, ed. Paul F. Lazarsfeld.

Ashworth, C.E. "Sport as Symbolic Dialogue." In *The Sociology of Sport*, ed. Eric Dunning, pp. 40-46.

Atkin, Charles; Bradley Greenberg; Felipe Korzenny; and Steven McDermott. "Selective Exposure to Television Violence." *Journal of Broadcasting*, vol. 23, no. 1 (1979), pp. 5-13.

Barthes, Roland. *S/Z*. Trans. Richard Miller. New York: Hill and Wang, 1974.

_____. "The World of Wrestling." In *Mythologies*. Trans. Annette Lavers. New York: Hill and Wang, 1972.

139

_____. "Upon Leaving the Movie Theatre." In *Apparatus*, ed. Theresa Hak Kyung Cha. New York: Tanam Press, 1981.

Barlett, Donald, and James B. Steele. *Empire*. New York: W.W. Norton, 1978.

Baudrillard, Jean. *L'Echange symbolique et la mort*. Paris: Gallimard, 1976.

Baudry, Jean-Louis. "Cinéma: effects idéologiques produits par l'appareil de base." *Cinétique* 7-8 (1970). Trans. Alan Williams as "Ideological Effects of the Basic Cinematographic Apparatus." *Film Quarterly*, vol. 28, no. 2 (1974-75), pp. 39-47.

_____. "Le Dispositif: approches métapsychologiques de l'impression de réalité." *Communications* 23 (1975), pp. 56-72. Trans. Bertrand Augst and Jean Andrews as "The Apparatus." *Camera Obscura* 1 (1976), pp. 97-126.

_____. *L'Effet cinéma*. Paris: Albatross, 1978.

Bazalgette, Cary, and Richard Paterson. "Real Entertainment: The Iranian Embassy Siege." *Screen Education* 37 (1980-81), pp. 55-67.

Ben-Horin, Daniel. "Television Without Tears: An Outline of the Socialist Approach to Popular Television." *Socialist Revolution*, vol. 7, no. 5 (1977), pp. 7-35.

Benjamin, Walter. "On Some Motifs in Baudelaire." In *Illuminations*. Trans. Harry Zohn. New York: Schocken Books, 1969.

_____. "The Work of Art in the Age of Mechanical Reproduction." In *Illuminations*.

Bettetini, Gianfranco. *The Language and Technique of the Film*. The Hague: Mouton, 1973. (Includes some reference to television technique.)

Bittner, John R. *Mass Communication*. Englewood Cliffs, N.J.: Prentice-Hall, 1977.

Brecht, Bertolt. *Brecht on Theatre*, ed. John Willett. New York: Hill and Wang, 1964.

Brown, Stanley. "That Old Villain TV Comes to the Rescue and Hollywood Rides Again." *Fortune*, November 1966, pp. 270-73.

Bruck, Peter. "The Social Production of Texts: On the Relation Production-Product in the News Media." *Communication-Information*, vol. 4, no. 3 (1982), pp. 92-124.

Brunsdon, Charlotte, and David Morley. *Everyday Television: 'Nationwide.'* BFI Television Monographs No. 10. London: British Film Institute, 1978.

Cater, Douglas D., and Richard Adler, eds. *Television as a Social Force: New Approaches to TV Criticism*. New York: Praeger, 1975.

Caughie, John, ed. *Television, Ideology and Exchange*. London: British Film Institute, 1978.

_____. "The World of Television." *Edinburgh Magazine*, 1977.

Cawelti, John. "Beatles, Batman and the New Aesthetic." *Midway*, vol. 9, no. 2 (1968), pp. 49-70.

Chandler, Arnold. *The Visible Hand*. Cambridge, MA.: Harvard University Press, 1977.

Chandler, M. "TV and Sports: Wedded with a Golden Hoop." *Psychology Today*, vol. 10, no. 11 (1977), pp. 64-76.

Chatman, Seymour. *Story and Discourse: Narrative Structure in Fiction and Film*. Ithaca, N.Y.: Cornell University Press, 1978.

Chodorow, Nancy. *The Reproduction of Mothering: Psychoanalysis and the Sociology of Gender*. Berkeley, CA.: University of California Press, 1978.

Clarke, Gerald. "Sanitizing the Small Screen." *Time*, 29 June 1981.

Comolli, Jean. "Machines of the Visible." In *The Cinematic Apparatus,* ed. Stephen Heath and Teresa de Lauretis. London: St. Martin's Press, 1980.

Comstock, George; Steven Chaffee; Natan Katzman; Maxwell McCombs; and Donald Roberts. *Television and Human Behavior.* New York: Columbia University Press, 1978.

Conant, Michael. *Antitrust in the Motion Picture Industry.* Berkeley, CA.: University of California Press, 1960.

Connell, Ian. "Ideology/Discourse/Institution." *Screen,* vol. 19, no. 4 (1979).

_____ . "Monopoly Capitalism and the Media: Definitions and Struggles." In *Politics, Ideology and the State,* ed. Sally Hibbin. London: Lawrence & Wishart, 1978.

Corliss, Richard. "Sex Stars of the Seventies." *Film Comment,* vol. 15, no. 4 (1979), pp. 27-29.

Coward, Rosalind. "Class, Culture and Social Formation." *Screen,* vol. 18, no. 1 (1977).

_____ , and John Ellis. *Language and Materialism: Developments in Semiology and the Theory of the Subject.* London: Routledge & Kegan Paul, 1977.

Curran, James, *et al.,* eds. *Mass Communication and Society.* London: Arnold, 1977.

Davidoff, Leonore; Jean L'Espérance; and Howard Newby. "Landscape with Figures." In *Rights and Wrongs of Women,* ed. Juliet Mitchell and Ann Oakley. Harmondsworth, U.K.: Penguin, 1976.

Doane, Mary Ann. "Misrecognition and Identity." *Ciné-Tracts,* vol. 3, no. 3 (1980).

Downing, John. "Communications and Power." *Socialist Review.* Forthcoming, 1983.

Downing, T. "Some Aspects of the Presentation of Industrial Relations and Race Relations in the British Media." Ph.D. dissertation, London School of Economics, 1974.

Drummond, Philip. "Structural and Narrative Constraints and Strategies in *The Sweeney.*" *Screen Education* 20 (1976), pp. 15-33.

Dundes, Alan. "Into the End Zone for a Touchdown: A Psychoanalytic Consideration of American Football." In *Interpreting Folklore.* Bloomington, IN.: Indiana University Press, 1980.

Dunning, Eric, ed. *The Sociology of Sport: A Selection of Readings.* London: Frank Cass and Co., 1971.

Dyer, Richard. *Light Entertainment.* London: British Film Institute, 1973.

_____ . "Victim: Hermeneutic Project." *Film Form,* vol. 1, no. 2 (1975), pp. 6-18.

_____ ; Terry Lovell; and Jean McCrindle. "Soap Opera and Women." *Edinburgh International Television Festival Programme,* 1977.

Eco, Umberto. *The Role of the Reader: Explorations in the Semiotics of Texts.* Bloomington, IN.: Indiana University Press, 1979.

_____ . *A Theory of Semiotics.* Bloomington, IN.: Indiana University Press, 1976.

_____ . "Towards a Semiotic Enquiry into the T.V. Message." *Working Papers in Cultural Studies* 3 (1972).

Elias, Norbert. "The Genesis of Sport as a Sociological Problem." In *The Sociology of Sport,* ed. Eric Dunning.

Elliot, Philip. *The Making of a Television Series.* London: Constable, 1972.

——————— . "Uses and Gratifications: A Critique and a Sociological Alternative." Leicester, U.K.: University of Leicester Centre for Mass Communications Research, n.d.

Ellis, John. "The Institution of the Cinema." *Edinburgh Magazine,* 1977.

Emery, Michael C., and **Ted C. Smythe,** eds. *Readings in Mass Communication.* Dubuque, IA.: W.C. Brown, 1974.

Epstein, Edward J. *News From Nowhere.* New York: Random House, 1974.

Eron, Leopoldo; L. Rowell Huesman; Monroe M. Lefkowitz; and **Leopold O. Walden.** "Does Television Violence Cause Aggression?" *American Psychologist,* vol. 27, no. 4 (1972), pp. 253-63.

Feuer, Jane. "The Self-Reflective Musical and the Myth of Entertainment." *Quarterly Review of Film Studies,* vol. 2, no. 3 (1977), pp. 313-26.

Fiske, John. "Television: The Flow and the Text." *Madog,* vol. 1, no. 1 (1978), pp. 7-14. (The Polytechnic of Wales.)

——————— , and **John Hartley.** *Reading Television.* London: Methuen & Co., 1978. (Contains a useful annotated bibliography.)

Fliegelman, Avra, ed. *TV Feature Film Source Book,* vol. 13, no. 3 (1972), pp. 10-15.

Fraleigh, Warren. "The Moving 'I'." In *The Philosophy of Sport: A Collection of Original Essays,* ed. Robert G. Osterhoudt, pp. 108-129. Springfield, IL.: Thomas, 1973.

Furlong, William Barry. "Football Violence." *The New York Times Magazine,* 30 November 1980, pp. 38-41, 122-134.

Furst, Terry, "Social Change and the Commercialization of Professional Sports." *International Review of Sports Sociology* 6 (1971).

Gans, Herbert J. *Popular Culture and High Culture.* New York: Basic Books, 1974.

Garnham, Nicolas. *Structures of Television.* BFI Television Monographs No. 1. London: British Film Institute, 1964.

Gerbner, George. "Ideological Perspectives in News Reporting." *Journalism Quarterly,* vol. 41, no. 4 (1964).

——————— ; **L. Gross;** and **W. Melody,** eds. *Communications Technology and Social Policy.* New York: John Wiley, 1973.

Gibson, William. "Network News: Elements of a Theory." *Social Text* 3 (1980).

Gitlin, Tod. "Media Sociology: The Dominant Paradigm." *Theory and Society* 6 (1978), pp. 205-253.

Glasgow University Media Group. *Bad News.* London: Routledge & Kegan Paul, 1976.

——————— . *More Bad News.* London: Routledge & Kegan Paul, 1980.

Gold, Herbert. "Television's Little Dramas: First the Verdict, Then the Show." *Harpers,* March 1977, pp. 88-89.

Gomery, Douglas. "Review—*The Movie Brats.*" *Screen,* vol. 21, no. 1 (1980), pp. 15-17.

Goodhardt, G.J.; A. Ehrenberg; and **M. Collins.** *The Television Audience: Patterns of Viewing.* Farnborough, U.K.: Saxon House, 1975.

Grealy, Jim. "Notes on Popular Culture." *Screen Education* 22 (1977).

Guttman, Allen. *From Ritual to Record: The Nature of Modern Sports.* New York: Columbia University Press, 1978.

Hall, Stuart. "Deviancy, Politics and the Media." In *Deviance and Social Control*, ed. P. Rock and M. McIntosh. London: Tavistock, 1974.

——————, and T. Jefferson. *Resistance Through Ritual*. London: Hutchinson, 1978.

——————, and Paddy Whannel. *The Popular Arts*. London: Pantheon Books, 1964.

Halloran, James D. "Understanding Television." *Screen Education* 14 (1975).

——————, ed. *The Effects of Television*. London: Panther, 1970.

——————, *et al. Demonstrations and Communications*. Harmondsworth, U.K.: Penguin, 1970.

Hartley, John, and John Fiske. "Myth—Representation: A Cultural Reading of *News at Ten*." *Communication Studies Bulletin* 4 (1977), pp. 12-33.

——————, and Terence Hawkes. *Popular Culture and High Culture*. Milton Keynes, U.K.: The Open University, 1977.

Harvey, Sylvia. *May '68 and Film Culture*. London: British Film Institute, 1978.

Heath, Stephen. "Screen Images, Film Memory." *Edinburgh Magazine*, 1976.

——————, and Gillian Skirrow. "Television: A World in Action." *Screen*, vol. 18, no. 2 (1977).

Heilman, Robert. "Football: An Addict's Memoirs and Observations." *Journal of American Culture*, vol. 4, no. 3 (1981).

Herzog, Herta. "On Borrowed Experience." In *Radio Research*, ed. Paul Lazarsfeld.

Hicks, Orton, and Haven Falconer. *MGM Television Survey: Interim Report*. Madison, WI.: Dore Schary Collection, Wisconsin Center for Film and Theatre Research, 1955.

Higgins, A.P. *Talking About Television*. London: British Film Institute, 1966.

Hirst, P. "Althusser's Theory of Ideology." *Economy and Society*, vol. 5, no. 4 (1976), pp. 385-412.

Hoggart, Richard. *The Uses of Literacy: Changing Patterns in English Mass Culture*. London: Chatto & Windus, 1957.

Holland, Norman. *The Dynamics of Literary Response*. New York: W.W. Norton, 1975.

Horowitz, Ira. "Market Entrenchment and the Sports Broadcasting Act." *American Behavioral Scientist*, vol. 7, no. 2 (1978), pp. 189-204.

Irigaray, Luce. "Ce sexe qui n'en est pas un." In *New French Feminisms*, ed. Elaine Marks and Isabelle de Courtivron, pp. 104-105. Amherst, MA.: University of Massachusetts Press, 1980.

Jameson, Fredric. "Reification and Utopia in Mass Culture." *Social Text* 1 (1979).

Jobs, Gertrude. *Motion Picture Empire*. Hamden, CT.: Anchor Books, 1966.

Johnson, William Oscar. "How Many Messages for This Medium?" *Sports Illustrated*, 19 February 1979.

——————. "Towering Babble and (SOB) Heidi." *Sports Illustrated*, 19 January 1970. (Part of a four-part series on the history of sport on television, beginning with 22 December issue.)

Johnstone, Sally M., and Robert C. Allen. "The Audience for Soaps: A Comparison of Two Popular Cultures." Paper presented at the Conference on Communication and Culture, University of Pennsylvania, 1981.

Katz, E. "Mass Communication Research and the Study of Popular Culture." *Studies in Public Communication* 2 (1959).

Kauffman, Helen. "The Appeal of Specific Daytime Serials." In *Radio Research*, ed. Paul Lazarsfeld.

Kitses, Jim, and E. Ann Kaplan. *Talking About the Cinema.* Rev. ed. 1974. London: British Film Institute, 1963.

Kostelanetz, Richard, ed. *Moholy-Nagy.* New York: Praeger, 1970.

Kress, G.R., and A.A. Trew. "Ideological Transformation of Discourse." *Sociological Review,* vol. 26, no. 4 (1978), pp. 755-776.

Lasch, Christopher. "Mass Culture Reconsidered." *democracy,* vol. 1, no. 4 (1981), pp. 11-14.

Lazarsfeld, Paul, ed. *Radio Research, 1942-1943.* Rev. ed. 1979. New York: Arno Press, 1944.

_____ , and Frank Stephen, eds. *Communication Research 1948-1949,* New York: Harper & Brothers, 1949.

Leavis, F.R., and Denys Thompson. *Culture and Environment.* London: Chatto & Windus, 1937.

Lee, Barrett A., and Carol A. Zeiss. "Behavioral Commitment to the Role of Sport Consumer: An Explanatory Analysis." *Sociology and Social Research,* vol. 64, no. 3 (1980), pp. 405-419.

Leech, Geoffrey N. *English in Advertising: A Linguistic Study of Advertising in Great Britain.* London: Longmans, 1966.

Levin, Harvey J. *Broadcast Regulation and Joint Ownership of the Media.* New York: New York University Press, 1960.

Leymore, V.L. *Hidden Myth.* London: Heinemann, 1976.

Lincoln, Melissa Ludtke. "Fancy Figures vs. Plain Facts." *Sports Illustrated,* 31 July 1978.

Livant, Bill. "The Audience Commodity: On the 'Blindspot' Debate." *Canadian Journal of Political and Social Theory,* vol. 3, no. 1 (1979), pp. 91-106. (Part of ongoing debate; see Smythe for start.)

Loewenthal, Leo. "Historical Perspectives on Popular Culture." In *Mass Culture: The Popular Arts in America,* ed. Bernard Rosenberg and David M. White.

MacCabe, Colin. "Realism and Pleasure." *Screen,* vol. 17, no. 3 (1976).

McCavitt, William E. *Radio and Television: A Selected Annotated Bibliography.* Metuchen, N.J.: Scarecrow Press, 1978.

MacDonald, Dwight. "A Theory of Mass Culture." In *Mass Culture,* ed. Bernard Rosenberg and David M. White.

McLuhan, H. Marshall. *The Mechanical Bride: Folklore of Industrial Man.* Rev. ed. 1967. New York: Vanguard, 1951.

_____ . *Understanding Media.* London: Routledge & Kegan Paul, 1964.

McQuail, Denis. *Communication.* London: Longmans, 1975.

Marc, David. *Demographic Vistas: Television in American Culture.* Ph.D. dissertation, University of Iowa, forthcoming.

Mendelsohn, Harold. *Mass Entertainment.* New Haven, CT.: College and University Press, 1966.

Merton, Robert K. *Mass Persuasion.* New York: Free Press, 1946.

_____ , ed. *Sociology Today*. New York: Free Press, 1959.

Metz, Christian. "The Fiction Film and Its Spectator." Trans. Alfred Guzzetti. *New Literary History*, vol. 8, no. 1 (1976), pp. 75-105.

_____ . *Film Language*. Trans. Michael Taylor. New York: Oxford University Press, 1974.

_____ . "The Imaginary Signifier." Trans. Ben Brewster. *Screen*, vol. 16, no. 2 (1975), pp. 14-76.

Meyer, Caroline. "The Rating Power of Network Movies." *Television*, vol. 25, no. 3 (1968), pp. 56, 84.

Meyersohn, Rolf. "The Sociology of Popular Culture: Looking Forward and Backwards." *Communication Research*, vol. 5, no. 3 (1978).

Miles, Rosalind. "Everyday Stories, Everyday Folk." Master's thesis, University of Leicester, 1980.

Modleski, Tania. "The Search for Tomorrow in Today's Soap Operas: Notes on a Feminine Narrative Form." *Film Quarterly*, vol. 33, no. 1 (1979), pp. 12-21.

Montgomery, Kathryn. "Television Criticism." *The AFI Education Newsletter*, vol. 6, no. 5 (1983).

Morin, Violette. "L'Information télévisée: un discours contrarié." *Communications* 28 (1978), pp. 187-202.

Morley, David. "Industrial Conflict and the Mass Media." *Sociological Review*, vol. 24, no. 2 (1976), pp. 245-268.

_____ . *The 'Nationwide' Audience: Structure and Decoding*. BFI Television Monographs No. 11. London: British Film Institute, 1980. (Includes a useful bibliography.)

_____ . "Texts, Readers, Subject." In *Culture, Media, Language*, ed. S. Hall; D. Hobson; A. Lowell; and P. Willis. London: Hutchinson, 1980.

Mulvey, Laura. "Visual Pleasure and Narrative Cinema." *Screen*, vol. 16, no. 3 (1975), pp. 6-18.

Murdock, G. "Blindspots About Western Marxism: A Reply to Dallas Smythe." *Canadian Journal of Political and Social Theory*, vol. 2, no. 2 (1978), pp. 109-119. (See Livant/Smythe.)

_____ . "Mass Communication and the Construction of Meaning." In *Reconstructing Social Psychology*, ed. N. Armistead. Harmondsworth, U.K.: Penguin, 1974.

_____ , and P. Golding. "For a Political Economy of Mass Communications." In *Socialist Register*, ed. R. Miliband and J. Saville. London: Merlin, 1973.

Neale, Steve. "Propaganda." *Screen*, vol. 18, no. 3 (1977), pp. 9-40.

Newcomb, Horace. *TV: The Most Popular Art*. New York: Doubleday/Anchor Books, 1974.

_____ , ed. *Television: The Critical View*. New York: Oxford University Press, 1979.

Nolan, Jack E. "Films on TV." *Films in Review*, vol. 17, no. 10 (1966). pp. 655-657.

_____ . "Films on TV." *Films in Review*, vol. 23, no. 6 (1973), p. 359.

Oriard, Michael. "Professional Football as Cultural Myth." *Journal of American Culture*, vol. 4, no. 3 (1981), pp. 27-41.

Ortega y Gasset, José. *The Dehumanization of Art*. Trans. Willard Trask. Garden City, N.Y.: Doubleday, 1956.

_____ . *The Revolt of the Masses.* New York: W.W. Norton, 1960.

Owen, Bruce; Jack H. Beeke; and Willard G. Manning, Jr. *Television Economics.* Lexington, MA.: Lexington Books, 1974.

Paterson, Richard. "Planning the Family: The Art of the Television Schedule." *Screen Education* 35 (1980), pp. 79-85.

Pepper, Robert. "The Pre-Freeze Television Stations." In *American Broadcasting,* ed. Lawrence W. Lichty and Malachi C. Topping, pp. 139-147. New York: Hastings House, 1976.

Pollock, F. "Empirical Research into Public Opinion." In *Critical Sociology,* ed. P. Connerton. Harmondsworth, U.K.: Penguin, 1976.

Porter, Dennis. "Soap Time: Thoughts on a Commodity Art Form." *College English,* vol. 38, no. 8 (1977).

Purdy, B. "Of Time, Motion, and Motor Racing." *Journal of American Culture,* vol. 4, no. 3 (1981).

Quigley, Martin, Jr. "11,325 Features for TV." *Motion Picture Herald,* 18 January 1967.

Rich, Robert. "Post '48 Features." *Radio-Television Daily,* 29 July 1960.

Rosenberg, Bernard, and David M. White. *Mass Culture: The Popular Arts in America.* Glencoe, IL.: The Free Press, 1957.

_____ . *Mass Culture Revisited.* New York: Van Nostrand Reinhold, 1972.

Ryall, Tom. *The Gangster Film.* British Film Institute Teachers Study Guide No. 2. London: British Film Institute, 1979.

Sage, George H. "Sport and the Social Sciences." *Annals of the American Academy of Political and Social Science* 445 (1979).

Schiller, Herbert. *Mass Communication and the American Empire.* New York: Kelley, 1970.

Schnapper, Amy. "The Distribution of Theatrical Feature Film to Television." Unpublished Ph.D. dissertation, University of Wisconsin, 1975.

Seiter, Ellen. "The Role of the Woman Reader: Eco's Narrative Theory and Soap Opera." *Tabloid* 6 (1981).

Sennet, Richard. *The Fall of Public Man.* New York: Alfred A. Knopf, 1977.

Sklar, Robert. *Prime-Time America.* New York: Oxford University Press, 1980.

Smythe, Dallas. "Communications: Blindspot of Western Marxism." *Canadian Journal of Political and Social Theory,* vol. 1, no. 3 (1977), pp. 1-27. (See Livant/Murdock.)

Spencer, Walt. "Now Playing at Your Neighborhood Movie House: The Networks." *Television,* vol. 25, no. 3 (1977), pp. 1-27.

Stamps, Henry. *The Concept of the Mass Audience in American Broadcasting.* New York: Arno Press, 1979.

Stedman, Raymond William. *The Serials: Suspense and Drama by Installment.* Norman, OK.: University of Oklahoma Press, 1971.

Steinberg, Cobbett. *Reel Facts.* New York: Random House, 1978.

Sterling, Christopher, and Sydney W. Head. *Broadcasting in America.* Boston, MA.: Houghton Mifflin Co., 1982.

_____ , and John Kittross. *Stay Tuned: A Concise History of American Broadcasting.* Belmont, CA.: Wadsworth, 1978.

Stone, Douglas. "TV Movies and How They Get That Way." *Journal of Popular Film and Television,* vol. 7, no. 2 (1979), pp. 147-149.

Stone, Gregory. "American Sports: Play and Display." In *The Sociology of Sport,* ed. Eric Dunning, pp. 47-59.

Television and Radio 1979. IBA Handbook. London: Independent Broadcasting Authority, 1979.

"Television's Hottest Show." *Newsweek,* 28 September 1981.

Thomas, Bob. *King Cohn.* New York: G.P. Putnam, 1967.

Thomas, Sari. "The Relationship Between Daytime Serials and Their Viewers." Ph.D. dissertation, University of Pennsylvania, 1977.

Thompson, E.P. *The Making of the English Working Class.* Harmondsworth, U.K.: Penguin, 1968.

Thompson, John O. "A Nation Wooed." *Screen Education* 29 (1978).

Tuchman, Gaye. "Television News and the Metaphor of Myth." *Studies in the Visual Anthropology of Culture,* vol. 5, no. 1 (1978).

Tullock, John. "Gradgrind's Heirs: The Quiz and the Presentation of 'Knowledge' by British Television." *Screen Education* 19 (1976), pp. 3-13.

Tunstall, Jeremy. *The Media Are American.* London: Constable, 1977.

Turner, Victor. "Frame, Flow and Reflection: Ritual and Drama as Public Liminality." In *Performance in Modern Culture,* ed. Michel Benamou and Charles Caramello, pp. 33-55. Madison, WI.: Coda, 1977.

Waldrop, Frank C., and Joseph Borkin. *Television: A Struggle for Power.* New York: William Morrow & Co., 1938.

Waters, Harry F., and George Hackett. "Sex and the Anchor Person." *Newsweek,* 15 December 1980, pp. 65-66.

Whannel, Paddy, and Peter Harcourt, eds. *Film Teaching.* London: British Film Institute, 1968.

Wicking, Christopher, and Tise Vahimagi. *The American Vein: Directors and Directions in Television.* New York: E.P. Dutton, 1979.

Willemen, Paul. "Notes on Subjectivity: On Reading Edward Branigan's 'Subjectivity under Siege,' " *Screen,* vol. 19, no. 1 (1978), p. 41-69.

Williams, Brien R. "The Tube's Eye View of Football: Network Coverage Imposes Its Own Ideology." *Human Behavior,* vol. 1, no. 3 (1978).

Williams, Raymond. *Culture and Society.* Harmondsworth, U.K.: Penguin, 1958.

_____ . *Television: Technology and Cultural Form.* New York: Schocken Books, 1975.

_____ . "There's Always the Sport." *The Listener,* 6 April 1970, pp. 522-523.

Williamson, Judith. *Decoding Advertisements: Ideology and Meaning in Advertising.* London: Marion Boyars, 1978.

Winship, Janice. "Handling Sex." *Media, Culture and Society,* vol. 3, no. 1 (1981), pp. 6-18.

Woods, R. "Discourse Analysis." *Ideology and Consciousness* 2 (1977).

Wolfson, C. "The Semiotics of Workers' Speech." *Working Papers in Cultural Studies* 9 (1976).

Worth, Sol, and Larry Gross. "Symbolic Strategics." *Journal of Communication,* vol. 24, no. 4 (1974), pp. 27-39.

Wren-Lewis, Justin. "TV Coverage of the Riots." *Screen Education* 40 (1981-82), pp. 15-33.